RELIGION TODAY: TRADITION, MODERNITY AND CHANGE

RELIGION AND SOCIAL TRANSFORMATIONS

Religion Today: Tradition, Modernity and Change – an Open University/Ashgate series

The five textbooks and Reader that make up this series are:

- *From Sacred Text to Internet* edited by Gwilym Beckerlegge
- *Religion and Social Transformations* edited by David Herbert
- *Perspectives on Civil Religion* by Gerald Parsons
- *Global Religious Movements in Regional Context* edited by John Wolffe
- *Belief Beyond Boundaries* edited by Joanne Pearson
- *Religion Today: A Reader* edited by Susan Mumm

Each textbook includes:

- an introduction to the issues and controversies relevant to the topic under discussion
- a series of detailed case studies, which allow readers to see the theories and debates at work today in the experience of religious practitioners from around the globe
- extracts from other publications, which address the same issue from different perspectives
- extensive references to other published material on the same topics
- supporting colour and black-and-white illustrations

The series offers an in-depth introduction to contemporary themes and challenges in religious studies. The contents highlight the central issues and ideas that are shaping religion today – and will continue to do so tomorrow. The textbooks contain plentiful contemporary case studies spanning many countries and religions, and seamlessly integrate methods of analysis and theoretical perspectives. They work to ensure that readers will understand the relevance of methodologies to lived experience and gain the ability to transfer analytic skills and explanatory devices to the study of religion in context. The textbooks focus on the following key issues in contemporary religious studies: representation and interpretation; modernity and social change; civil religion; the impact of globalization on religion; and the growth of alternative religion.

The accompanying Reader presents primary and secondary source material structured around these core themes. It will serve as an invaluable resource book, whether used to accompany the textbooks in the series or not.

RELIGION TODAY: TRADITION, MODERNITY AND CHANGE

RELIGION AND SOCIAL TRANSFORMATIONS

EDITED BY DAVID HERBERT

Ashgate

Aldershot • Burlington USA • Singapore • Sydney

in association with

The Open
University

This publication forms part of an Open University course AD317 *Religion Today: Tradition, Modernity and Change*. Details of this and other Open University courses can be obtained from the Call Centre, PO Box 724, The Open University, Milton Keynes MK7 6ZS, United Kingdom: tel. +44 (0)1908 653231, e-mail ces-gen@open.ac.uk

Alternatively, you may visit the Open University web site at http://www.open.ac.uk where you can learn more about the wide range of courses and packs offered at all levels by the Open University.

To purchase this publication or other components of Open University courses, contact Open University Worldwide Ltd, The Berrill Building, Walton Hall, Milton Keynes MK7 6AA, United Kingdom: tel. +44 (0)1908 858785; fax +44 (0)1908 858787; e-mail ouwenq@open.ac.uk; web site http://www.ouw.co.uk

British Library Cataloguing in Publication Data

Religion and social transformations. (Religion
   today : tradition, modernity and change ; v. 4)
    1.Religions 2.Religion and politics 3.Religion and social problems
   I.Herbert, David II.Open University
   291.1'7

Library of Congress Control Number: 2001095922

Co-published by

The Open University	Ashgate Publishing Ltd	Ashgate Publishing Company
Walton Hall	Gower House, Croft Road	Burlington, VT 05401-5600
Milton Keynes MK7 6AA	Aldershot, Hants GU11 3HR	USA

Ashgate web site: http://www.ashgate.com

First published 2001.

Edited, designed and typeset by The Open University.

Printed and bound in the United Kingdom by The Bath Press, Bath.

ISBN 0 7546 0745 3 (hbk)
ISBN 0 7546 0817 4 (pbk)

1.1

21702B/ad317b2introi1.1

Contents

Preface

Religion and Social Transformations is the second of a five-volume series entitled *Religion Today: Tradition, Modernity and Change*, published by Ashgate Publishing Ltd in association with The Open University. Like all the volumes in the series, *Religion and Social Transformations* has been compiled primarily with the needs of Open University undergraduate students in mind. However, it is hoped that the contents of the volume will also be of interest and value to other readers who would like to know more about the place of religion in the world today.

The authors have benefited greatly from the careful and constructive comments on the first drafts of their chapters by Professor Kim Knott of the University of Leeds (external assessor), Professor Ken Thompson of the Faculty of Social Sciences at The Open University (reader) and Dr Claire Disbrey (tutor consultant). Any inaccuracies or questionable judgements are the responsibilities of the authors alone. Thanks are also due to the writers and publishers who permitted the texts to be reprinted in Part Two of the volume.

The authors wish to acknowledge the contribution made to the production of this volume by: Adrian Roberts (course manager), Julie Bennett, Kate Clements and Peter Wright (editors), Paul Smith (picture researcher), Richard Hoyle (designer) and Pip Harris (compositor).

The authors of the four chapters in the volume are:

- David Herbert Department of Religious Studies at The Open University
- Susan Mumm Department of Religious Studies at The Open University
- Helen Waterhouse Department of Religious Studies at The Open University

Introduction

DAVID HERBERT

Historically, religions have played a major role in both the gradual changes and the major upheavals that have transformed societies. This historic role can be witnessed from the Christianization of the Roman Empire (third century to sixth century CE) and the Islamization of the Middle East (seventh century to tenth century CE) to the European Reformation (sixteenth century), the Wars of Religion (sixteenth/seventeenth centuries CE) and the colonization of the Americas (sixteenth century to nineteenth century). But what of the twentieth century? Arguably, the forces that have most shaped the twentieth century – caused wars and revolutions, and moulded the patterns of global interaction – are capitalism, nationalism and communism. The first and last of these are either indifferent to or hostile to religion, even though arguably both have been influenced by religious ideas (capitalism by the 'Protestant work ethic', Marxism by Jewish/Christian eschatology). And while religion has remained a potent mobilizing force for nationalism in some cases (e.g. Poland, Serbia), this association has declined, at least in Europe through the twentieth century. Furthermore, in the '"brave new world" in the wake of the French Revolution', according to conventional sociological theory, religion is not just rejected ideologically but functionally superfluous (Wilson, 1991, p.23). On this understanding, religious justification and support for institutions is no longer needed in societies integrated through modern functional systems – economic, administrative, educational and political. Religion, under these circumstances, becomes a private option, even a leisure pursuit.

Yet the last quarter of the twentieth century suggests that the rise and fall of the social influence of religion may not be a simple matter. In Iran in 1979 the world witnessed a 'social revolution in the name of God', arguably the first major twentieth-century revolution to reject the secular traditions of both the French Revolution (1789) and the Russian Revolution (1917) (Hobsbawm, 1995, plate 30). In other cases, Islam has been influential in social transformation without a revolution. Since 1970 in modern Muslim societies as diverse as Tunisia, Egypt, Pakistan and Indonesia Islam has gradually increased its influence throughout the social system (e.g. in education, politics, law, health and social welfare). But the social impact of Islam is just one particularly striking example of the changing social significance of religion in the last third of the twentieth century. Religion also played a part in the major political upheavals in Eastern Europe in 1989–90, and has been involved both ideologically and institutionally in arguments about the role of women in society and the relationship between humanity and the environment. Religious motivation was not so dominant in the revolutions of 1989 as in that of 1979 – rather, perhaps, the main demand was for freedom. But, strangely for western Europeans not accustomed to associating religion with freedom, this demand was often made through religious figures and organizations, and using religious symbolism. Rebelling against communism as an ideology, this was in some ways an anti-ideological revolution (Garton-Ash, 1999, pp.134–5). But in the cases of Poland and East Germany the role of the churches was more than that of institutional midwife, making space for opposition forces to emerge. Religious and religiously inspired ideas and ideals also played a role. So too did religious symbolism, from Papal masses that supported Solidarity to Leipzig's and Berlin's candlelit vigils. Indeed, one of the lessons of 1989's predominantly bloodless revolutions is that symbols completely lacking in instrumental force can sometimes overcome the powerful systems of control harnessed by the modern state. In Chapter 1 we examine the contribution of religion to these processes, as well as in the aftermath of the fall of communism.

Thus, in Poland and East Germany, religion made a positive and highly influential contribution to the peaceful demise of communism, as Chapter 1 argues; and the Burgess text in Part Two details the case of two theologians' contrasting roles in the renewal of political institutions. But since 1989 the Catholic Church in Poland has been accused of undemocratic behaviour and of trying to impose its morals on society, and even of attempting to establish a 'para-religious state',[1] while in East Germany church officials have been implicated as collaborators with the *Stasi* (secret police). The latter has called into question the whole policy of 'the Church in Socialism' on which the role of the churches in the opposition movement was based.

But societies do not change only through political revolutions. Just as the revolutions of 1989 were in part a victory of words and symbols over physical strength, so words and symbols play a crucial ongoing role in shaping societies and people's lives within them. One of the

---

[1] In the words of Tadeusz Zielinski, and independent official concerned with human rights monitoring, in 1992. Zielinski defines a para-religious state as one in which religious institutions dictate to governments on matters of policy that touch on moral issues (in Brzezinski, 2000, p.199).

main legacies of the French Revolution of 1989, and of the American Declaration of Independence and the whole Enlightenment culture that influenced both, is the language of human rights. In the wake of the Second World War, and especially since the formation of the United Nations (1948) and the UN's Universal Declaration of Human Rights, the discourse of human rights has become a powerful medium of communication, but one that has proved controversial since the collapse of European colonial empires, particularly with the resurgence of Islam since the 1970s. In Chapter 2 we examine the complex encounter between Islam and human rights.

One of the major social transformations of the twentieth century was in the role of women in society, and, as Susan Mumm argues in Chapter 3, perhaps the most noticeable change in the sphere of religion in the last half of that century has been in the role of women. However, religion has mostly played a reactive rather than a pro-active role in advancing feminism, and this presents both religions and women in them with considerable challenges, which we examine in Chapter 3.

Such a reactive role is also sometimes ascribed to religions – especially 'Western' ones – in relation to another key transformation in the late twentieth century – or perhaps a revolution still waiting to happen – the transformation in environmental consciousness. There has been an increase in awareness of the human impact on the environment, and of the environment as a finite, fragile system that humanity can damage and even destroy. The revolution threatened here is one that replaces the pyramid with humanity at its apex with a web in which all life and the non-living environment are inextricably bound in a process of continual change. Some argue that such a vision is already present in 'Eastern' religious traditions, but in Chapter 4, in relation to Buddhism, Helen Waterhouse argues that the situation is not so straightforward. Rather, the monastic ethic in Buddhism that encourages 'living lightly off the land' is oriented not to saving the planet from environmental degradation, but to developing the spiritual practice of the individual monk or nun. Indeed, things could hardly be otherwise, for as Keown says:

> The earliest Buddhist canonical literature is well over two thousand years old, and many problems we face today are the result of modern social, economic and technological development which could scarcely have been imagined in ancient times.
>
> (Keown, 2000, p.1)

This gap between the world in which sacred texts were written (or received) and the contemporary one presents profound challenges to the current followers of each of the religions considered here

(Buddhist, Christian, Hindu, Islamic and Jewish). This is especially so because followers do not regard their scriptures simply as historical documents, but rather as 'storehouses of transforming, timeless visions of the cosmos' (Beckerlegge, 2001, p.1).

The interpretative bridge between past and present that contemporary followers build to bring to life the visions given in their sacred texts is 'hermeneutics' and is discussed in Chapter 3. But it is a task that concerns religions in all the chapters of this book, especially if one broadens its meaning from interpretation of written texts to the whole range of media in which religious traditions are transmitted, including symbols, rituals, songs and institutions. Religious traditions face this task in the context of a globally dominant 'cultural modernity' associated with Western societies, the features of which include increasing material wealth, gender equality, democratization and individual autonomy, but also often increasing economic inequality and public disorder. Furthermore, in many of the cases considered here, religious institutions face the task of renewing their traditions in contexts in which they have been implicated in oppressive acts and systems.

Thus, according to feminists, virtually all religions have helped perpetuate 'patriarchy', a system of male domination (Chapter 3). Mernissi and Gupta in Part Two present feminist readings of Muslim and Hindu traditions (with respect to women's rights and the goddess Kali respectively) that are highly controversial within those traditions. Gupta in particular raises the question of continuity of tradition in an acute form, when she interprets Kali, who might be seen as the male projection of all that is 'Other' onto the female form, as a source of women's liberation in a post-patriarchal context.

Not all responses to contemporary challenges involve religion changing in order better to 'fit' new contexts, in the sense of corresponding with dominant global systems and their core values. We shall consider a Buddhist and a Muslim example below, but first Peter Beyer's text on religion and environmentalism introduces some ideas that can help us make sense of them. Beyer in Part Two names the dominant global systems as: 'a world capitalist economy and the system of sovereign states... [and] the world-wide scientific-techno-logical systems, health systems and education systems' (Beyer, Part Two, p.265 below). A key aspect of these systems is their 'instrumental orientation' (ibid.), that is, people and things are treated as objects to be manipulated for their use value, rather than revered and respected as having their own interests or intrinsic value. Thus natural and social worlds are 'objectified'. In such a world-view:

> Action is conceptualised as the intentional, self interested behavior of individuals in an objectivated world, that is, one in which objects and other individuals are related to in terms of their possible manipulation. The rationality of action is correspondingly conceptualized as the efficient linking of actions-seen-as-means to the attainment of individual goals.
>
> (White, 1988, p.10)

Beyer names three of the 'main cultural values' spread by these instrumentally based systems in the process of 'globalization': freedom, equality and fraternity – the same as those of the French Revolution of 1789 (Beyer, Part Two, p.267 below). Each of these values conflicts to some extent with the instrumental orientation of the systems that transmit them. Thus seeing individuals as having their own freedom clashes with seeing them as objects to manipulate, and so on. These conflicts show no sign of diminishing with the advance of globalization, though they do not seem to be impeding its progress. It is in this context that we need to consider the relationship of religions to globalization.

Take, for example, two cases of religious response that fit neither with the instrumental orientation of dominant global systems, nor with the values of political and cultural modernity (freedom, equality, fraternity). First, a Buddhist approach to environmentalism, which challenges the instrumental character of these systems. Second, a Muslim response to human rights, which challenges global values. It should be noted at once that these are the responses of particular Buddhists and Muslims rather than of the traditions as a whole –religious responses to contemporary social transformations are characterized by their diversity.

Given this important caveat, let us briefly consider each in turn. In Chapter 4, Waterhouse contrasts the sociologist Beyer's verdict that 'religion cannot do anything direct about environmental problems... the... solutions are going to be political, educational, scientific, economic, and medical' (Beyer, Part Two, p.280 below), with a western Buddhist's view that:

> The only true solution to the problem, in a Buddhist analysis, will be neither technological nor legal.... It must involve the evolution of a sufficient number of beings to a higher level of awareness, to a higher ethical sensibility.
>
> (Sponberg, accessed 2001)

For Beyer, religions can only impact on the environment indirectly, by motivating people to take action, action which is itself defined in non-religious, instrumental terms. In contrast, for Sponberg, while instrumental action can be a 'stop-gap measure' (ibid.) it is 'the mystical transformation of individuals' that is the real key to change. Thus Sponberg rejects, at least as a first priority, the instrumental orientation of the major global social systems.

Then, in Chapter 2, David Herbert considers the responses of different Muslim groups to the concept and institutions of human rights. One central issue here is the *hadd* penalties (amputation of a hand for theft, flogging for adultery, etc.) and the unequal treatment of women in certain spheres, for example, in inheritance and legal competence, all stipulated in the Qur'an. For some Muslims these need to be reconsidered in the light of historical experience (An-Na'im, 1998, p.227), whereas for others these are non-negotiable, leading to the rejection of some values favoured by the dominant world systems:

> The democratic system prevailing in the world does not suit us in the region... Islam is our social and political law. It is a complete constitution of social and economic laws and a system of government and justice.
>
> (King Fahd of Saudi Arabia, *International Herald Tribune*,
> 15 March 1992; quoted in Halliday, 1995, p.138)

Furthermore, while the Gulf States may be exceptional in that the influx of oil wealth has arguably enabled an élite to retain political power while pacifying a small population with 'petrodollars' (Inglehart, 1997 pp.280–92), the Islamization of legal systems has occurred in several Muslim countries with large populations, complex societies and economic problems (e.g. Egypt, Pakistan, Iran). Such cases exemplify the rejection of key values of the dominant global systems, yet also exhibit an acceptance of the instrumental orientation of such systems – thus, for example, *sharia* law is administered through modern bureaucratic legal systems.

These two examples together – a Buddhist rejection of instrumentality and an Islamic rejection of core global values – suggest that religions can adopt a range of strategies to cope with modern global conditions. Beyer in Part Two points to another role that religions can play in relation to global systems. Religions are holistic systems which are not easily absorbed into any one functional system. Therefore, they provide alternative perspectives from which to view and to criticize the so-called 'residual problems' of the dominant global systems, which include environmental damage, inequalities and social problems (Beyer, Part Two, p.281 below). Examples of religious responses to the challenge of these residual problems include feminist re-readings of sacred texts, especially when they connect up with other 'liberation' issues, the East German churches' support of alternative movements campaigning for 'peace, justice and the integrity of creation', and at least some kinds of Buddhist environmentalism.

These reflections on religion and global systems can help us to address one of the key questions raised by this book: is religion still relevant? Without prejudging the arguments, this brief introductory tour suggests a cautious 'yes' may be the appropriate response. Religion in a world dominated by global systems remains relevant in three main ways. First, because religion can sometimes work well within specialized functional systems, for example, in health and social welfare systems, especially where the state fails or struggles to meet people's needs . Examples of such successful functionalization – religion finding work to do – in contemporary societies, include Catholic worker's welfare organizations in Poland (Chapter 1), the Islamization of law (Chapter 2) and the mobilization of environmental projects on Buddhist grounds (Chapter 4).

Second, religion can also be relevant even when it isn't directly performing a practical function. Because of its holistic vision, religion can raise awkward questions about the consequences of the dominance of instrumental systems, whether for the environment (Chapter 4), women (Chapter 3), the universality of ideas originating in the West (human rights, Chapter 2), or the sanctity of human life (Polish Catholicism and abortion, Chapter 1). In these moral controversies, religious voices often appear on both sides of an argument (e.g. for and against abortion); but that doesn't make them any less important. Third, religions can sometimes combine these first (practical) and second (critical) roles, successfully challenging instrumental systems by non-instrumental means, as in the symbolic challenge led by the Polish and East German churches which contributed in crucial ways to the downfall of communist governments (Chapter 1).

Yet in other situations religion fails or struggles to be relevant. Patriarchal religion fails to be relevant in any positive sense for women who may be less oppressed in society than in church, synagogue or mosque; and women (and sometimes men) struggle to reform it (Chapter 3). The East German church struggles to be relevant in a highly secularized, reunited Germany, and the Polish church finds itself out of line with social values, no longer the unchallenged voice of the nation in a post-communist system (Chapter 2).

So, to return to our opening question, what role have religions played in the social transformations of the late twentieth century? Obviously, the examples collected here are only a small sample, but they enable us to make two preliminary suggestions. First, the big anti-religious ideologies, especially communism, have sharply declined in influence in the latter part of the twentieth century. However, it is questionable how important this is for religion's capacity to play a significant social role, for communism's impact on the vitality of religion appears to have been varied. It attacked religion's institutional capacity to reproduce itself, but at the same time its own failure to meet people's needs materially and politically created new roles for religion.

Second, the view that religion is no longer necessary for the operation of societies dominated by modern global systems requires qualification. Religion may be less necessary to legitimize social order, but the world system comprised of these dominant global systems continues to produce 'residual problems' to keep holistic systems such as religions busy, responding to them practically and critically. Furthermore, religion has shown an unexpected capacity to adapt itself to modern systems, at the same time as attacking those systems' values. Thus the role of religion in social transformations has changed and diversified, retreating in some areas of social life, expanding in others, leading change in some areas (the transition from communism in Poland and East Germany), following in others (the rise of feminism).

In conclusion, the chapters in Part One and the texts in Part Two are designed to enable the reader to reflect across religious traditions in a range of contexts on two themes: the changing roles of religion in contemporary societies, and the challenges posed by contemporary social transformations for the reading and use of sacred texts and other sacred traditions. Contrary to some expectations, the emerging pattern seems less one of decline and increasing irrelevance than of adaptation and transformation.

References

An-Na'im, A. (1998) 'Shari'a and basic human rights concerns' in C. Curzmann (ed.) *Liberal Islam: a Sourcebook*, Oxford: Oxford University Press.

Beckerlegge, G. (ed.) (2001) *From Sacred Text to Internet*, Aldershot: Ashgate/Milton Keynes: Open University.

Brzenzinski, M. (2000) *The Struggle for Constitutionalism in Poland*, 2nd edn, Basingstoke and London: Macmillan.

Garton-Ash, T. (1999) *The Magic Lantern: The Revolution of '89 Witnessed in Warsaw, Budapest, Berlin and Prague*, 3rd edn, New York: Vintage.

Halliday F. (1995) *Islam and the Myth of Confrontation*, London: IB Tauris.

Herbert, D. (2001) 'Representing Islam: the Islamization of Egypt 1970–2000', in Beckerlegge, 2001.

Hobsbaum, E. (1995) *Age of Extremes: The Short Twentieth Century*, London: Abacus.

Inglehart, R. (1997) *Modernization and Postmodernization: Cultural, Economic and Political Change in 43 Societies*, New York: Princeton University Press.

Sponberg, A. (accessed 2001) 'The Buddhist conception of an ecological self', *Western Buddhist Review*, vol.2 (http://www.westernbuddhistreview.com/vol2/ecological_self.html).

White, S. (1988) *The Recent Work of Jürgen Habermas: Reason, Justice and Modernity*, Cambridge: Cambridge University Press.

Wilson, B. (1991) *The Changing Functions of Religion: Toleration and Cohesion in the Secularized Society*, Maidenhead: Institute of Oriental Philosophy.

PART
ONE

Religion and the 'Great Transformation' in Poland and East Germany

DAVID HERBERT

Introduction

> It is not important whether there will be capitalism in Poland. It is not important whether there will be welfare – the most important thing is that Poland should be Catholic.
>
> (Deputy Polish Prime Minister Henryk Goryszewski, 1993, quoted in Brzezinski, 2000, p.197)

> As East Germans and East German Christians adjusted to a new way of life, many of them fell silent, unable to say exactly who they were and where they fit in a new Germany.
>
> (Burgess, 1997, p.140)

These quotations suggest something of the contrast between the roles that religion has played in the cases of Poland and East Germany since the 'Great Transformation': the collapse of communist regimes across the region in the autumn and winter of 1989–90, and in their place the emergence, in most cases, of fledgling democracies and market economies (Ramet, 1995). While Catholicism, as the first quotation suggests, has been supported by some of Poland's post-communist governments as central to the identity of the Polish nation at the highest level, the second quotation reflects the German churches' experience of disorientation. Furthermore, Poland has the highest rate of church attendance in post-communist Europe, East Germany amongst the lowest.[1]

---

[1] Eighty-five per cent and 20 per cent respectively claim to attend 'at least once a month' (Bruce, 1999, p.90).

However, in spite of these differences there are also parallels and similarities both in the history and contemporary situation of the Christian churches in each country. First, for both, World War II marked a change from a relatively plural religious situation to one in which a single church became dominant. Thus, although historically Poland had a large Jewish population and straddled the border between Eastern Christianity (Orthodoxy) and Western Christianity (Catholicism and Protestantism), after World War II border changes and the destruction of Poland's Jews, Poland was left with a 95 per cent Roman Catholic population, with only small Greek Catholic, Orthodox, Protestant, Jewish and Muslim minorities. Germany, the home of the European Reformation, also straddles a division between mostly Catholic southern Europe and predominantly Protestant northern Europe. However, the division of Germany following World War II created an East German state (German Democratic Republic, **GDR**) in which approximately 90 per cent of the population was nominally Protestant, with most belonging to the Lutheran dominated Evangelical Church (*Evangelische Kirche Deutsche*, **EKD**), leaving a Catholic minority of fewer than ten per cent. Second, in both countries Christian institutions (Catholic and Protestant respectively) share a similar legacy from the communist period, including communist hostility to and attempts to exclude religion from public life. Third, in both societies religion played a significant role in the transition from communist to democratic regimes, which we shall examine in further detail below. Fourth, in the post-communist period, the major church institutions have struggled to face up to the challenge of a dramatically altered role, from being the principal institutional channel of opposition to communist regimes, and hence a focus for national unity, to becoming one group among many competing for this role in the more open civil and political societies of a democracy. Symptomatically, in both cases coalitions of interest groups united through the churches fell apart almost as soon as the communist regimes collapsed. Complexities for religion's role in post-communist society in each case also arise from the fact that adjustment is occurring not just on a national level, but as part of the increasing integration of these societies, economies, and polities into regional (e.g. European) and global systems. Reunification has made eastern Germany part of the German federal system and the European Community (EC), while Poland has joined **NATO** and also seeks EC membership.

As a result of these different yet related histories, religious traditions in Poland and eastern Germany face complex challenges for traditional Christian models of the relationship between church, state and society. The Polish Catholic Church (**PCC**) and the EKD in eastern Germany illustrate two such models.

The PCC illustrates the 'national church' model in which the church assumes an identity between church and nation. Thus it seeks to influence society by playing a major, indeed dominant, role in the mainstream of society. Since 1989, it has sought to shape attitudes and behaviour and to exercise power through the state (e.g. in law and the constitution, and public education in schools), political society (some direct involvement in political campaigning), and **civil society** (through charities, publishing, radio, and local and national voluntary organizations). The pluralism of contemporary societies challenges this model both at a practical and ideological level. Practically, increased movement of people across national boundaries and the diversity this brings makes any monopolistic identification between church and nation difficult to sustain, even in Poland. Ideologically, the concept of pluralism, which underlies modern constitutional democracy favours the separation of powers (state, judiciary and party political) and of church and state, which sit uneasily with a concept of a national community united by religion. As we shall see, this has led to conflict between the church and those favouring a more secular model of democracy.

In contrast, the EKD in East Germany made a virtue of its enforced separation from the state under communism, favouring a second traditional model of church/state/society relations which might be called the 'prophetic minority model'. As a powerless minority, the church saw itself as able to exercise an independent voice, at one level at least, unencumbered by the compromises that wielding political power brings. The growth of opposition groups on church premises (the only public space available) contributed to this self image, and the church was able to identify itself with the early Christian church as a powerless, persecuted minority. However, the new relationship to the state and western churches in a reunited Germany has proved intensely problematic, compromising an understanding of church as an independent 'prophetic' witness on the margins of a largely secularized society. In particular, the church has been confronted with the extent of its compromises with the state under communism (collaboration with the secret police, the *Stasi* or **Staatssicherheitdienst**), and the extent of its financial dependence on the western churches.

Thus the opening of their national frontiers to wider regional and global forces has not proved an entirely comfortable experience for Christians in either Poland or the former East Germany, raising questions about the traditional models of church–state–society relations they had adopted and adapted for their own contexts.

In this chapter we are concerned to find out what these two cases can tell us about the relationship between religion and social change in the contemporary world. Two strands will run through our account of Poland and Germany: first, the relationships between religion, state and society, and second, Christian understanding of these relationships (because Christianity is the major religious tradition in these societies). We begin with a brief examination of the relationships between religion, state and society in the formative period of Christianity, because this informs and provides models for later Christian thinking and action. We then outline the role of religion in the history of Poland and East Germany leading up to the 'Great Transformation' of 1989–90, and finally examine in more detail the challenges of the post-communist period.

Church and state in early Christianity

> You know that those who are supposed to rule over the Gentiles [non-Jews] lord it over them, and their great men exercise authority over them. But it shall not be so among you; but whoever would be great among you must be your servant, and whoever would be first must be slave of all.
>
> (Mark 10:42–4, **RSV**, 1973)

> Let every person be subject to the governing authorities. For there is no authority except from God, and those that exist have been instituted by God.
>
> (Romans 13:1, RSV, 1973)

These two passages suggest tensions within the New Testament concerning attitudes to ruling authorities. The first, attributed to Jesus in Mark's gospel, implies some criticism of the Roman style of rule, and reflects the experience of living in an occupied territory. The second, from the highly influential early convert to Christianity Paul, attributes divine legitimacy to the ruling authorities, and encourages obedience to them.

However, both need to put into context: both men were, according to Christian tradition, executed by the Roman authorities, and Paul in particular was continually harassed by them, as both his letters and the record of his journeys in the Acts of the Apostles indicate. Admonition to obedience then, does not imply approval, any more than criticism of style implies rebellion. None the less, the fact remains that Romans 13:1 has become a pretext through history to provide legitimacy for theories of the state to permit anything that a ruling authority does or commands its subjects to do, an understanding which was to prove particularly influential in mainstream German

Protestant theology, at least until controversies leading up to and during World War II (Krusche, 1994, p.324). In reaction, later German theologians have turned to the counter-tradition associated with Jesus' statement: 'it shall not be so among you', and this second tradition proved influential in the peace movement in both parts of the divided Germany (see for example Wengst, 1987).

Jesus' words can be related to the context of the early Christian movement. Christianity began in Judea, a province of the Roman Empire. Jesus and his first followers were Jewish, and Christianity first emerged as a movement within Judaism, but had become a clearly separate group by the end of the first century CE. One reason for this was the failed Jewish rebellion against Rome (66–70 CE), which led to the destruction of Jerusalem and the dispersion of the Jewish people. Another reason for the split with Judaism was that as Christianity spread along the trade routes of the Roman Empire, it made converts from other religious groups, so that these soon began to outnumber Jewish followers. Tensions over the Jewish identity of early followers are already found in Paul's letters (e.g. Corinthians 1:8-9; Galatians 5), probably written between 45 and 60 CE, the earliest documents in the New Testament. None the less, the split with Judaism did not improve the early Christian movement's standing with the authorities, and Christians experienced intermittent persecution over the next two hundred and fifty years.

Thus emerging from a minority religion (Judaism) within the Roman Empire has made Christianity's relationship to state power problematic from the beginning. As the German New Testament scholar Klaus Wengst comments – as a supporter of the West German peace movement during the 'Cold War' – with regard to Mark 10:42–4:

> Both a sober and critical view is taken of the central feature of the Pax Romana ['Peace of Rome'], the way in which rule is exercised... Here there is no mincing of words, but it is clearly stated that the existing 'order of peace' is based on the oppressive rule of force... The alternative which Jesus puts forward shows that he is not resigned... peace based on an oppressive force is not what Jesus wants.
>
> (Wengst, 1987, pp.56–7)

None the less, private criticism shared with his disciples does not imply public confrontation, and Jesus appears to have tried to avoid confrontation with the Roman authorities (Matthew 22:21). However, a central theme in Jesus' teaching, the concept of the kingdom of God/heaven (in Mark and Luke/Matthew respectively) may also be seen as presenting an implicit challenge to the ruling authorities. Scholars have argued extensively about the meaning of the phrase, but the most widely shared view at present is that it refers to some kind of alternative order – God's rule – and is thus at least implicitly threatening to political authorities. Furthermore, while the present dimension of this alternative order is present in ways which may not directly confront the Roman authorities – in changed relationships, in healings, etc. – Jesus also envisaged a future in which the kingdom would break into the present order in a more forceful way.

Thus the idea of 'the kingdom' presented, at least at an implicit level, a two-fold challenge to the Roman authorities – as an alternative system of values and social practices in the present, against which secular authorities could be judged lacking, and as a threat for the future. In this way the question mark over the loyalty of Christian subjects which later led to Christian persecution can be seen as having its origins in the teaching of Jesus. Certainly the crucifixion of Jesus suggests he was perceived as a threat by the Roman authorities (Sanders, 1985). However, as we shall see below, on the basis of Jesus' sayings such as 'my kingdom is not of this world' (John 18: 36), Luther constructed a doctrine of **'two kingdoms'** that made a clear distinction between spiritual and temporal spheres, strongly legitimizing secular authorities in the latter sphere.

The Romans passage has, as already stated, been used to legitimate governing authorities regardless of their behaviour. The context is one in which Paul is admonishing Christians to non-retaliatory behaviour, much in the style of Jesus: 'Bless those who persecute you... never avenge yourselves, but leave it to the wrath of God... if your enemy is hungry, feed him' (Romans 12:14–21; parallels in Matthew 5:44 and Luke 6:27–8). The main intention then is not to expound a theory of the state. Rather, obedience to the ruling authorities may be a way to avoid persecution as far as possible, as may the other recommendations Paul makes. Furthermore, such behaviour clearly places limits on responses to the authorities by Christians. Thus, some commentators argue, the justification of state power should always be considered in the context of the primary aim of ensuring the viability of Christian life. This implies that, ultimately, the Christian cannot simply go along with whatever the state does: the Christian life might come before life itself, and did so for Paul. None the less, as Wengst argues, by stating that:

> ... those in authority are virtually appointed by God to their function... without caveat, qualification and dialectic, he [Paul] at least exposes himself to the danger of providing theological legitimation for *de facto*

> power no matter how it may have come into being and how it may be used.
>
> (Wengst, 1987, pp.83–4)

However, such an unqualified legitimization of state power is in tension with other Pauline passages. For example, I Thessalonians 5:3–4 describes those who see the present order as one of 'peace and security' as 'in darkness', unaware of the imminence of the other order – here Paul's **apocalyptic**[2] imagery is strongly reminiscent of Jesus'. Criticism of the state which preaches 'peace and security' is clearly implied.

It is important to note from this discussion that the proper relationship between governing authorities and the Christian community is a disputed one within the New Testament, enabling subsequent generations to draw different conclusions. Little support for outright rebellion is given, but criticism of the authorities is implied in the Christian vision of an order based on different values. Christianity continued to grow within the Roman Empire, suffering intermittent persecution during the first three centuries of its existence; that is, until the Emperor Constantine converted to and legalized Christianity early in the fourth century, paving the way for Christianity to become the official religion of the Empire.

Both of the texts we have examined reflect a situation in which Christians were relatively powerless; however, this was to change with the conversion of Constantine. The relationship between the earthly kingdom and the heavenly kingdom had to be worked out in a new way, and not surprisingly it was texts that are more supportive of ruling authorities – such as Romans 13:1 – that came to be favoured over more ambivalent or potentially subversive texts such as Mark 10:42–4. None the less, the rejection of state authority has also surfaced at times in Christian history, as we shall see. Between the two paths of co-option and confrontation, Christian churches in majority situations have faced the task of negotiating some kind of critical solidarity with the state and with modern development of national identity.

The main purpose in this chapter is to examine the role that the Christian religion has come to play in east central Europe under the particular circumstances of the late twentieth century. In fact, in contrast to the Islamic case in Egypt and elsewhere (Herbert, 2001 and Chapter 2 below), arguments over the meaning of sacred texts have had little direct impact on political practice in either Poland or eastern Germany during this period. However, the New Testament is

---

[2] Referring to God's intervention at the end of the world.

one of the main sources of political theology in all Christian traditions, and political theology has influenced political behaviour in both these countries. Thus arguments in political theology did effect the role of the churches in Germany in World War II, and have continued to have an influence in the communist and now the post-communist periods. In particular, there are strong parallels between the task of the church in helping society to come to terms with the past after the World War II and the communist period (*Vergangenheitbewältigung* – 'mastery of the past').

In Poland, one could argue that it is the pattern of identification of God with the chosen nation Israel in the Hebrew scriptures (Old Testament) that is most significant for shaping the relationship between church and nation. But other developments in political theology have also influenced events in Poland – in particular, the Second Vatican Council (1963–5) which led the Catholic church into a constructive engagement with modernity, and importantly the adoption of the discourses of human rights and democracy. But scripture and political theology alone are not enough to make sense of contemporary developments in church–society–state relations in Poland and eastern Germany: for this, we must look also at key developments in their histories.

Religion, state and nation in Poland and Germany to 1989

Poland to 1989

> Hail, O Christ, Thou Lord of Men!
> Poland in Thy Footsteps treading
> Like Thee suffers, at Thy bidding
> Like Thee, too, shall rise again
>
> (Nineteenth-century Polish hymn; quoted in Davies, 1996, p.826)

In Poland, religion, nation and state have been closely intertwined from the foundation of the Polish nation – the baptism of Prince Miesko the First in 966 is traditionally regarded as the beginning of both Polish statehood and Polish Christianity. The hymn above shows the identification of the Polish nation with the suffering Christ, but even stronger is the association of the fortunes of the Polish nation with the Virgin Mary, especially in the form of the Black Madonna of Częstochowa:

> The title 'Queen of the Nation' bestowed on Our Lady of Częstochowa already in the second half of the fourteenth century, reflects her

position as the Patroness and defender of Polish sovereignty, national identity and culture.

(Kubik, 1994, p.110)

Legend holds that the icon was painted by the apostle St Luke, but what is well documented is that the painting was given as a gift to the monastery at Jasna Gora ('bright mountain') at Częstochowa shortly after its foundation in 1382. The symbolic identification of the Black Madonna with the Polish nation was later to prove crucial in Polish resistance to Swedish imperialism in the seventeenth century, in nationalist mobilization in the nineteenth century, and in the PCC's symbolic confrontations with the communist authorities from the mid-1950s. Arguably too, it was the development of confrontation on this symbolic ground which contributed to the success of the Solidarity movement in the 1980s (Figure 1.1).

Figure 1.1 Preaching in front of the Black Madonna at Częstochowa. Bruno Barbey/Magnum.

Poland was not greatly affected by the upheavals of the Reformation that convulsed the neighbouring German-speaking lands in the sixteenth century, nor by the wars of religion that followed in the seventeenth, and only to a limited extent by the eighteenth-century Enlightenment. Poland's relative isolation from these developments, in particular the idea of church–state separation and political toleration of religious difference as the founding principles of liberalism, is significant for the development of church–state relations in the twentieth century.

However, Polish Catholicism was not entirely isolated from the rest of the Catholic world, nor indeed from the influence of the Vatican. In the theory of church–state relations, late sixteenth-century Catholic thinkers developed the medieval idea that legitimacy of rulers depends on their service to the common good of the people into the view that subjects had the right to resist rulers who did not serve the common good (De Gruchy, 1995, p.81). This has led to them being described as 'the main founders of modern constitutionalist and even democratic thought' (Skinner, 1978, vol.2, p.174). For example, in *De Rege et Regis Institutione* (1599) the Spanish Jesuit Juan de Mariana wrote that if princes oppress the people:

> Their position is such that they can be killed not only justly but with praise and glory.
>
> (quoted in De Gruchy, 1995, p.81, n.127)

Such an argument was soon to find its implementation in Poland, for by the seventeenth century Poland's power had begun to decline, so that in 1655 the Swedish army was able to break a truce with Poland and virtually destroyed the Polish army. The turning point in the Swedish campaign illustrates the connection between the Black Madonna and the Polish nation. Province after province was forced to surrender, until, unexpectedly, the monastery at Jasna Gora, housing the Black Madonna, held out for forty days. Then:

> Polish soldiers carrying the Holy Icon into battle forced the Swedes to retreat for the first time during the war. After this victory, King Jan Kazimerz made a solemn vow. 'In the name of the whole nation he proclaimed that the Blessed Virgin should henceforth be venerated as "Queen of the Crown of Poland". The Polish nation would never be false to that promise. The cult of Our Lady remained its supreme consolation through epochs of the anguish that surpassed that of 1655.'
>
> (Halecki, 1956, p.159)

That anguish included the disappearance of the Polish state from the political map between 1772 and 1918: Poland was partitioned three times between 1772 and 1795, carved up between the Russian and Austrian Empires, and the Prussian state. Again in nineteenth-century nationalism, the Black Madonna proved an important symbolic inspiration, described by the partitioning powers as the 'Main Revolutionary', because of its mobilizing power to inspire nationalist uprisings (Kubik, 1994, p.109).

Poland's nationalist movement, however, faced a long and largely unsuccessful struggle:

> The Polish national movement had the longest pedigree, the best credentials, the greatest determination, the worst press, and the least success. It traced its origins to the anti-Russian confederations of the eighteenth century; and it bred an armed uprising in every generation between the Partitions and the Second World War – in 1733, 1768, 1794, 1830, 1848, 1863, 1905, 1919, 1944. It nourished a precocious brand of nationalism which was already maturing in Napoleonic times. At heart this had little to do with economic rationale, everything with the will to preserve culture, identity, and honour.
>
> (Davies, 1996, p.826)

Poland finally secured independence in the Treaty of Versailles (1918) which concluded World War I. But it was not until the Poles had defeated the Soviet Red Army in 1920 that this independence was secure. However, Polish independence was to last fewer than 20 years: in 1939 the Germans under Hitler invaded, precipitating British entry into what became World War II. The German occupation was to last six years, during which time most of Poland's three million strong Jewish population was killed.[3] Poland also suffered the highest rate of civilian casualties (some 18 per cent) of any country in World War II. Liberation in 1945 was not followed by national independence because Poland fell under the Soviet sphere of influence. Soviet-supported members of the Communist Party took power, and their successors were to remain in control until 1989. Stalin also redrew Poland's borders, extending them approximately 100 km west into Germany, and took Polish territory in Belorussia in the east. The result, together with the loss of the Jewish population, was to create an almost ethnically and religiously homogeneous Poland for the first time in history – 95 per cent of Poles were Roman Catholics, with small minorities of Russian Orthodox, Greek Catholics and Muslims in the east, and a remnant of Jews in the major urban centres. It is in this context that post-war developments in Poland need to be understood.

---

[3] After the Holocaust, Poland's Jewish population was reduced from some three million (Davies, 1996, p.1023) to a few hundred thousand, and was reduced further to a few thousand (mostly by Jews leaving) by a series of pogroms ending in 1968.

In spite of an agreement between the Polish episcopate and the government in 1950, the 1950s were perhaps the toughest period for the Catholic church under communism. There were widespread arrests of clergy between 1951 and 1953, among them the Polish Primate Cardinal Wyszynski (Ramet, 1995, p.183; Kubik, 1994, p.110). The government also undertook other measures to try to control or, if not, divide the church. As in other communist countries, such as Yugoslavia (Ramet, 1999, pp.87–9), alternative 'patriotic priests'' associations were set up with an aim to divide loyalties; there were direct appeals to the Vatican above the heads of Polish leaders, and attempts were made to interfere with church appointments (Ramet, 1995, p.183; Gilarek, 1997, p.114). The church responded in several ways. One was to increase control over its own clergy:

> Wyszynski drew two complementary lessons from this experience: the chaos produced by intra-institutional freedom can produce weakness and uncertainty, leaving the institution vulnerable to assault; and the vigorous assertion of authority builds power and institutional strength.
>
> (Ramet, 1995, p.184)

Another was to mobilize church support among the people, a strategy which led the church into conflict with the state not on a directly political ground – which probably would have led to their immediate repression – but over the symbolic representation of the nation. While still interned (1953–6), Wyszynski hatched plans for the 'Great Novena': a decade of celebrations leading to the dual millennium of Polish statehood and conversion to Christianity in 1966. The nation was to renew the vow of King Jan Kazimerz to the 'Mother of God, Queen of Poland'. Thus a million pilgrims attended the opening mass on 26 August 1956, with the imprisoned Wyszynski standing before his copy of the Madonna and reciting the vow at the same time as Bishop Klepacz led the pilgrims. As Kubik comments:

> It was this spectacular ceremony that defined the cultural frame of the conflict between the Church and the state for decades to come.
>
> (Kubik, 1994, p.111)

This cultural frame was important because it gave symbolic structure to the protests which were developing in the country. In June, protesters from a factory in Poznan had gone to Warsaw to demonstrate over working conditions: a party official was sent to Poznan, but once there refused to investigate conditions; the infuriated workers marched to the city centre to express their views. This led to three days of street fighting and confrontations with the authorities in which hundreds died. To the initial cries of 'bread' the protesters added demands for freedom and the release of

Wyszynski (Osa, 1997, p.350). The celebrations for the Great Novena enabled the development of a religious nationalism independent of political parties, fuelled by Wyszynski's synthesis of 'Polish legends, folklore, and peasant mysticism with the intellectual products of the Polish Romantic poets, and elements of Catholic theology to create a Mariological vision of the nation and Polish history' (ibid., p.353). One important aspect of the Great Novena was the idea that a copy of Black Madonna should tour all parishes. As a result, between 1957 and 1980 (a second Novena took place from 1966 to 1980), the Madonna was seen by virtually all Polish Catholics, with the effect that:

> These direct encounters with the Black Madonna strengthened social integration on both local and national levels and rejuvenated the religiosity of Poles: countless incidents of conversion were reported from all over the country; there were massive returns to the sacramental life.
>
> (Kubik, 1994, p.112)

The state's celebration of a millennium of Polish statehood, which portrayed the communist system as the 'crown of the road traversed by the Polish Nation through history towards freedom and progress' (Gomulka, the communist leader, 1966; quoted in Kubik, 1994, p.114) could not compete. The clash of church and state celebrations at Gniezno on 15 April 1966 established a pattern to be repeated across the country as people broke through police barriers to escape from the secular celebrations to attend the sacred ones. (ibid., p.115). The widespread dissemination through the Novena of this cultural frame meant that:

> The initial public presentation of Solidarity in the Gdansk shipyards in August 1980 – with its crosses, flowers, religious pictures, Masses – [was] instantly comprehensible to a mass public. Such a religious/ historical format both enhanced Solidarity's potential for mass mobilization, and constrained it in its move toward increasingly instrumental, and away from expressive, ends.
>
> (Osa, 1997, p.352 (see Figure 1.2 and Colour Plate 3))

Furthermore, the church provided more than a language of protest capable of uniting otherwise disparate groups in Polish society: it also mobilized social networks through which collective action became possible. Thus the Great Novena stimulated 'the expansion of parish social networks that integrated urban workers and intellectuals, and rural factory workers and farmers, into moral communities' (ibid., p.361).

Figure 1.2 Gdansk 1980. A priest dispenses communion to striking shipyard workers. Peter Marlow/Magnum.

From the late 1960s and through the 1970s the church complemented these networks by expanding its other activities in civil society. From an international perspective, this can be seen as part of the revitalization of the church – and particularly the greater value placed on secular activities and the advocacy of human rights, espoused by the Second Vatican Council (1963–5). This Council, the first held by the church for nearly a century, marked a watershed in Catholic thinking. In particular, the Council endorsed the sacred significance of secular activity in a new way, giving rise to new forms of political activism and of political and liberation theology (Milbank, 1990, pp.206–7), and paving the way for the church to play a new role as global advocate of human rights (Casanova, 1994, p.72). In Poland, in particular, human rights, with their implicit invocation of international support, were to become a useful tool with which to pressurize the communist regime during the 1970s and 1980s.

The Polish church's increased activity in civil society from the mid 1960s included the development of clubs and student centres for the Catholic intelligentsia, and the expansion of the Catholic press, with *Tygodnik Poweszechny* ('Weekly Public') providing a significant dissenting voice. For example, during the anti-Jewish campaign of 1968 it continued to publish the work of Jewish authors, and when the Jewish poet Antoni Slonimski was blacklisted for criticizing official anti-semitism, the editor Jerzy Turowicz invited him to join the staff (Ramet, 1995, p.181). More money was put into church building, and a network of social services, including day-care facilities for children and pharmacies, were developed. More broadly, a range of cultural activities which grew into an 'alternative culture' developed: art exhibitions, poetry readings and theatre groups were sponsored throughout Poland.

The church developed high-level contacts with two of the associations which came together in 1980 to form the Solidarity trade union: the developing workers' groups and The Workers' Defence Committee (KOR) – actually a group of disaffected left-wing intellectuals. The succession of a Polish pope (John Paul II) in 1978 was also a considerable stimulus to resistance, and added international pressure. The Pope's visit in 1979 (see Colour Plate 1) mobilized the myth of St Stanislaw similar to the way that the Great Novena had mobilized traditions surrounding the Black Madonna. Stanislaw, Bishop of Krakow, was slain by King Boleslaw the Bold in 1079, and had become a symbol of state persecution of the church. In 1978, Cardinal Wyszynski used this legend to address a contemporary theme:

> The conflict between Boleslaw and Stanislaw revolved around the issues of justice and human rights. It proves that already nine hundred years ago the Church struggled for human rights and already nine hundred years ago there was in Poland a man of the Church who fought for human rights.
>
> (*Tygodnik Poweszechny*, 21 May 1978; quoted in Kubik, 1994, p.133)

Figure 1.3 The Pope in Poland: Papal Mass, 1979. Bruno Barbey/Magnum.

Up to three million people celebrated the final mass led by the Pope during his first visit in 1979 (Figure 1.3). Through this generation of national solidarity, backed up by organizational and networking support, the church provided much of the infrastructure, symbolism and vocabulary for the Solidarity movement that shook the communist regime in 1980–1, and survived through the years of martial law to negotiate its downfall in 1989. Thus it was that:

> During the memorable strike of 1980, the first thing the Gdansk workers did was to affix a cross, an image of the Virgin Mary, and a portrait of John Paul II to the gates of the shipyards. They became the symbols of victory.
>
> (Wałęsa, 1982, p.10)

During the 1980s the Catholic church continued its expansion into civil society. After the 1981 suppression of Solidarity, it greatly expanded its role in education, offering range of courses across the curriculum. For example, at the Institute of Christian culture in Lubochnia, the adult education provision included lectures on 'Non-communist resistance in World War II' and 'Citizen's Protection under the Law' (Ramet, 1995, pp.180–1). The church also expanded its operation in the welfare sector, with the Rural Pastoral Communities Association and Pastoral Service to Workers Association established to cater to the needs of rural and urban workers. The church continued its close connections with the underground Solidarity movement, while at the other end of the spectrum the Pope maintained the pressure with public statements and a visit. An economic crisis coincided with the political one for the communist government. In February–April 1989, round-table talks between the government and Solidarity led to the latter's legalization and that of other groups in the 'parallel society'.[4] Changes in the law on property and religion were to follow (Ramet, 1995, p.118). Finally:

> In August Poland's bewildered communists invited Solidarity to form a government under their own continuing... state presidency. Tadeusz Mazowiecki, a devout Catholic, was accepted as premier ... The Soviet bloc was no longer a bloc.
>
> (Davies, 1996, p.1123)

Shortly we shall consider how the PCC has coped with the challenges that the post-communist period has brought. First, let us look at the churches' role in the process that brought Germany to a similar point.

---

[4] The phrase 'parallel society' refers to the development of networks, organizations and cultural phenomena (ranging from informal gatherings to the underground press to church welfare organizations) that developed in parallel to official (state sanctioned) society from the 1970s.

Germany to 1989

Origins to 1933

The German-speaking tribes converted to Christianity at the end of the eighth and the beginning of the ninth century (Davies, 1996, pp.281–2). The first distinctive development in terms of church–state–society relations, especially in the northern merchant cities of the Hanseatic League, is the late medieval establishment of an early and long-running (fifteenth to eighteenth-century) example of self government under a charter or compact. This strong tradition of local independence and devolved government also influenced the princes and monarchs who ruled the rest of Germany (Everett, 1997, p.29), and this spirit of local autonomy played a part in the resentment of and resistance to papal authority crucial to the sixteenth-century Reformation. The 'radical Reformation' of the fifteenth and early sixteenth century which preceded it also drew on this tradition, but to an extent that the mainstream reformers, especially Martin Luther (1483–1546), would not tolerate. The various **anabaptist** movements took Jesus' saying in Mark 10:42–5[5] very seriously, and attempted to establish their own autonomous communities of believers (De Gruchy 1995 pp.85–7).

Less radical than the anabaptists in his attitude to secular authority, but more influential in the long term, the French reformer John Calvin (1509–64) argued that in certain circumstances subjects had the right to overthrow unjust rulers, an argument taken further by later Calvinists, such as Oliver Cromwell, Parliamentarian leader in the English Civil War (1649–60) (De Gruchy, 1995, p.78). However, while Calvinist theology has had some influence in Germany, the more dominant influence has been that of Luther. Luther sought to restore the direct link between believers and God which he felt had been corrupted and distorted by the intermediary role the Catholic church had adopted for itself. Under the principle of *sola scriptura* ('only scripture') he sought to make the Christian scriptures the sole arbiter in religious matters, and encouraged people to read the scriptures in their own language and interpret them for themselves.

However, Luther did not extend such autonomy to the political sphere – as already indicated, he rejected the radical readings of the anabaptists, and in 1525 supported the princes in the brutal crushing of the Peasant's Revolt (Davies, 1996, p.485). He developed the doctrine of the 'two kingdoms', in which a clear distinction is made between spiritual and temporal matters, with the church responsible

---

[5] Arguing that relationships amongst Jesus' followers should not follow the pattern of domination found in Roman society.

for the former, the governing authorities the latter. As Everett comments, for Luther:

> Christian freedom was to be focussed on the inner freedom of the individual believer. To protect spiritual freedom from democratic excess as well as Roman intervention, church leaders after Luther sought external governance by princes and monarchs... Like the parental God who seeks to nurture and protect the inner spirit, the prince would care for the church's [that is the antipapal Evangelical church's] external form.
>
> (Everett, 1997, p.30)

This system was consolidated in the Treaty of Westphalia (1648) which concluded the Thirty Years War, under the principle of *cuius regio, eius religio*: the religion of the ruler is to be the religion of the people under his or her jurisdiction. The churches remained under the care of the princes until the late nineteenth century, when most became state churches, part of the emerging state bureaucracy.

A somewhat different relationship between churches and state emerged after World War I (1914–18) in the new German constitution of 1919. This declared a formal separation of church and state (Article 37), but continued the system of church taxes for those churches recognized as public corporations – the EKD and the Catholic church. The church tax system enabled these churches to raise income from their members through the state's tax system. Public corporation status also carried a number of other privileges: the right to run hospitals and social services, to run religious education in government schools, and later to have representatives on the boards of radio and television stations (Everett, 1997, p.32). In contrast, other churches were merely private associations with legal standing but no special privileges. This church tax system has continued in West Germany to the present, but was stopped in the East under the communists. Its reintroduction was to become a major point of contention in post-reunification East Germany.

The German churches and the Third Reich (1933–45)

> We repudiate the false teaching that there are areas of our life in which we do not belong to Jesus Christ but to another Lord.
> (Second thesis of the **Barmen Declaration** (1934), foundation document of the Confessing church; quoted in Krusche, 1994, p.323)

> As Christians, expressing thanks to God, we respect every state structure and authority even when they are a distortion... and therefore, as believing Christians, we thank God our Lord that he

has given the Führer to our people in their need as a 'pious and faithful ruler' (Luther).

(Lutheran theologians Werner Elert and Paul Althaus in response to the
Barmen Declaration (1934), ibid.)

Whoever raises race or nation or state... or the agents of state authority or other values of human communal life... to the highest norm of all, taking it out of the merely temporal scale of things to turn it into a religious value, making it the object of idolatry, inverts and adulterates the God-created and divinely ordained scheme of things.

(Pope Pius XII (1937); quoted in Ramet, 2000, pp.115–6)

The Nazification of German society posed a major challenge to all the churches, as the Nazis sought to extend their influence into all areas of life. In the sphere of religion one example was the Nazi sponsored German Christian movement, which used 'neo-pagan trappings and racist ideology' (ibid., p.115). The Nazis also acted against traditional Christian institutions, for example, imprisoning Catholic priests and closing Catholic schools. The above quotations indicate something of the diversity of Christian responses to these events. Such responses were complex both at the level of theology and practice, and the brief account here will focus only on aspects that were to resurface in more recent controversies.

In particular, amongst Protestants we see another stage in the development of trajectories in church–state relations in the German tradition stemming from the Reformation. In the sixteenth century anabaptists at one extreme had rejected the authority of the state entirely, Lutherans at the other extreme strongly legitimized it, especially through the doctrine of the 'two kingdoms'. While no major groups in Germany in 1933–45 rejected the legitimacy of the state wholesale,[6] continuities can be seen between the some theologies that developed in the Confessing church that broke way from the mainstream EKD in 1934 in protest at the Nazi regime, and the peace movements of 1978–89 that eventually challenged the legitimacy of the communist state of the GDR. The idea of society, as distinct from both church and state, as a category of theological importance can also be seen in currents developing from the Confessing church; such an idea becomes of particular importance in an increasingly secularized, plural German society in the post-communist period. However, during the Nazi period the majority of the EKD continued to support the state, a position which was also to have repercussions in the post-communist period.

---

[6] The Mennonite *Brüderhof*, descendants of the anabaptists, left Germany for Robertsbridge in Sussex in 1933.

Three basic categories of response to these challenges can be discerned. First, the majority of the EKD under Reichsbischof Ludwig Müller accepted the Nazi innovations, Müller describing National Socialism in 1934 as 'a healthy corrective' that 'corresponds with our history' (ibid., p.117). This proved unacceptable to another wing of the EKD, led by Martin Niemöller and including the influential theologians Karl Barth (1886–1968) and Dietrich Bonhoeffer (1906–45). They refused Müller's line, and broke away to form the Confessing church (*Bekennenden Kirche*), issuing the Barmen Declaration (1934) stating their opposition to Nazism. Barth was particularly influential in the wording of the Barmen Declaration. He had been a major force in German Protestant theology since World War I, when his experience as an army chaplain had turned him against religion that uncritically supports nationalism, and led him to insist on the sovereignty of the Word of God over and against any secular ideology, and on the independence of the church from the state to safeguard its role as mediator of that Word.

In some ways, the Confessing church's rejection of Nazism resembles the Catholic position, as the first and third quotations above illustrate. The fundamental ground for rejecting Nazism in both cases is that Nazism is idolatrous: it sets up nation and party in place of God. Both begin from a position which is basically affirmative of state authority. However, when the state begins to interfere with core 'mission interests' of the church – freedom of worship, religious education, the churches' authority over their clergy – the church begins to resist. Thus the Barthian approach within the Confessing church and the Catholic approach provide a second kind of response to Nazism.

However, some in the Confessing church represented a third response arguing that resistance to a phenomenon like Nazism ought to begin before the churches' core interests are threatened. Bonhoeffer, for example, argued that it is not good enough for the church to be independent of the state, for the church also needs to be actively involved in dialogue with other groups in society:

> whilst the story of the German Church struggle of the 1930s is in many ways a very vivid illustration of the strengths of Barthian confessional intransigence, it can also be seen in another light, as no less a dramatic illustration of its major weakness. For the question of theological method is, very largely, a question of *with whom* one chooses to be in dialogue, and on what terms. The Barthian approach dictates that the theologian is chiefly in dialogue with his or her fellow church members, and only secondarily, or incidentally with any part of the outside world... One is far more likely to have some sentiment of

solidarity with people with whom one is already engaged in dialogue, as fellow citizens and equals.

(Shanks, 1995, pp.82–4)

Such an approach shapes political priorities. Barth stressed church independence – but the first and main victims of Nazism were not Christians but Jews, and then communists. The persecution of the Jews only produced strong resistance from the churches when the Nazis prohibited the ordination of clergy of Jewish ancestry: in other words, only when the churches' independence from the state was affected. In other words, because the primary reference of the Confessing church under the influence of Barth's theology was to its 'mission' interests, like the Catholic church it did not act until these were threatened.

Bonhoeffer took a rather different approach. He argued against the use of religion as an excuse to evade the responsibilities of faith by claiming that the church plays by different rules to any secular organization – and thus avoids being judged like any other political actor. Instead, Bonhoeffer argues for:

> a direct correlation of theological truth with the believing community's *demonstrable* capacity to resist the sort of evil represented by the Third Reich.

(ibid., p.85)

Hence his involvement in the 1944 plot to kill Hitler, and his subsequent execution on the gallows at Flossenburg. Such a position arises because Bonhoeffer, unlike Barth, places solidarity with other groups in society first, no longer subordinate to church loyalty. What is significant about it for our purposes is that it theorizes society beyond church and state in a positive way, a particularly important concern in an increasingly secular Germany (enforced in the East, evolving in the West), and also in plural, post-communist Poland. In some ways, it parallels the shift we have observed in Catholic thinking initiated by the Second Vatican Council, which placed a new value on secular activities and thus led to new political activism and theologies, and the advocacy of human rights. Like those Catholic developments, however, it also carries the risk that the church loses sight of its mission in the process of political engagement.

Allied occupation and the communist period (1945–89)

In the aftermath of the war, during the allied occupation (1945–9) the Catholic and Evangelical churches took different paths on the issue of responsibility for atrocities committed by the Third Reich. It was to be decades before there was a significant change in the Vatican's

position. The Catholic line was to deny its tendency to accommodate
National Socialism by stressing the positive aspects of its resistance to
it (Ramet, 2000, p.119). The Evangelical Church, its mainstream
accommodationist leadership disgraced, and unwilling to be
compromised again, took a more radical line, drawing up what
came to be called the 'Stuttgart confession of guilt' in October 1945,
and which marked the beginning of era of 'political protestantism'.
Part of the text ran:

> We accuse ourselves of not having been more courageous, of not
> having prayed more sincerely, of not having believed more joyously,
> of not having loved more burningly.
>
> (Stern, 1992, p.33; translated in Ramet, 2000, p.120)

While, as Ramet comments, this may seem 'tepid' by today's
standards, it was too much for many at the time, leading to calls for
the church to keep out of politics. However, some, such as Niemoller,
went further, telling a student gathering in 1946 that 'We Christians
must accept and recognize our guilt', and calling for German
Christians to come to terms with the reality of six million Jews
murdered, responsibility for which cannot simply be placed entirely
on a few leaders (Ramet, 2000, p.120). As such it created an important
precedent for the EKD in the period since World War II, when it has
attempted to act as the conscience of the nation both under
communist rule and in the post-communist period.

In 1949, the separation of the West's and the Soviet spheres of
influence led to the creation of two German states: the Federal
Republic of Germany (FDR) in the west, and the German Democratic
Republic (GDR) in the east. After the division, the balance altered
between Protestants and Catholics in each country: numbers of
Protestants and Catholics became roughly equal in West Germany
(46.7 per cent and 43.8 per cent respectively), whereas East Germany
became almost 90 per cent Protestant (De Gruchy, 1995, p.195).
Official separation of church organizations amongst the Evangelical
churches did not occur until 1969, eight years after the construction of
the Berlin Wall (ibid., p.197). However, the churches in East Germany
were increasingly isolated from outside influences, and subject to one
of the most aggressively atheistic regimes in communist Eastern
Europe.

The course of church–state relations between 1949 and 1989 can
be divided into two main phases. Between 1949 and 1978 the
communist government sought to undermine the church and secure
a total monopoly on public life. After 1978, in response to pressure
from secular opposition forces, the state sought a rapprochement
with the church and eased restrictions on it; a liberalization that in fact

gave the churches the opportunity to nurture opposition movements that were eventually to topple the government.

The period from 1950–5, as with Poland, saw some of the most severe persecution, as both communist regimes sought to consolidate their authority: pastors, church workers and students were arrested for alleged subversive activities. Church influence on the youth was targeted, in particular, by a committee under the future communist leader Eric Honecker, set up in 1953 to subvert the church youth movement. Under the constitution, church schools and religious holidays were abolished.

However, already in 1953, the state was beginning to experience opposition from other sources, with the workers' uprising of 17 June. In this context, the regime decided to release its grip on the church a little, releasing many of those imprisoned, and switching instead to a policy of providing communist alternatives to the social functions of the churches. For example, in 1955 the ***Jugendweihe*** ('youth dedication') was introduced as an alternative to Christian confirmation, submission to which was made a pre-requisite for secondary education: by the mid 1980s more than 97 per cent of young people were participating in the rival ritual (Burgess, 1997, p.154, n.28). In 1956, the state stopped collecting the church tax, and with falling membership the church found it increasingly difficult to survive financially. Then in 1958 all religious instruction in school was banned. Relations with the West German church became strained after the latter began to supply chaplains to NATO forces stationed in the FDR.

In 1968 all official relations with the West German church were banned. Isolated, the church responded by gradually accepting the formula of the 'church in socialism' (*Kirche im Sozialismus*) proposed in 1969 by Hans Seigewasser, Secretary for Church Affairs. This formula was to prove a double-edged sword for both the regime and the Evangelical churches. On the one hand, the church risked being perceived to have sold out; on the other, it gained the possibility of some influence and the easing of restrictions. The meaning of the phrase 'church in socialism' was also strongly contested. More conservative forces advocated a total acceptance of the regime, but others, such as Bonhoeffer's former pupil Albrecht Schönherr, understood the phrase as a challenge to active involvement in public life, with the risk of conflict with the authorities. (Moses, 1996, p.242).

By 1978 the churches' gamble appeared to be paying off: new leader Eric Honecker was worried by secular social movements concerning peace and the environment as a potential threat to the state's legitimacy, and offered an easing of restrictions and some privileges (delegates were allowed to travel abroad to ecumenical gatherings; some religious broadcasting was allowed on state television) in return for the church statements of loyalty to the state (Ramet, 2000, p.129). Such international connections enabled the fostering of peace movements on both sides of the 'iron curtain'. The new rapprochement did not, however, prevent the state from introducing pre-military training in schools, which the churches saw as a further step to militarize society.

Such objections need to be seen in the context of the massive state security apparatus established by the **GDR** government, to which we shall return when we consider the issue of church collaboration with the Stasi (secret police). The church continued to lead protest against compulsory military training in schools, which proved a successful rallying point. This proved to be the starting point of a new confidence, as the churches began to take advantage of the relative lifting of restrictions and their relative autonomy in an otherwise police state by allowing alternative groups to meet and to organize on their premises. As Ramet explains:

> Over the succeeding eleven years (from 1978) the Protestant Churches increasingly became active in protest against pre-military training and discrimination against conscientious objectors, in sheltering independent pacifists and environmental groups, and in pressing for a liberalization of restrictions on travel to West Germany. The State Security Service (Stasi) was able to recruit collaborators among clergy involved in the independent pacifist and environmentalist groups, but failed to stop their activity; indeed, the same clergy often worked in both directions – encouraging and supporting critical opposition to the regime while passing information to the Stasi.
>
> (Ramet, 2000, pp.129–30)

In mid 1987 members of the state and church youth movements, joined by various peace groups across the GDR, took part in a march for peace. In November arrests were made after a raid on an environmental library and a rally to commemorate Rosa Luxemburg and Karl Liebnecht (Marxists who had none the less insisted on the necessity of democracy). This led to the first big public demonstration – a four-day vigil on church property at the Zionskirche in Berlin. The authorities were forced to back down, and the prisoners were released. Thus by 1988 the state was beginning to question the wisdom of its 'partnership' with the church, and began another crackdown – but by then it was too late: the GDR began to lose its control. The churches maintained the pressure: three ecumenical councils representing nineteen communions, including the Catholic church, convened in 1988 and in 1989 agreed to and published a

Figure 1.4 2 November 1989, German Democratic Republic. Thousands of people gathered in churches all over the country, such as here in Geras Johannis Church, to pray for peace and to participate in rallies demanding democratic reforms. Popperfoto.

twelve-point manifesto calling for democratic reform and addressing the issues of peace, justice and the integrity of creation (Moses, 1996, p.244).

Revelations of electoral fraud in May 1989 proved that the regime could not be trusted to reform (De Gruchy, 1995, p.202). Again, the churches played a leading role in the final months of the communist regime (Figure 1.4). What became known as the 'Monday demonstrations' began in Leipzig in September 1989 (Colour Plate 4), and soon spread across the GDR (Wollenberger, 1991, p.207). On 24 October 1989 Bishop Gottfied Forck of East Berlin addressed the nation on West German television, demanding the re-establishment of political pluralism in East Germany (Ramet, 2000, p.130). Following the protests in support of liberalization in Tiananmen Square, Beijing, and the Chinese authorities' brutal repression of them in June, Soviet leader Gorbachev told Honecker that Soviet intervention in Eastern Europe could no longer be relied on. On 12 November 1989 East German troops stood by as thousands demolished the Berlin Wall (Colour Plate 5) (Davies, 1996, p.1216). Over the winter of

1989–90 the churches played a critical role in the round-table processes that were set up to mediate the transition to democracy.[7] In the first democratic elections in March 1990, 21 Protestant pastors won seats, testimony to their role in the struggle for democracy (De Gruchy, 1995, pp.203–4).

But what of the future? Below we consider the challenges facing the churches in the former East Germany and Poland since 1989.

The post-communist period

Introduction

After the leading role and high esteem the churches had gained in the overthrow of communism, several factors quickly damaged this standing in both countries, quite different in each case.

In Poland, the church campaigned strongly (and with success) for the introduction of stricter abortion laws and for a favoured status for religious instruction in schools. At the same it failed to come to terms with the considerable social consequences of Poland's economic 'shock therapy' – a very sharp transition to a market economy. Suddenly, queues disappeared and there were goods in the shops – but many people had no money to buy them. Both situations damaged the image of the church, making it seem overly concerned with its 'mission' interests and the regulation of sexual ethics. Yet while most Poles were dedicated to the church, they had also become used to the more liberal abortion laws and widespread availability of contraception under the communist regime. At the same time the church seemed to be ignoring its wider programmatic interests at a time when the people experienced these as pressing.

More broadly, at an institutional level, the role of God's representative of the nation pitted against a hostile atheistic state is not the best preparation for the role of one interest group among others in a plural democracy. The mass of Catholics in Poland has been selective in what they had picked up from the Second Vatican Council – the concern for human rights for example, was less readily extended to minority groups such as the Jews, towards whom widespread anti-semitic attitudes persisted (Ambrosewicz-Jacobs, 1999), in spite of the changes in the church's official teaching (e.g. the papal encyclical Nostra Aetate in the late 1980s), and the work of Catholic intellectuals such as Jerzy Turowicz at *Tygodnik Poweszechny* ('Weekly Public').

---

[7] We shall discuss this further below.

Our account will focus on two issues in particular: first, church–state relations as reflected in the controversy between the church and the ombudsman for citizens' rights over the legality of changes in religious education introduced by the government under church pressure; second, attitudes to ethnic and religious minorities, both at grass-roots and official levels.

In Germany, the causes of the damage to the churches' reputation were different. Reunification followed rapidly after the transition to democracy (1991), and East German Christians, having played such a radical, visible public role in the transition process found themselves part of a church they regarded as conservative. Furthermore, East German Christians soon discovered they had been financially dependent on subsidies from the West German churches, and that the West German churches were not willing to continue these subsidies in the post-reunification situation. The slogan 'peace, justice and the integrity of creation' that had been used by the churches in their support of the peace movement seemed less compelling as many pastors and their congregations faced unemployment. Another severe blow was the opening of the *Stasi* files, which revealed the extent of church collaboration with the regime. And, in addition, the rate of decline in church membership and attendance increased, causing not only a financial crisis but an identity crisis. For Catholics, church tensions have grown between a church keen to reform and a conservative pope who has described German Catholics as 'decadent': a survey in 1994 showed that 68 per cent of Catholics leaving the church did so over the church's stance on sexual ethics (Ramet, 2000, pp.138–9). Of these issues, we shall focus on those arising from reunification and the opening of the Stasi files.

Poland since 1989

As we have seen religion, and in particular the Polish Catholic Church, has played an important role in Polish national identity throughout history, but an unusually important one in political and public life of the nation in the twentieth century. Three factors may account for this historical role – the disappearance of the Polish state, leaving the Catholic church (and the Polish language) as central repositories of national identity throughout the nineteenth century, the continued denial of Polish independence under Soviet domination, and the virtual monopoly (*c.* 95 per cent) of the Roman Catholic Church on Polish religious life since 1945. Surveys from the early 1990s show Polish society to have, alongside Ireland, the highest rate of religious attendance in Europe: 85 per cent of Poles indicated that they attended church at least once a month (Bruce, 1999, p.90). Given this, how has the PCC responded to the new challenges of democracy? How has the institution which helped bring about democracy through its role in mobilizing the Solidarity movement coped with playing the democratic game?

What kind of church–state relations?

> I cannot understand... how anyone could bring the case of religion before the Tribunal – the religion in which the vast majority of Poles believe, which so often helped the nation free itself from oppression throughout its history. In the name of what constitution is religion being taken to court? In the name of that Stalinist constitution with its many amendments? Are we not more in need of an ombudsman capable of telling us that a given action is inconsistent with the will of the nation[,] for in the long run it is that nation and its will which decide what shape the law will take?
>
> (Polish Primate Cardinal Glemp in reaction to the challenge of the Ombudsman for Citizens' Rights to a government directive on religious education, 24 August 1992; quoted in Pawlik, 1995, p.34)

> I am deeply disturbed by the evolution of opinions concerning the relationship between the state and the Catholic church. The church is actually interfering with all three spheres of power: legal, executive and court. I am afraid that we are standing at the gateway of a denominational state... Church officials cannot claim the right to the privilege of putting pressure on the judges of the Constitutional Tribunal, who should announce their verdicts according to their own consciences and legal knowledge.
>
> (Ombudsman for Citizen's Rights Tadeusz Zielinski in response to the PCC's lobby of the Constitutional Tribunal over his challenge to the government directive on religious education, 15 April 1993; quoted in ibid., pp.35–6)

In the early 1990s, a highly public conflict erupted between church officials and the Ombudsman for Citizens' Rights (OCR), a kind of constitutional watchdog originally set up by the communists under pressure from Solidarity in 1987. The disagreements centred on new arrangements for religious education pushed through by the Solidarity government in consultation with the Catholic church. But the controversy raised far broader questions about the nature of Poland's democracy and the role of the Catholic church in post-communist society.

The church had already considerably extended its educational role in society in the 1980s. Indeed, in 1987 there were more than 22,000 places of religious teaching in Poland (Gilarek, 1997, p.128). But religious instruction was not part of the state school curriculum.

Hence the Conference of the Polish Episcopate published rec-ommendations for its reintroduction in May 1990, followed by discussions between church officials and the government. The result, in August, was the issuing of instructions by the Ministry of Education, authorizing the Catholic church and 'other interested churches' to offer religious instruction in state schools. Appointments were to be made by church authorities but financed by the state, and parents were required to enrol their children in order for them to receive this instruction.

From the perspective of the role of the church in the new democracy, several points about these developments are worth noting. First, the kind of curriculum proposed was not the non-confessional approach[8] to a variety of religious traditions which is usual in Britain,[9] but rather a confessional, specifically Catholic (Colour Plate 2), education.[10] Second, although in theory provision is made for non-Catholic confessional education, in practice the small numbers of non-Catholics have made this very difficult to implement. Furthermore, other Christian denominations in Poland, represented by the Ecumenical Council, were not consulted. Third, the instruction was issued without debate in Parliament (the *Sejm*) or in other public forums, but rather on the basis of private discussions between ministers and the Catholic church. Fourth, the arrangements arguably violated church–state separation as specified in the constitution and other legislation. It was on this basis that the instruction was challenged by the OCR, first, unsuccessfully, in 1990, and then, following a further instruction, with some success in 1992–3.

The role of the OCR was first proposed by the Solidarity National Congress in 1981, and introduced by the communist government in July 1987. It was the first official position in the communist world designed to protect human rights and to be independent of

[8] The non-confessional approach aims to provide a neutral or objective description of religious beliefs and practices, so that a person may understand something about religions without being inducted into them.

[9] Although this is complicated in England and Wales by the requirement for a 'mainly Christian' act of daily worship in the 1988 Education Act.

[10] Indeed, more generally in eastern Europe, the concept of non-confessional religious education is treated with great suspicion after years of communist propaganda about religion, so that the introduction of religious education in schools is seen primarily in terms of allowing religious professionals or other representatives into schools to teach children about their particular tradition. However, in higher education, groups such as the Institute for the Study of Religion at Jagiellonian University, Krakow, Poland, pioneered a non-confessional, non-Marxist approach under communism, and in contemporary Bosnia there is interest in developing a non-confessional multi-faith curriculum in schools.

government, and, as such, represented a major concession to the democratic opposition. Although the ombudsman cannot compel the state authorities to follow his or her recommendations, he or she can to make recommendations to the *Sejm* for changes in legislation, can petition the Constitutional Tribunal[11] to review state action, and can initiate proceedings in the courts, up to the Supreme Court if necessary, on behalf of individuals or organizations (Brzezinski, 2000, p.79).

The first two holders of this post (Ewa Letowska, 1987–91 and Tadeusz Zielinski, 1991–5; see Gilarek, 1997, p.129) both became controversial figures in Polish public life, largely because they raised difficult questions about the nature of the new democracy in Poland. In particular, their actions exposed tensions between two models of democracy: a 'majoritarian' model in which the values of the majority (or organizations that claim some special relationship with the nation (e.g. the PCC)) are reflected in law (and hence sometimes imposed on those who disagree), and a 'constitutional' model in which the state attempts to be neutral on questions of value and emphasis is placed on legal procedure. Whereas the first depends on the political will of the majority, the second depends on the legitimacy of the constitution and of law more broadly; and in the Polish case this legitimacy was questionable because the laws and constitution had been drawn up under the communists. In fact, between 1989 and 1997, Poland's constitution was undergoing reform. In 1989 changes were made to enshrine the rule of law and remove references to the Communist Party and the Soviet Union, but the old constitution was otherwise retained largely intact. A 'small constitution' was agreed in 1992, but, slowed by the fragmentation of Solidarity into splinter parties and by several changes of government, a full new constitution was not agreed until 1997 (Brzezinski, 2000, p.123).

It was in this context that in 1990 the ombudsman challenged the Ministry of Education's directive on religious education, on the basis of its incompatibility with the Religious Education Act of 1961 (which ruled on the secular character of state schools), and with two articles in the 1989 constitution relating to freedom of conscience and the separation of church and state (Article 82, Sections 1 and 2) (Gilarek, 1997, p.129; Brzezinski, 2000, p.178). However, her petition was rejected by the Constitutional Tribunal. The 1961 act, passed in the communist period, was considered inconsistent with the directive; but the tribunal's reaction was to petition the *Sejm* to pass a new law to replace it – which it did. Second, it was argued that state support

---

[11] Another concession to democratic pressure in 1982, though initially extremely limited in its powers (Brzezinski, 2000, p.77)

for religious education provided by the church under church appointment did not violate the separation clause, whereas state appointment of teachers of religion (as in Britain, for example) or a state curriculum (also as in Britain at a local level) would. Third, it was argued that the requirement for parents to opt their children into this system did not violate freedom of conscience, because it did not force parents to make a public declaration of faith – they could remain silent and children need not receive this education.

A further government instruction on religious education in April 1992 again produced a challenge from the ombudsman. This instruction introduced ethics as an alternative to religious education and required children (rather than their parents) to volunteer for religious education. Both of these changes was challenged by the ombudsman, as was the inclusion of grades for religious education and ethics on school reports, the payment of priests by the state to teach religious education, and the right of priests to sit on school boards (Gilarek, 1997, p.130). In April 1993, the ombudsman's objections were partially upheld – in particular, the requirement for children to provide written declarations of their willingness to take religious education was declared illegal. For the purposes of understanding the relationship between the Catholic church and Polish society, the principles involved here are more important than the specifics of the legislation, so we shall concentrate on the former, and then consider public reaction to the whole affair.

First, the affair raises questions about the legitimacy of modern legal systems. Modern legal and social theories tend to see law as a kind of autonomous self-regulating sphere, which should operate impartially without political interference. Zielinski's comments quoted at the beginning of this section are consistent with this opinion. On the other hand, in a democracy, law is created through the political process (as Cardinal Glemp argued), so there is always a tension when the logic of a legal system contradicts political will. This tension was particularly strong in this case because the political system under which the law was created is regarded as illegitimate by most Poles, and had been decisively rejected at the ballot box, although it should be noted that the constitution had been significantly modified by this stage.

Second, the affair raises questions about the role of the church in relation to the state and to political processes. For church officials, certain matters are regarded as so fundamentally favourable (e.g. basic religious instruction) or unfavourable (e.g. abortion) to the good functioning of society that their requirement (or prohibition) by law is justified over any considerations of freedom of choice. In fact, the case of religious education is complex in this respect, because the government directives required either parents or children to request the instruction. The requirement in this case was not for everyone to receive Catholic instruction (cathechesis), but rather for it to be available to those who wanted it. The availability of cathechesis is thus viewed by the PCC as a fundamental right. As Cardinal Glemp comments:

> It is quite unacceptable to bring the case of cathechesis, which reveals the redeeming power of the Crucifix, before the Constitutional Tribunal. Intolerance of the Crucifix was characteristic of Hitler's times [and] communism, but today we are free.
>
> (9 April 1993; quoted in Pawlik, 1995, p.35)

In the eyes of the ombudsman, such an insistence compromises the secular character of state schools. Furthermore, there are also examples where the PCC has not been content to allow people to decide for themselves. Abortion, which had been permitted for both 'social and medical' reasons under the communist system, was greatly restricted in 1993 to circumstances when 'a woman's health is in danger, when the fetus is severely deformed, or when the pregnancy results from incest', largely due to pressure from Catholic groups (Brzezinski, 2000, p.181). Furthermore, when Zielinski challenged a move by the governing body of the Polish medical profession to tighten its regulations on abortion beyond the law, restricting permitted circumstances to rape or threat to the woman's life or health alone, he was sharply attacked by the Catholic church (again, Zielinski's petition was rejected). In this context, we may consider Zielinski's claim that Poland was in danger of becoming a 'para-religious' state:

> As opposed to a theocracy, which is a political system where there is near total rule by the clergy... a para-religious state is a political system in which there exists a formal differentiation between church and secular authority and in which the church has no intention to replace civil governments, but claims pretences in the control of all its doings if these have a moral significance, and in moral judgement it is the highest arbiter. In such a state the church authorities demand that law impose under the threat of penalty the observance of all the rules that the Church demands of its faithful, and also that which is a sin in the eyes of the church also be an offence according to state law.
>
> (August 24 1992; quoted in Brzezinski, 2000, p.199)

The evidence suggests that while the PCC was not attempting to make Poland a 'para-religious' state in the sense Zielinski describes here, it did (and continues to) insist that certain matters are beyond compromise, and that, where the political system permits, it will use whatever means are available to ensure that its view of these matters prevails. The actual scope of these matters is relatively limited, but includes the right to transmit religious tradition, freedom of worship and the autonomy of clergy, and insistence on certain restrictions on technologies that effect reproduction (e.g. abortion, genetic engineering). In the case of religious education in Poland, in the eyes of the PCC its close association with the nation further justifies the use of the state system to deliver religious education.

However, it should also be noted that both sides in this controversy behaved as if some things, although very different things in each case, are so important that they are simply non-negotiable. For the ombudsman, these were legal and constitutional process, and the individual rights enshrined within these. Thus certain basic rights (e.g. freedom of conscience) of dissenting minorities must respected, even though the majority may disagree. For Catholic officials, rather different rights, such as the foetus's right to life, are non-negotiable. One may, however, argue that the two approaches are fundamentally different because, for the ombudsman, laws and even the constitution can be changed through the political process, whereas the Church appeals to a sacred principle, beyond the political process. Yet in response it may be argued that any form of liberal democracy rests on some non-negotiable basic rights.

Whatever the ethics of the case, opinion polls indicate that church officials paid a considerable price in popularity for their clashes with the ombudsman. From a highest-ever rating of 87.8 per cent in May 1989, approval of the functioning of the Catholic church slumped to 41 per cent by January 1993, at the height of the controversy with the ombudsman concerning both abortion and religious education, and there is good evidence that the controversy was influential in this result: a slightly later survey (May 1993) showed that 87 per cent of respondents knew something of the ombudsman's work, half of these had heard of the motion to dismiss him, and 80 per cent disagreed with it.

The ombudsman controversy exposed tensions between two forms of legitimization of public activity: that based on the views of the majority or the 'will of the nation' as invoked by the church, and that based on legal principles and citizens rights as invoked by the ombudsman (Pawlik, 1995, p.40). This tension becomes particularly evident in popular and church attitudes to some minority religious and ethnic groups in Polish society, for example, new religious movements (NRMs), Greek Catholics (who are often ethnically Ukrainian) and Jews, and it is to the issue of the treatment of minorities that we now turn.

Religious and ethnic minorities in post-communist Poland

As we noted earlier, the combination of the Holocaust and post-war pogroms resulted in a very small Jewish population in Poland, so that most people have no first-hand contact with Jewish people or Jewish culture. As a result, images of Jews are based on cultural stereotypes, which are predominantly negative:

> In a large part of Polish society, the word 'Jew' (like the word 'Gypsy') is used to label an enemy... . For example, anti-Jewish graffiti in recent years often referred to the 'Jewish-communist system' (*zydo-komuna*) of the Democratic Left Alliance. Or the word is used to insult an enemy such as the members of an opposing football club.
>
> (Ambrosewicz-Jacobs, 1999, p.394)

Such negative stereotypes of Jews have been part of popular culture in Europe for hundreds of years, but in many parts of western Europe such attitudes have been challenged since World War II, so that they are no longer an acceptable part of public discourse. But in central eastern Europe, in spite of its official rhetoric, the communist system seems to have been largely ineffective in tackling prejudice. Furthermore, Ambrosewicz-Jacobs shows that such attitudes are being reproduced amongst teenagers who have grown up under the post-communist system. Her survey was conducted in June 1996 amongst 173 fourteen-year olds in six schools in different areas of Krakow in southern Poland.

Ninety per cent of the sample did not know any Jew, and had never met one: yet 42.9 per cent agreed with the statement that 'Polish culture needs to be protected from Jewish influence', 61.5 per cent did not find anti-Jewish graffiti 'disturbing or shameful' and 22.4 per cent even found it 'amusing' (ibid., pp.392–7). Some 37.8 per cent would 'probably not vote for a Jewish political candidate' (ibid. p.394). On the specific point of 'majority identity' versus 'citizenship rights' highlighted by the ombudsman controversy, 42.9 per cent agreed with the proposition that 'a Jew cannot be a true Pole', and 46.4 per cent agreed that 'the Jews have Israel, so Poland should be for Christians'. However, on a positive note (if rather inconsistently), most students thought it was not good to have a negative opinion about Jews, and agreed with the proposition that Jews are the same as everyone else. Furthermore, 65.5 per cent said schools were not teaching enough about the Jewish people, and 64.6 per cent that 'the whole question of Poland and the Jews is important to them', indicating at least a willingness to learn (ibid. p.392).

Negative attitudes persist in spite of official Catholic teaching on anti-semitism (there was a special letter from the episcopate to be read in all parishes in 1991 condemning anti-semitism), and the leading role of the Catholic intelligentsia in attempting to combat it (including publications and exhibitions promoting knowledge about Jewish culture (ibid. p.395)). The government has also taken action, creating a Presidential Commission on Anti-Semitism. In view of the controversy concerning religious education, it is also interesting to note that students perceived their religious education teachers (i.e. priests, under the arrangements described above) to have unusually positive opinions about Jews (22.6 per cent very positive, 40.5 per cent positive, 17.3 per cent slightly positive), compared with the 2.4 per cent very positive and 18.6 per cent positive attributed by the students to the adult population as a whole (ibid.). However, the curriculum in both religious education and history contains little information about Jews, Jewish history or Judaism (Kapralska, 1995). Ambrosewicz-Jacobs further argues that the opinions of religious education teachers have considerable influence on students (Ambrosewicz-Jacobs, 1999, p.390). Therefore, if the church authorities made more effort to ensure that Catholic teaching since the Second Vatican Council was actually taught in schools, it seems likely that this could have a strong positive effect, alongside curriculum developments in history and literature that reflect the contribution of Jews to Poland's history and culture.

Consider now the case of other minorities, for if the knowledge about Judaism conveyed in the state education system is limited, that of other religious and ethnic minorities is even more so (Kapralska, 1995). Negative attitudes towards non-Catholic NRMs such as Jehovah's Witnesses, **ISKCON**, and the Unification Church are evidenced in surveys, the media and amongst church officials (Urban, 1999, p.173; Doktor, 1999, p.182). There is also increasingly restrictive legal regulation of NRMs in line with developments both elsewhere in post-communist Europe, and in western Europe, under the influence of the Council of Europe and European Community (Doktor, 1999, p.188), as Poland moves further away from an American-style religious free market (albeit one in which the Catholic church is dominant) towards a European-style, state-regulated religious market.

Hann describes the situation facing Greek Catholic minorities (who are also ethnically Ukrainian) in south-eastern Poland, drawing on anthropological fieldwork conducted in and around the town of Przemyśl (Hann, 1997, p.27). Greek Catholics practise the Greek rite

of the Eastern Orthodox liturgy, but are in communion with the
Roman Catholic church (Keleher, 1992, p.289).[12] Several factors are
relevant to escalating tensions between ethnic Poles and ethnic
Ukrainians. First, new movements of goods and people as eastern
Europe's borders have become more porous: in particular, prejudice
against Ukrainians has been exacerbated by the flood of traders from
neighbouring Ukraine anxious to sell their goods in comparatively
well-off Poland, and by ethnic Ukrainians (displaced by Stalin in
1948) returning with money from Poland's relatively rich western
border with Germany and seeking to reclaim and buy property.
Second, a backlash was provoked by the central government's efforts
to promote local Ukrainian identity (and strengthen political ties with
the Ukraine) by holding the biannual festival of Ukrainian culture in
Przemyśl. The festival went ahead despite obstruction from the local
council, but was marred by an arson attack on the Ukrainian club and
anti-Ukrainian graffiti (Hann, 1997, p.41). Third, tensions have been
increased by controversy over the Orthodox-style cupola of the local
Carmelite convent, which had been a Greek Catholic cathedral until it
was confiscated and handed over to the Carmelites (a Roman
Catholic religious order) by the communists in 1946. Local Polish
nationalists led a successful campaign to replace the cupola with a
'western-style' tower, and cost the protesting conservation officer (an
ethnic Pole) his job in the process.

Hann's conclusion is that in south-east Poland the breaking down
of national frontiers and the arrival of a democratic political system
has not liberalized culture, but rather 'unleash[ed] forces that
exaggerate and strengthen national and confessional barriers'
(ibid., p.29). Taken together with the evidence on anti-semitic
attitudes, religious education and the controversies over the
ombudsman, we can see that many conflicting and complex
processes are at work in Poland's post-communist social transformation, and that religion has played an important if controversial role in
it.

In analysing this, it is important to distinguish different elements of
democratization. Let us consider four:

1   support for a popularly elected government

2   the ability to unite and to make effective an opposition
    movement against an authoritarian regime

---

[12] The re-emergence of Greek Catholic communities which had been suppressed
under communism has caused tensions in Catholic–Orthodox relations, especially
in the Ukraine and Russia.

3   the ability to manage political and social change, effectively to implement policy on a day-to-day basis

4   support for individual rights (even if the actions or beliefs of those protected are not popular) and for legal process.

The Catholic church unanimously supports (1), and it was particularly effective at (2). However, the strength of the church in unifying and mobilizing opposition (2) may also be its weakness in the practical politics of the post-communist period (3). As Osa argues:

> Polish Catholicism managed to relocate its confrontation with Leninism from the substantive ground of public policy to a higher plateau of symbolic politics, where the Church and society *could win*... Ironically, the creation of religiously tinged ideological and solidary frameworks then constrained the movement from transcending the field of symbolic politics.
>
> (Osa, 1997, p.365)

Thus the church was able to get away with challenging the communist regime because it did so at a symbolic, not a practical, level. The church was in no position to offer a practical alternative to communist rule, and the communists found it difficult to refute or repress the church's symbolic claims. But symbolic unity does not easily translate into practical compromise. The apparatus of resistance is not the best for implementing policy. As we shall see, opposition movements organized on a similar basis in East Germany also faced similar difficulties. Mobilization on the basis of a religiously rooted national identity is also one factor contributing to difficulties with support for individual rights and legal process above the will of the majority (4).

Care is needed in assessing the role of religion here. On the one hand, the Catholic intelligentsia has played a leading role in seeking to combat popular prejudice, and insofar as it follows Vatican teaching the Catholic hierarchy supports this position. However, in claiming to speak for 'the people' in opposing the ombudsman (in spite of the opinion polls suggesting that the majority of the people did not in fact agree), the Catholic hierarchy opted for a populist rather than a constitutional model of democracy. Furthermore, it may be argued that successful opposition to the communist regime in the 1980s depended not only on the organization of élites, but also crucially on the mobilization of a popular Catholicism wedded to precisely the identification of church and nation that is antithetical to constitutional democracy. In different circumstances, such mobilization can have very dangerous consequences, as in the case of the Serbian Orthodox church in Yugoslavia (Sells, 1996).

We now turn to consider the challenges that have faced East German Christians in the post-communist period.

East German Christianity since 1989

There used to be rigid state control, and now we get just as much control from bureaucracy... We had lots to give, but decisions were made above our heads; we were never asked. The GDR systems were often evil, but at least sometimes they were truly social.

(Pfarrer Kwaschik, Pastor in the former East Germany, on the reintegration of East German Protestant churches with the German Protestant Church (EKD).

Quoted in Cantrell and Kemp, 1995, p.286)

It has been argued that the strength of the Catholic church in Poland in shifting political confrontation to a symbolic level was a key element in the success of Poland's democratic movement, but also a source of weakness because it did not provide a training in practical political compromise, and because the symbolic unity of the nation in the church stands in tension with the principles of constitutional democracy. In East Germany, the symbolic identification of the Protestant churches with the nation was never so great, partly because focusing on German unity in the East German state would have been political suicide, and partly because the discourse of nationalism was so profoundly discredited by World War II. However, as the only relatively free space within East German society, the churches, like the PCC, were also the breeding ground for opposition groups, especially after restrictions on church activities were eased in 1978. For similar reasons to the Polish case, the opposition provided by these groups tended to take a symbolic form, especially in public protest, because on these grounds they could delegitimize the East German state in a way that could never have been achieved through open confrontation. The youth march for peace in 1987 and the candle lit vigils of 1989 provide examples of the translation of political conflicts into symbolic forms.

One might therefore expect that East German churches would face similar difficulties to the Polish church in adapting to post-communist life, and to some extent this has been the case. But other factors were also at work. One is the specifically Protestant character of the East German churches (c. 90 per cent of East Germans were nominally Protestant at partition). This Protestant heritage shaped the way in which East German opposition movements thought about and organized themselves, in particular their opposition to hierarchy and advocacy of forms of radical, egalitarian democracy, which had the added advantage of also appealing to elements within communist discourse, if not practice. These ideas fed into the round-table discussions (December 1989 – March 1990), which were convened by the churches, and served to smooth the transition process leading up to the first democratic elections. Two representatives of every major social and political organization took part in these talks, which discussed a wide range of issues. Indeed, once the communist government joined the talks in mid-January, the Round Table:

> essentially assumed legislative powers, both vetoing government proposals and setting forth its own agenda, including measures relating to economic reform, environmental protection, property rights and immigration.
>
> (Burgess, Part Two, p.198 below)

For some Protestants, such as the theologian Wolfgang Ullman (see Burgess's text in Part Two), 'the Round Table represented a new way of doing politics' (ibid.), because – in contrast to majoritarian democracies in which either centrist parties tend to dominate and power swings between a small number (usually two) of large parties, or small parties hold the balance of power and exercise dispro-portionate influence – the limiting of all interest groups to a couple of representatives created the conditions for a more balanced debate. Furthermore, such a system of co-opting representatives can achieve a much broader representation of opinion than most elected systems, in particular, favouring the participation of minority groups. It is also, however, undemocratic, in the sense that the composition of the group does not reflect the balance of opinions in society, but rather the decision of whoever convenes the groups, and hence may be subject to manipulation by an élite. The Round Table group also produced a draft constitution for a new East German state, which sought to incorporate into the political system the benefits of opposition movements' experience of popular participation.

In the event, however, the election was won by a party favouring rapid unification with West Germany, so although the draft consti-tution fed into debate on a new constitution for the reunified state, its influence in practice was minimal. This is the second factor which serves to differentiate East German from Polish experience: reflecting the change in the slogan of the crowds over the winter of 1989–90 from '*Wir sind das Volk*' ('we are the people') to '*Wir sind* ein *Volk*' ('we are *one* people') (Garton-Ash, 1999, p.72). Thus, unlike the Poles, the East Germans never got the experience of forming their own state, but rather were reunited with West Germany, a process in which the larger, wealthier and undiscredited western institutions often tended to dominate. This general trend was also reproduced in the reunification of the Protestant church. East German Christians felt that their experience of surviving communism and taking a leading role in bringing about its downfall gave them something to bring to a reunited church – in particular, an openness to democratic participation and an orientation to social relevance. But in fact the experience of reunification of the church appears to have been a disappointing and disillusioning experience for many (Cantrell and Kemp, 1995, p.288).

In addition to the greater size and strength of the West German branch of the EKD, the vitality of East German contributions to the terms of reunification was sapped by two aspects of life under the old communist system that came back to haunt the former East German church. Both stemmed from the institutionalization of secrecy and deception within that system. The first is the funding of the church, the second the infiltration of the church by agents of the secret police or Stasi.

In the case of funding, East German churches were proud that they were supported by voluntary contributions, as opposed to the church tax system in West Germany, whereby revenue for the churches is raised by a tax collected by local authorities on behalf of the churches. They were proud that they could support themselves, and proud of the independence this gave them from the state. But in fact it turned out that East German churches had actually been dependent on contributions from the West, something that the leadership has understandably kept secret, because the state would have portrayed the churches as agents of western propaganda. Furthermore, after reunification the western churches were unwilling to continue this subsidy, so the eastern churches were forced to reintroduce the church tax, and even with this still faced church closures and job cuts (Burgess, 1997, pp.139–40). To make matters worse, the East German clergy were over-ruled in their wish to opt for a lower level of pay – 70 per cent of the wage of their western counterparts – with the money saved going to the parish: the western churches insisted on parity of salary (Cantrell and Kemp, 1995, p.281).

But if the affair of the church finances was humiliating, the opening of the Stasi files struck at the roots of trust in the churches, trust which had enabled them to play a leading role in nurturing opposition under communism and then mediating between parties during the transition. Particularly damaging to the churches' reputation was the publication at the end of 1991 of an edited collection of Stasi records entitled *Pastors, Christians and Catholics*. This documented the extent to which the Stasi had aimed to manipulate the church, while the editors 'suggested that the church's efforts at rapprochement and "critical solidarity" had played into the hands of the state' (Burgess, 1997, p.112). This struck at the heart of the policy of 'the church in socialism', as well as raising questions about the actions of particular individuals.

These accusations need to be placed in context. The state security system in East Germany was one of the most invasive in the communist world. It pervaded every aspect of life: it is estimated that 300,000 people (two per cent of the population) were involved in its intelligence-gathering operations. Husbands and wives were recruited to spy on each other, parents on children and children on parents (Spülbeck, 1996, pp.66–71). Even beyond it is the Stasi's actual infiltration, psychological damage stemmed from the fear or suspicion that one was being watched or followed, whether by the men in leather jackets on the street corner or the person in the next pew. People assumed their telephones were bugged, their mail read. Arbitrary arrest and interrogation added to this fear. Furthermore, when the Stasi files were made public and revealed something of the actual extent of infiltration there was a tremendously demoralizing and divisive effect on social life,[13] whatever the benefits of openness. We shall return to the ethical issues raised for the churches by this process, but first it should be noted that, while the Stasi files tended to be accepted at face value by the media, in a system pervaded by lies it is likely that much of this material is unreliable, and it is certainly incomplete since many records were destroyed.

The experience of the opening of the Stasi files challenged the churches at several levels. First, at a practical level, how is such material to be judged, and in particular what were churches to make of accusations of collaboration aimed at prominent church leaders? Under communism, churches were aware that a certain level of contact with the authorities were unavoidable, and since the Stasi worked covertly it was not always possible to tell to whom information was being passed on. Church guidelines stipulated some rules to regulate pastors' contact with the authorities: they were not to report private conversations with parishioners or enter into secret conversations with the Stasi, and were required to report any attempts to recruit or interrogate them to the church authorities (ibid., p.113). But some leaders were given wider discretion to negotiate with the authorities, at which the Stasi were particularly likely to be present. Such leaders were sometimes classified as informants by the Stasi, who were under pressure to prove their success at recruiting informants. Given the biased and incomplete nature of the main source of evidence, and the discretion given to such leaders, how could their cases be fairly assessed?

---

[13] See Spülbeck, 1996 for an account of the effects of this on one East German village.

One example illustrates the problem. Heinrich Fink had been dean of the theology faculty at Humbolt University before reunification, had close ties with the Christian Peace Conference and took a strong interest in Marxist–Christian dialogue both in the communist world and in Latin American liberation theology. He had also influenced church and state officials to support the small Jewish community in East Berlin (Burgess, 1997, p.110). After reunification he became rector of the university with a mandate for democratic renewal. However, although Fink's own files had been destroyed by the Stasi, in December 1990 evidence came to light in other files that he had been an 'IM' (*inoffizieller Mitarbeiter,* 'unofficial collaborator') for twenty years, providing information on church officials and policies and seeking to influence them in the interests of the state (ibid., p.111). In 1991, the government minister responsible for the university dismissed Fink, who protested his innocence. No voluntary declaration of independence was ever found, and Fink argued that while he had been interviewed by the Stasi on these topics, such meetings 'were no different from the kind of contact with the Stasi that every church leader could expect to have' (ibid.). Fink went to court to try to get his job back, but in spite of the support of leading East German intellectuals he lost his case.

Such cases raise more general questions about the difficult process of *Vergangenheitbewältigung* ('mastery of the past', or 'coming to terms with the past'; Burgess, 1997, p.105). These also affect other former communist states and had already greatly affected Germany after World War II. Is a difficult past best dealt with by being made public, or, as was tried in Poland initially, by drawing a 'thick line'[14] under the past in the interests of present reconciliation? If the past is to be subject to public scrutiny, what form should this take? Should it be a legal process, or a truth commission of the kind which has operated in post-apartheid South Africa? And what role should the churches play, whose core mission is concerned with repentance, forgiveness and reconciliation?

There are both political and moral dimensions to these questions. Politically, what kind of process will best promote democratic renewal in society and restore trust in the church? Morally, how is the churches' mission to be understood? Should the church emphasize mercy or justice, advocate forgiveness on the part of victims to release themselves from the bondage of the past, or stress the need for confession and repentance to precede any possible forgiveness? Different groups in the churches have answered these questions in

[14] Garton-Ash, 1999, p.165, quoting Poland's first post-communist Prime Minister, Tadeusz Mazowiecki.

different ways, some giving priority to the political task of getting on with the new arrangements, others to the moral need for an open process of facing up to the past as an essential prerequisite for moving on.

The churches in Eastern Germany face these difficult questions in a context of rapidly declining numbers and public trust. Between 1989 and 1995 the EKD lost 1.5 million members across the whole of Germany, the Catholic church about 800,000 (Ramet, 2000, pp.133–4). On a scale of +5 (total trust) to –5 (no trust) the churches in Eastern Germany scored –0.5 in 1992, lower than 'corporations, television, the federal government and banking concerns; and far lower than the police or constitutional court' (ibid., p.134). None the less, in spite of these problems the churches remain:

> One of the few places in the former East Germany where people and communities would be able to undertake the arduous work of trying to understand the lives that they had lived under the Marxist–Leninist regime.
>
> (Burgess, 1997, p.120)

At a practical level, the churches have taken the lead in organizing mediation between victims and former victimizers, for example, between former Stasi and dissidents (ibid., p.121). The churches have also sought to play a reconciliatory social role in the new Germany, for example, in taking the lead in discussing the issues raised by Germany's asylum policy and the growth of attacks on asylum seekers, Turks, Jews and Jewish sites (synagogues, graveyards) by right-wing groups (Ramet, 2000, p.136; Cantrell and Kemp, 1995 p.282)[15]. Indeed, ironically, with their loss of numbers and social status the churches may once again find themselves in the role of 'prophetic minority', this time on the broader German stage.

Conclusion

What do Poland and Germany tell us about the role of religion in contemporary societies? First, examination of the period of transition to democracy shows the perhaps surprising degree to which religious institutions, symbols and ideas can continue to influence modern European societies, at least under some circumstances and particularly by providing a sense of cohesiveness to society in opposition to a repressive state. The fact that one church (the PCC) or church

---

[15] Although Cantrell and Kemp (1995, p.282) report big differences among their respondents on how important and relevant to them this question was seen as being.

organization (the EKD) in some sense claimed the allegiance[16] of a high proportion of the population (95 per cent and 90 per cent respectively) probably helped make this possible.

Yet, surprisingly, given the extent of church involvement in the events that led to the downfall of communism, the role of religion in the transition to democracy has tended to be neglected as a causal factor in analyses of these political processes. Even Poland is no exception:

> The role of this institution [the PCC], its members and hierarchy, social networks and symbols – has not been systematically considered in any of the arguments over Solidarity's emergence... The question of religion and its relation to the emergence of Solidarity is consistently downplayed in the literature, despite frequent references to religion's role in sustaining Polish national identity.
>
> (Osa, 1997, p.340)

Even those who do consider the church's role incline to treat it as either an abstract belief system or in terms of episcopal decisions, rather than as set of social networks and symbols embedded in culture. This has tended to produce a static image of church involvement as providing 'consolation' or a 'bedrock of ethical belief' but not significant social mobilization (ibid.). However, a more dynamic understanding of the relationship between religion, culture, social movements and politics is possible. In particular, religion can be seen as contributing to a critical mass of protest which can lead to innovations in other parts of the social system – for example, the relationship between the Pope's visit in 1979 and the formation of Solidarity in 1980. The fact that the church may not come up with specific 'strategic or tactical ideas' does not mean that it did not have an important causal role in the development of the democratic movement.

A similar blind spot to the role of religion is apparently also found in accounts of the East German case:

> By the mid 1980s the Evangelische Kirche in East Germany consistently represented the major ideological and political alternative to the Communist Party and the socialist state... [Yet a] review of recent literature on the democratization of Marxist–Leninist states provides little insight into how and why religion played such and important role.
>
> (Burgess, 1997, pp.45, 61)

The Polish and East German cases can help us to arrive at a more dynamic understanding of the relationship between religion, culture, social movements and politics. In these cases, the churches

---

[16] Or, at least, that no other religious organisation did, to present a rival allegiance.

Figure 1.5 Symbolic warfare in Poland. Sacred and secular authorities line the route during the papal visit of 1983. Bruno Barbey/Magnum.

contributed to the democratic transition in four different ways (Herbert, 1999, pp.279–82).

First, they provided an institutional space in otherwise totalitarian societies within which it was possible to organize various forms of opposition, or at least preserve the possibility of thinking differently, to the communist state (Pollack, 1995, p.102; Cantrell and Kemp, 1993, p.288, 1995, p.289).

Second, religion provided a symbolic resource, or fund of collective memories, which was mobilized to oppose or subvert state-imposed communist ideologies. The role of Christian symbolism in the opposition movements in Poland is particularly striking, whether in the Great Novena, at the papal visits, or in the symbols and imagery of Solidarity (Kubik, 1994, pp.129–238; Figure 1.5). But religious symbolism also played an important, if lower key, role in East Germany (Figure 1.6). Here religion entered into the fabric of the symbolic structure through which people interpret political and social reality.

Third, religion functioned as an institutional and ideological connection with an international order which stretched beyond both the state and the communist bloc. This is particularly evident in the case of the Catholic church, especially after the appointment of a Polish pope, but links between the EKD in East and West Germany, even after their organizational separation in 1968, remained signifi-

Figure 1.6 Symbolic warfare in the GDR. Demonstrators light candles on the steps of the ex-headquarters of the secret police (Stasi) in Leipzig to commemorate the victims of Stalinism, 18 December 1989. Popperfoto.

cant, as witnessed in the nurturing of peace movements on both sides of the iron curtain (De Gruchy, 1997, pp.193–205). Again, it is true that these international connections are paralleled by secular organizations, although the operations of the most obvious secular analogy, multinational corporations, were limited in the Eastern bloc. There is an important symbolic dimension to the mobilization of these connections: sacraments such as communion, for example, provide a sense of unity that transcends state boundaries. The Christian belief in a universal church, past, present and future, helped people to transcend the boundaries of communism, first psychologically, and eventually politically.

This leads on to the fourth and final role of religion as an intellectual force, from which opposition thinking and identities could be self-consciously constructed. Here one can point to the influence of Catholic intellectuals on KOR, the Worker's Defence Committee in Poland (e.g. Luxmoore and Babiuch, 1995),[17] and such influences were also present in East Germany (discussed at length in the Burgess text in Part Two below. Although confined to élites, this influence was significant in the events of 1989–90, thus providing a channel for religion to have a social effect.

[17] Similar connections can be traced in Czechoslovakia with the production of Charter 77 (Luxmoore and Babiuch, 1995).

But if religion can be so influential at times of national crisis or transition, why does it seem to have difficulty sustaining that effectiveness during the consolidation period? For a while the PCC exerted enormous influence in post-communist Poland; it had apparently done so at the expense of its popularity, even if this had not yet translated into loss of membership or a decline in attendance. And, in East Germany, citizens' movements began to move away from the churches as soon as public space opened up, and long before the opening of the Stasi files (Pollack, 1995, pp.103–4). In our discussion of Poland, we have already argued that the same two features – a symbolic mode of engagement and an identification of church and nation – that enabled the church to successfully challenge the communist regime, now presents massive problems for it in the post-communist period; for the first is not readily translated into practical action (precisely why it was so difficult to combat), while the latter is in many ways opposed to constitutional democracy. The churches in Germany do not face the second problem to the same extent; but equally the lack of identification of church and nation also explains why their support is so much lower.

So, are the churches in democratic modernity bound to decline in numbers and influence, as the East German church has experienced, in line with most of northern Europe? Will Polish Catholicism's confrontation with the secular values of modern constitutional democracy undermine its popularity as Poles rejoin the European mainstream?

The answer would seem to be 'not necessarily', for two main reasons. First, studies in Brazil and the United States suggest that Catholicism does not necessarily decline under democratic modernity (Casanova, 1994, pp.114–210). As we have seen, church teachings are no longer opposed to most aspects of modernity, although there are tensions between Catholic teaching on the sacredness of life which conflict with some liberal understandings of rights (e.g. abortion, euthanasia and genetic experimentation). Rather, evidence from Brazil and the United States suggests that the Catholic church can continue to play an influential public role where it accepts that it is only one voice amongst others in civil society, and does not attempt to exercise influence undemocratically at the level of the state, or risk becoming partisan by supporting particular political parties. Such evidence suggests that 'the church in civil society' model may provide a better future than the 'national church model' for Poland.

Second, however, in Poland one can already see the development of a right-wing within popular Catholicism. This group is unhappy with many aspects of the post-communist system, including unemployment, increasing economic inequalities and social diversity (e.g. immigration, especially from other less prosperous post-communist societies, and the growth of NRMs, which are seen as a threat to a social order held to be rooted in Catholicism), and the liberalization of society. The popular radio station *Radio Maria*, though opposed by the Church hierarchy, broadcasts a form of xenophobic Polish nationalism to which popular or folk Catholicism is central. As society liberalizes but inequalities widen, a religious right in Poland could arise with similar characteristics to the American right, but focused on different issues – for example, opposition to European integration.

Glossary

anabaptist Christian groups stemming from the late fifteenth century, who rejected the authority of the state in favour of autonomous pacifist Christian communities.

apocalyptic to do with 'the end times', referring in Jewish–Christian–Muslim belief in the dramatic intervention of God at the end of history.

Barmen Declaration (1934) A Statement agreed between dissenting members of the German Protestant church, which declared their reasons for opposing Nazism and splitting from the main organization (EKD) to form the Confessing Church.

civil society definitions differ, but typically a part of society situated between the state and the family (and usually not including the economy), consisting of voluntary associations, informal groups and social networks. The existence of such an independent sphere of association is often thought to be important for the development of democracy.

EKD *Evangelische Kirche Deutsche* alliance of Protestant churches in Germany, predominantly Lutheran.

ISKCON International Society for the promotion of Krishna Consciousness, or 'Hare Krishna' movement.

Jugendweihe 'youth dedication' introduced in 1955 by East German communists as a rival ritual to Christian confirmation. It was made a prerequisite for secondary education.

GDR German Democratic Republic. Communist East German state (1949–89).

NATO North Atlantic Treaty Organization. Military alliance between the United States and European states.

PCC Polish Catholic church.

RSV Revised Standard Version of the Bible – a translation widely accepted across Christian denominations.

Sejm Polish Parliament.
Staatssicherheitdienst 'state security service' East German secret police or Stasi.
'two kingdoms' Lutheran doctrine of separation of the powers of church and state.

Bibliography

Ambrosewicz-Jacobs, J. with Mirski, A. (1999) 'The influence of religious instruction on the attitude of Krakow youths towards Jews', in Borowik (1999) pp.388–402.

Bernhard, M. (1993) *The Origins of Democratization in Poland,* New York: Columbia University Press.

Borowik, I. (1997) 'Institutional and private religion in Poland 1990–1994', in Borowik (1999) pp.235–55.

Borowik, I. (ed.) (1997) *New Religious Phenomena in Central and Eastern Europe*, Krakow: Nomos.

Borowik, I. (ed.) (1999) *Church–State Relations in Central and Eastern Europe*, Krakow: Nomos.

Bruce, S. (1999) *Choice and Religion: a Critique of Rational Choice Theory*, Oxford: Oxford University Press.

Brzezinski, M. (2000) *The Struggle for Constitutionalism in Poland,* Basingstoke: Macmillan.

Burgess, J. (1997) *The East German Church and the End of Communism*, Oxford: Oxford University Press.

Cantrell, B. and Kemp, U. (1993) 'The role of the Protestant churches in eastern Germany: some personal experiences and reflections', *Religion, State and Society*, vol. 21, nos 2 and 3, pp.277–88.

Cantrell, B. and Kemp, U. (1995) 'East Germany revisited', *Religion, State and Society*, vol. 23, no. 3, pp.279–89.

Casanova, J. (1994) *Public Religions in the Modern World*, Chicago: Chicago University Press.

Davies, N. (1996) *Europe: a History*, Oxford: Oxford University Press.

De Gruchy, J. (1995) *Christianity and Democracy*, Cambridge: Cambridge University Press.

Doktor, T. (1997) 'State, church and new religious movements in Poland' in Borowik (1997) pp.165–77.

Everett, W. (1997) *Religion, Federalism and the Struggle for Public Life: Cases from Germany, India and America*, Oxford: Oxford University Press.

Garton-Ash, T. (1999) *The Magic Lantern: the Revolution of '89 Witnessed in Warsaw, Budapest, Berlin and Prague*, 3rd edn, New York: Vintage.

Gautier, M. (1997) 'Church attendance and religious belief in post-communist societies', *Journal for the Scientific Study of Religion*, vol. 36, no. 2, pp.289–96.

Gilarek, K. (1997) *Coping with the Challenges of Modernity. The Church of England in Great Britain and the Catholic Church in Poland*, unpublished MA thesis, University of Exeter/Jagiellonian University Krakow.

Gilarek, K. (1999) 'Coping with the challenges of modernity. The Church of England in Great Britain and the Catholic Church in Poland', in Borowik (1999) pp.189–203.

Halecki, O. (1956) *A History of Poland*, New York: Roy Pubishers.

Hann, C. (1997) 'The nation-state, religion, and uncivil society: two perspectives from the periphery', *Human Diversity*, vol. 126, no. 2, pp.27–45.

Herbert, D. (1999) 'Christianity, democratization and secularization in eastern Europe', *Religion, State and Society*, vol. 27, nos 3 and 4, pp.277–94.

Herbert, D. (2002) *Religion and Civil Society: Rethinking Public Religion in the Contemporary World*, Aldershot: Ashgate.

Herbert, D. (2001) 'Representing Islam: the Islamization of Egyptian society 1970–2000', in G. Beckerlegge (ed.) (2001) *From Sacred Text to Internet*, Aldershot: Ashgate/Milton Keynes: Open University.

Kapralska, L. (1995) *Jewish Topics in the History Curriculum of Polish Schools*, unpublished report for TEMPUS programme 'Ethnic identity in Europe after Auschwitz: the case of Polish–Jewish relations (post 1989)'.

Keheler, S. (1992) 'The church in the middle: Greek-Catholics in central and eastern Europe', *Religion, State and Society*, vol. 20, nos 3 and 4, pp.289–302.

Kubik, K. (1994) *The Power of Symbols Against the Symbols of Power: the Rise of Solidarity and the Fall of State Socialism in Poland*, University Park, PA: Pennsylvania State University.

Krusche, G. (1994) 'The church between accommodation and refusal: the significance of the Lutheran doctrine of the "two kingdoms" for the churches of the GDR', *Religion, State and Society*, vol. 22, no. 3, pp.324–32.

Luxmoore, J. and Babiuch, J. (1995) 'In search of faith: the metaphysical dialogue between Poland's opposition intellectuals in the 1970s', *Religion, State and Society*, vol. 23, no. 1, pp.75–95.

Michel, P. (1992) 'Religious renewal or political deficiency: religion and democracy in central Europe', *Religion, State and Society*, vol. 20, nos 3 and 4, pp.339–44.

Moses, J. (1996) 'The church policy of the SED regime in East Germany, 1949–1989: the fateful dilemma', *Journal of Religious History*, vol. 20, no. 2, pp.228–45.

Musial, S. (1989) 'Sprawa karmelu w oswiecimiu' 1–3, in *Niedziela Tygodnik Katolicki*, 32:27–9.

Osa, M. 'Creating Solidarity: the religious foundations of the Polish social movement', *East European Politics and Societies*, vol. 11, no. 2, Spring 1997, pp.339–65.

Pawlik, W. (1995) 'The church and its critics: the spell of the Polish ombudsman', *Polish Sociological Review*, vol. 109, no. 1, pp.31–45.

Pollack, D. (1995) 'Post Wende citizens' movements', in E. Kolinsky (assisted by S. Wilsdorf) (eds) (1995) *Between Hope and Fear: Everyday Life in Post-Unification East Germany, A Case Study of Leipzig*, Keele: Keele University Press, pp.101–22.

Ramet, S. (1995) *Social Currents in Eastern Europe: Causes and Consequences of the Great Transformation*, London: Duke University Press.

Ramet, S. (2000) 'Religion and politics in Germany since 1945: the Evangelical and Catholic churches', *Journal of Church and State*, Winter 42: 1, pp.115–45.

Robertson, R. (1992) *Globalization: Social Theory and Global Culture*, London: Sage.

Rowland, C. (1987) *Radical Christianity*, London: SPCK.

Saunders, J. (1985) *Jesus and Judaism*, London: SCM.

Sells, M. (1996) *The Bridge Betrayed: Religion and Genocide in Bosnia*, Berkeley and Los Angeles: University of California Press.

Shanks, A. (1995) *Civil Society, Civil Religion*, Oxford: Blackwell.

Skinner, Q. (1978) *The Foundations of Modern Political Thought*, vols 1 and 2, Cambridge: Cambridge University Press.

Spülbeck, S. (1996) 'Anti-semitism and fear of the public sphere in a post-totalitarian society: East Germany', in Hann, C. and Dunn, E. (eds.) *Civil Society: Challenging Western Models*, London: Routledge, pp.64–78.

Stern, F. (1992) 'Evangelische Kirche zwischen Antisemitismus und Philosemitismus', *Geschichte und Gesellschaft*, 18, no. 1, p.33.

Tibi, B. (1998) *The Challenge of Fundamentalism: Political Islam and the New World Disorder*, Berkeley: University of California Press.

Tischner, J. (1992) 'Christianity in the post-communist vacuum', *Religion, State and Society*, vol. 20, nos 3 and 4, pp.331–7.

Urban, K. (1997) 'A selection of issues related to the process of new religious associations in Poland between 1977 and 1997', in Borowik (1997) pp.165–77.

Wałęsa, L. (1982) *The Book of Lech Wałęsa*, London: Allen Lane.

Wecławowicz, G. (1996) *Contemporary Poland: Space and Society,* London: University College London.

Wengst, K. (1987) *Pax Romana and the Peace of Christ*, London: SCM.

CHAPTER 2

Islam and human rights

DAVID HERBERT

Introduction

> To those who argue that attaining full human rights is a universal human aspiration, others may respond that the notion of human rights is simply a product of one particular civilisation's history ... many Middle Easterners have ideas about human rights that ... must be understood in the context of the sustained engagement between the Middle East and the West going back to the time of Muslim penetration into Spain and Europe in the eighth century, through the Crusades of the eleventh century and beyond, and into the more recent colonial and post-colonial periods. This context has forged complex, many-tiered, starkly ambivalent, and often actively hostile attitudes in many Middle Easterners towards Western traditions, Western forces, and Westerners themselves. The idea of 'human rights', closely associated with the West over the last few decades, is prey to the same complexity.
>
> (Dwyer, 1991, pp.1–2)

The relationship between Islam and human rights is an emotive and complex one. To tackle it, this chapter will argue that we need to be aware of five different but related sets of factors: historical, socio-economic, cultural, religious and philosophical. Our focus will be on religious factors and their interaction with the other four, but first it will be useful to outline the most important factors in all five areas.

First, as the above quotation argues, is the often troubled history of the relationship between Muslim majority societies[1] (from Morocco to Indonesia) and the Christian (or post-Christian) societies of Europe and 'the West'. Occupied by western European colonial powers since the early-mid nineteenth century, many Muslim societies only achieved their independence from colonial rule in the post-war

---

[1] Most societies in which Muslims form the majority also contain minorities, whether secular or from another religious group, especially Christians or Jews. Hence the phrase 'Muslim majority societies' is most accurate. However, for the sake of brevity, 'Muslim society' will be used.

period, (e.g. Egypt in1952; Pakistan in 1948 (both from Britain), Tunisia in 1956, Algeria in 1963 (both from France)). In the Middle East, in particular, post-colonial administrations mobilized around nationalist and socialist ideologies have failed to meet the expectations of their fast-growing populations for either economic improvements or political participation. This failure, together with a humiliating military defeat by Israel in the Six-Day War (1967), has led to widespread disillusionment with secular solutions to contemporary problems, and to a return to Islam as an alternative source of inspiration, leading to an Islamization[2] of society (Herbert, 2001, pp.169–76). As Dwyer argues, this history means that Muslim attitudes to the West and ideas associated with the West, including human rights, have become complex.

Second is the socio-economic transformation which modernization has brought to Muslim societies during the last 200 years, and the changing attitudes to human rights reflects this troubled history. Urbanization and industrialization have transformed life in many Muslim societies, breaking up traditional communities, transforming patterns of work, bringing new wealth and health care but also new poverty, over-crowding and unemployment. New attitudes to the relationship between the sexes have been brought about both by changes in the division of labour and by contact with the cultural modernity of western Europe and its white majority former colonies (especially the USA). Local economies were distorted by having to supply the primary product needs of colonial powers, later to become the 'First World' (although some countries, including several Muslim ones, have been able to turn this to their advantage through the formation of the oil cartel OPEC (Organization of Petroleum Exporting Countries) in 1973, which dramatically transformed the wealth of the Gulf states.

Third, there are cultural factors. Socio-economic transformations have had repercussions for culture, intensifying the process of Islamization. Thus later industrialization and urbanization than in Europe and North America has in many cases meant that new and cheaper communications and transport technologies were available during modernization, in contrast to the West. Arguably, this has permitted the retention of closer kinship networks and the more effective transmission of culture, including religion (see Herbert, 2001, p.192). However, in spite of this effective retention of modified forms of traditional culture and religion, western products and media are also highly influential, so that many in Muslim societies feel 'a

---

[2] 'Islamization' is defined here as 'the increasing influence of Islamic symbols and discourse (speech and writing) on the social systems of a society'.

Figure 2.1 British UN soldier at the destroyed mosque in Ahmnici, Bosnia. Western refusal to lift the arms embargo on Bosnia, which left Bosnian Muslims vastly out-armed by the Serbia-backed Bosnian Serbs, confirmed Western Islamophobia in the eyes of many Muslims. Roger Hutchings/ Network.

numbing awareness of the power and pervasive nature of the western media which are perceived as hostile' (Ahmed, 1992, p.32). Furthermore, the West continues to wield great political and military power (consider the Gulf War, 1991).

Fourth, there are the religious factors. As indicated in the previous paragraph, religion has remained an important factor in Muslim societies. Indeed, the importance of religion as a political factor has increased since 1970[3] (ibid.). The political oppression and economic failure of many governments in Muslim societies, combined with regional factors such as the defeat of Arab nations by Israel in the Six-Day War, has meant that many in Muslim societies have turned to Islam as a solution to contemporary problems, increasing the emphasis placed on religion. Of particular relevance to debates about human rights is the turn to **sharia** (Islamic law), which derives from the Qur'an and traditions about the Prophet Muhammad

[3] 1970, the death of the Egyptian President Nasser, is an important turning point in Arab political history. After Nasser, the influence of Arab nationalism declined and came to be rivalled by political Islam. Reflection on Arab humiliation in the 1967 Six-Day War with Israel began to surface, favouring political Islam, and in 1973 the formation of OPEC, led by Saudi Arabia with its militant form of Islam, further boosted Islamic political identity.

(*hadith*), as a source of law in contemporary Muslim societies. Arguably, some features of *sharia* contradict modern human rights principles, creating problems for the implementation of human rights where *sharia* functions as a source of law. However, there is debate about what *sharia* requires in contemporary societies. (Both of these points are dealt with later in the chapter.) Besides the law, religion and culture interact in ways which can affect prospects for the implementation of human rights, whether it is religious texts which shape cultural attitudes or culture which shapes the reading of religious texts (see Chapter 3, below).

Fifth, there are philosophical factors. In the midst of this history, these social transformations and arguments over sacred texts, there also lie several philosophical questions, which centre around this one: what is the relationship between human rights and culture? Can we assume that human rights are universal, and therefore that we can judge all cultures and religions by the one standard? Or are rights but the invention of particular human cultures, and therefore subject to local variation in their applicability, or are they even irrelevant in some contexts? These questions provoke strong reactions from different sides of the debate: in western societies, where the cultural dominance of the Christian tradition has to varying extents broken down, human rights provides a secular guide to social relations in increasingly religiously and culturally plural societies. Challenges to the universality of human rights then, are in a sense challenges to the moral order of that society, a threat to its common humanity. In Muslim majority societies where, in many places, the cultural dominance of Islam has increased during the last thirty years, Islam is widely understood as the foundation of social order, and as a universal religion. Challenges to Islam's universality are therefore similarly seen as a threat to moral order and to a common humanity rooted not in secular Enlightenment principles but in God's word revealed finally in the holy Qur'an.

The topic of Islam and human rights therefore places considerable demands on the student of religion: to cope with the emotional intensity which debate in this field generates, to grasp something of the history and the social transformations shaping the Muslim world (and to some extent 'the West'), to understand something of the Islamic tradition, its relation to law, and the modern concept of human rights, and to engage in philosophical debate (to which anthropologists and others have also made contributions) on the universality of human rights. But the rewards may also be considerable: what topic could be more important than to tackle the pressing problem of how to live together peaceably and in mutual respect in our increasingly inter-connected world?

To introduce these issues, the chapter is structured in the following way. First we present a sketch of the widely perceived dichotomy between Islam and human rights, including a look at some of the most difficult texts from the Qur'an with respect to human rights. How do Muslims deal with the apparent tension between the two? Responses to this tension are structured by one's understanding of the relationships between Islam, *sharia*, and modern law, which is dealt with next. It will be seen that in spite of the authority that all Muslims ascribe to the Qur'an and other early sources, the relation of these sources to modern legal systems and modern societies is disputed. In this context, we then go on to examine some of the different theoretical positions that Muslims have adopted on the relation between Islam and human rights. Next we look at this relationship in practice, examining the ways that human rights **discourse** has been used by different groups in one Muslim society: Tunisia. In particular, we shall focus on the struggle of the Tunisian Human Rights League to agree a charter of human rights based on the Universal Declaration of Human Rights (UDHR), a struggle which illustrates the complexities of the relationship between Islam and human rights in practice. Finally, we examine the relationship between human rights and culture in general. Like the relationship between Islam and law, this is also disputed. First, following from the Tunisian example, this examination considers the importance of culture for the legitimization of rights in local contexts. It then examines the separate issue of whether human rights are only the product of local cultures, or whether they really are universal in some sense that transcends culture. This last issue has importance not just for Muslim societies but for all. It will be argued that while it is difficult to demonstrate the universality of human rights in the full modern sense, all cultures produce ethical norms that, given appropriate conditions, can be developed to support human rights. It will be further argued that global conditions justify such developments. In particular, the transformation of the world into a system of states connected by various global networks, and the transformation of traditional communities into societies of anonymous strangers, have created both modern individuals and a series of threats to them, and hence the need for human rights to defend individuals from these threats.

Islam and human rights: a 'clash of civilizations'?

In the West, concern, fear or animosity towards Islam is often linked to issues of human rights: examples include the right to free speech (e.g. Muslim reaction to Salman Rushdie's novel *The Satanic Verses*), the right of women to equality, and the right of the individual against communal conformity (e.g. consumption of alcohol, dress code). Also in the West, human rights are widely regarded as universal, that is valid for all individuals in all times and places, regardless of historical or cultural circumstance, or indeed the moral worth of the individual. The Universal Declaration of Human Rights (UDHR, 1948, in Mumm, 2001), produced in the aftermath of the Second World War, has played a key role in the promotion of this concept of human rights. When such a view comes into contact with another which also sees itself as universally valid, conflict is likely.

The Moroccan feminist scholar Fatima Mernissi portrays the relationship between Islam and human rights in this way.

> The majority of Muslim states have signed this covenant [i.e. the UN Charter, incorporating the UDHR], and thus find themselves ruled by two contradictory laws. One law gives citizens freedom of thought, while the *shari'a*, in its official interpretation based on *ta'a* [obedience] condemns it. Most Muslims, who are familiar with the Koran [sic] from very early in life, have never had occasion to read the United Nations Charter or become acquainted with its key concepts... It has come to our shores folded away in the attaché cases of diplomats and, like a harem courtesan, has never succeeded in getting out.
>
> (Mernissi, 1993, p.60)

Such a contrast may be developed by arguing that in Islam all knowledge of human nature and right conduct ultimately derives from the final revelation of God to Muhammad, the 'Seal of the Prophets', given in the Qur'an. In contrast, the universality of human rights in the liberal tradition of western thought springs from the independence of the concept from any particular religious revelation.

The contrast may be further developed by considering some of the punishments (***hadd*** penalties)[4] specified in the Qur'an:

> As for the man or woman who is guilty of theft, cut off their hands to punish them for their crimes. That is the punishment enjoined by Allah.
>
> (**Surah** 5:38)

---

[4] In only a few cases does the Qur'an specify penalties. These are known as the *hadd* punishments, and are given for theft, adultery (and false accusations of), armed robbery, wine drinking and apostasy.

> The adulterer and the adulteress shall each be given a hundred lashes;
> let no pity on them cause you to disobey Allah.
>
> (Surah 24:2)

The penalty of amputation runs contrary to many understandings of Article 7 of the Covenant on Civil and Political Rights: 'no one shall be subjected to cruel, inhuman, or degrading treatment or punishment' (An-Na'im, 1992, p.29). Under modern law adultery is regarded as a moral matter, and only the concern of the law if it impinges on divorce proceedings. Similarly, discrimination between the sexes runs contrary to modern concepts of gender equality:

> The male heir shall inherit twice as much as the female.
>
> (Surah 4:12)

> When you contract a debt one upon another for a stated term, write it down... And call in two witnesses, men; or if the two be not men, then one man and two women... that if one of the women errs, the other will remind her.
>
> (Surah 2:282)

> Men have authority over women because Allah has made the one superior to other and because they spend their wealth to maintain them. Good women are obedient. As for those from whom you fear disobedience, admonish them and send them to bed apart and beat them. Then if they obey take no further action against them.
>
> (Surah 4:34)

At first sight, then, there is a strong case for seeing the relationship between Islam and human rights in terms of a 'clash of civilizations', to use Samuel Huntingdon's (1993) controversial phrase. However, there are good reasons to think that the situation is not quite so straightforward as this contrast suggests. For both in Muslim majority societies and in the West, Muslims adopt a range of positions on issues of human rights, and in so doing interpret the Islamic tradition in a variety of ways. Central to each of these interpretations are the relationships between Islam (literally, 'submission to Allah (God)'), *sharia* (usually translated 'law', but originally meaning 'path' or 'way') and what each of these means in the contemporary world, in particular in terms of modern political and legal systems. We therefore begin our discussion of Muslim approaches to human rights with discussion of these relationships.

Islam, sharia and law

> Whatever the differences in orientation and agenda, central to Islamic
> revivalism throughout the Muslim world has been the demand for
> more Sharia law. The rule of thumb employed to judge the Islamic
> commitment and character of Muslim society has been the presence or
> absence of Islamic law. Moderates and radicals alike see the un-
> Islamic nature of their societies, as epitomized by Western-inspired
> legal codes, and clamour for the implementation of Islamic law.
> Countries as different in degree of modernization and Westernization
> as Egypt, the Sudan, Libya, Iran, Pakistan, Nigeria, Malaysia and
> Mauritania have all had to face this issue.
>
> (Esposito, 1994, p.202)

The demand that contemporary Muslim societies should be made
more Islamic, specifically by the implementation of *sharia* law
derived from the Qur'an and other early Islamic sources, is a central
defining characteristic of Islamic revival across the Muslim world. The
term '**Islamist**' (*Islami* in Arabic) may be used to describe Muslims
who seek such a revival, turning to Islam as a solution to modern
political, social and economic problems. Given the nature of the
punishments and inequalities between the sexes in the Qur'anic
passages considered above, demands for the implementation of
sharia seem bound to come into conflict with the international
human rights treaties to which the governments of these countries are
also signatories. However, there is considerable disagreement on
what the implementation of Islamic law means. There are several
sources of this disagreement, of which we shall discuss three major
types. First, the meaning of *sharia*, and specifically whether its
prescriptions should be regarded as primarily moral or legal. Second,
the authority of the post-Qur'anic development of *sharia*, and the
diversity within this tradition. Third, the question of whether *sharia*
should constitute an entire legal system, or whether it is properly
more limited, and may sit alongside other systems. We shall consider
each of these in turn.

The Arabic word *sharia* is usually translated as 'law'. However,
some commentators argue this is misleading, because in the Qur'an
(45:18; 42:13; 5:48; 42:21), *sharia* refers to a way or path, literally to a
watering hole, the source of life in a desert environment. Thus it
originally meant something like 'a righteous way of life', an
understanding which is broader than the modern concept of 'law',

understood as a set of rules of human origin collected together in the legal system of the state.[5] In contrast, the original sense of *sharia* includes also the whole field of ethics (Al-Azmeh, 1993, p.12). Therefore – unlike the western conception of the law – because law and morality are not clearly distinguished, when the Qur'an gives a command or prohibition, there is a question of whether its enforcement should be a matter of personal conscience or legal requirement.

Second, there is disagreement over the authority of the development of *sharia* after the death of Muhammad. While he was alive, Muhammad could be consulted on what God's way was on a particular point, but after his death Muslims needed to find another method to discern this. The instructions given in the Qur'an are quite limited, so a lot of discernment was needed:

> The Quran is not a law book. About six hundred of the six thousand verses in the Quran are concerned with law, and many of them covering matters of prayer and ritual. Approximately eighty verses treat legal topics in the strict sense of the term: crime and punishment, contracts, family laws.
>
> (Esposito, 1994, p.77)

The early caliphs[6] shared some of Muhammad's authority, and were therefore able to take over his guiding role to some extent. Some even had the authority to override some of the instructions given in the Qur'an; for example, 'Umar increased the penalty for adultery from flogging to stoning, and for wine drinking from 40 to 80 lashes (Ruthven, 1991, pp.140–1). However, over time the religious authority of the caliphate declined, and so the task of discerning (*fiqh*, 'understanding') God's way (*sharia*) became the job of a specialized group of religious scholars called **ulama**. The *ulama* set about defining rules and procedures for *fiqh*: they limited the sources that could be drawn on (in the Sunni[7] case, to the Qur'an and traditions about the Prophet, called *sunna*) and the methods of discernment that could be used. For Sunnis, **ijtihad** (intellectual struggle) became

[5] This is still a rather narrow view of the West's modern concept of law – it sets aside the continuing debate between legal positivists, advocates of natural law (to which I refer later in the chapter) and discourse ethicists (Habermas, 1996).

[6] Leaders of the Muslim community after the death of the Prophet; the title means 'God's deputy on earth'.

[7] The Muslim world is divided into two parts: Sunni, comprising *c.* 90 per cent, and Shi'a, comprising *c.*10 per cent of the world Muslim population. The origin of differences lie in the controversy over the succession to Muhammad as leader of the Muslim community, but other differences, in sources of law and festivals have developed over the years. Shi'ites are concentrated in Iran and Lebanon. Here we shall concentrate on Sunni Islam.

limited to **qiyas** (reasoning by analogy) – a controversial decision to which we shall return. *Qiyas* works in the following way:

> When faced with a new. situation or problems, scholars sought a similar situation in the Quran and Sunna. The key is the discovery of the effective cause or reason behind a Sharia rule. If a similar reason could be identified in a new situation or case, then the Sharia judgement was extended to resolve the case. The determination of a minimum rate of dower (payment to a bride's parents on marriage) offers a good example of analogical deduction. Jurists saw a similarity between the bride's loss of virginity in marriage and the Qur'anic penalty for theft, which was amputation. Thus, the minimum dower was set at the same rate that stolen goods had to be worth before amputation was applicable.
>
> (Esposito, 1994, p.83)

Two points are important here for the issue of authority of the post-Qur'anic discernment of *sharia*. First, the example of the setting of the dower gives us some insight into the male-dominated context in which the process of *fiqh* was carried out. Liberal commentators argue that this means that the whole post-Qur'anic development of *sharia* needs to be re-thought. **Islamist** commentators, however, while being selectively critical of the post-Qur'anic development of *sharia*, often also accept it, and in doing so fail to distinguish between the Qur'anic and post-Qur'anic senses of *sharia*:

> Today, when... some fundamentalists call for the implementation of shari'a, what they really have in mind is the implementation of the jurisprudence (theory of law – in this case, *fiqh*) formulated by the early jurists. This jurisprudence has now been extracted from its historical and political context, and endowed with everlasting, essentialist qualities. The point is thus overlooked that this jurisprudence was in the first place a human improvisation meant to address certain political and social issues in a certain historical, geographical and social context.
>
> (Ayubi, 1991, p.2)

Thus the original Qur'anic sense becomes confused with the profane sense of the whole legal tradition which has subsequently developed. This is important because, whereas in the early Muslim community this developing tradition was seen as a matter of debate and argument applying the relatively scant resources of revelation to existing conditions, a sacred status has subsequently been conferred on this tradition itself, thus preventing further debate and argument in the spirit of the original tradition.

Second, the traditional limitation by Sunni *ulama* of the exercise of reason in the discernment of *sharia* to analogy has been rejected by most modern commentators. From radical revivalists to liberals, many argue that the wider intellectual struggle (*ijtihad*) needs to be rejoined, arguing against the original (fourteenth-century) decision to 'close the gates of *ijtihad*':

> No one, in fact, had a right to put a stop to the process of *ijtihad*.
>
> (Rahman, 1984, p.69)

This means that there is a widespread consensus amongst contemporary Muslims that the traditional limitations on new interpretation should be lifted. We shall see the importance of *ijtihad* in practice in the Tunisian case later in this chapter. For now, we may note that if *ijtihad* is freely practised, new possibilities open up for the reconciliation of Islamic tradition with human rights, although new interpretation may also lead in other directions.

Other legal principles also challenge the traditional limitation of the use of reason to analogy. For example, **istihsan**, which literally translates as 'to approve, or deem something preferable' (Kamali, 1991, p.246). This involves recognizing that the fundamental intention of a law may conflict with the letter of the law, and hence the former may be invoked to override the latter (ibid., p.249) in particular cases. This is a controversial principle, but is widely used in practice (ibid., p.259). For example, Islamic legal tradition is very limited in the kind of evidence which it considers authoritative, which is largely confined to oral testimony. However, modern scientific forensic evidence, such as photography, audio recording and DNA analyses are increasingly being recognized using this principle (ibid., p.249). Thus the letter of the law (limitation of valid evidence to oral testimony) is overruled in favour of what is discerned to be the fundamental intention (to use the most reliable form of evidence available).

We can also consider how *istihsan* might be applied to two of the texts from the Qur'an introduced on pages 70–1, and which appear incompatible with the equality of the sexes found in contemporary understandings of human rights:

> The male heir shall inherit twice as much as the female ... Men have authority over women because Allah has made the one superior to the other and because they spend their wealth to maintain them.
>
> (Surah 4:12–34)

One reason given for male authority is economic: 'they spend their wealth to maintain them'. In a context in which males have the responsibility of economic provision for dependants, they need to inherit a larger share. The deeper principle behind the law on inheritance is, one might argue, the need to ensure adequate economic provision for everyone. But, it may be argued, if the economic system changes so that women are no longer economically dependent on men, the basis of this division of inheritance becomes questionable; more profoundly, male authority becomes question-able. Such a reading is only suggestive of the potential of this kind of method for developing interpretations of *sharia* more compatible with human rights. It does not, for example, deal with the phrase 'Allah has made one superior to the other'. The whole question of women and Islam in early Islamic sources and their reading today is addressed more fully in Fatima Mernissi's text in Part 2 of this volume. The point to note here is that *istihsan* opens up new possibilities of interpretation which may impact on the relationship between Islam and human rights.

In fact, a range of means has been used to allow for a degree of flexibility in interpreting instructions found in the Qur'an. One is appeal to a tradition attributed the Prophet (*sunna*) which states that if there is any doubt (**shubha**), the *hadd* penalties should not be applied. Traditionally, this has included not only doubt about whether the person accused actually committed the offence, but also some mitigating circumstances (e.g. theft should not be punished by amputation when food is stolen to survive in time of famine). Reformers have suggested these could be extended further, for example to include psychological conditions such as kleptomania (An-Na'im, 1992, p.36). Another traditional strategy is to argue that the *hadd* penalties are intended for the ideal Islamic community, but are inapplicable in today's corrupt societies. This move may reconcile *sharia* with human rights on a practical level because the penalties are never used, but obviously does not reconcile them on a theoretical level.

Traditionally, a further source of flexibility has been that local judges (**qadis**) have traditionally been able to exercise considerable discretion in the implementation of *sharia*. Contrary to some western stereotypes (Makdisi, 1985), Rosen (1987) has shown in relation to Moroccan *sharia* courts that the practice of such *qadis* is not arbitrary, but governed by a distinctive legal rationality, one which is arguably closer to the logic of local cultural systems than western legal systems are to the logic of local western cultural systems (Rosen, 1987). All these sources of flexibility (*ijtihad, istihsan, shubha,* the discretion of the *qadi*) give rise to disagreements over what it means to implement *sharia*. They show that *sharia* is not a monolithic system that can simply be implemented in a mechanistic way. However, while many Muslims are prepared to be flexible in their interpretation and application of Qur'anic injunctions, few are prepared to challenge them head on. We shall shortly consider one example, the Sudanese legal scholar and human rights activist An-Na'im.

A third area of disagreement over the meaning of *sharia* is whether the *sharia* should, if properly interpreted, constitute a whole legal system, or whether it is more limited in scope, and hence increasing the scope of compatibility with other legal systems. Part of the argument here is historical. The historian Ira Lapidus argues that two patterns of the relationship between *sharia*, law and society have been influential in Muslim history:

> The Middle Eastern Islamic heritage provides not one but two basic constellations of historical society, two golden ages, two paradigms, each of which has generated its own repertoire of political institutions and political theory. The first is the society integrated in all dimensions, political, social, and moral, under the aegis of Islam. The prototype is the unification of Arabia under the leadership of the Prophet Muhammad in the seventh century ... The second historical paradigm is the imperial Islamic society built not on Arabian or tribal templates but on the differentiated structures of previous non-Islamic societies... By the eleventh century Middle Eastern states and religious communities were highly differentiated ... Thus, despite the common statement that Islam is a total way of life defining political as well as social and family matters, most Muslim societies ... were in fact built around separate institutions of state and religion
>
> (Lapidus, 1992, pp.14–5)

For radical Islamists, the imperial version of Islam is seen as a corruption of the pure, undifferentiated Islamic state. But such a view has to come to terms with the fact that neither the Qur'an nor *hadith* specify any form of government through which the relatively few laws they specify should be enforced (Ayubi, 1991, pp.1–2). Furthermore, historically it has been the more complex, differentiated form of imperial Islam that has proved enduring and influential. In this setting, *sharia* composed only a small part of public law:

> Though in theory the *sharia* was the only officially recognized system of law, in practice a parallel system of caliphal laws and courts existed from the earliest times ... *sharia* courts ... were increasingly restricted to family law and the handling of religious endowments ... Grievance courts dealt with public law (criminal, land and commercial regulation).
>
> (Esposito, 1994, pp.87–100)

Thus while the scope of *sharia* was increasingly restricted by the encroachment of western legal systems in the colonial period, it is important to note this restriction does not originate then, but stems from a much earlier period. Thus liberal Muslims argue that limiting the scope of *sharia* represents a practical and appropriate response to the demands of complex societies, a response with many historic precedents.

In conclusion, Islamic revivalism has forced Muslim societies to reconsider the relevance and meaning of *sharia*, which had become relatively marginal in the legal systems of Muslim countries until the 1970s. Since then, there have been Islamization programmes in countries as diverse as Egypt, Pakistan and Nigeria, as well as Islamic revolutions in Iran and Sudan, each of which have controversially sought to 'implement *sharia*'. Debates triggered by these developments have centred around whether *sharia* is primarily a moral or legal phenomenon, the authority of *fiqh* developed to discern *sharia* in the post Qur'anic period – particularly acute given the scarcity of legal material in the Qur'an – and the place that *sharia* should occupy in contemporary legal systems, given historic precedents. These debates shape Muslim responses to human rights, and hence to part of the international system of modern law, and it is to these responses that we now turn.

Muslim responses to human rights

> The democratic system prevailing in the world does not suit us in the region... Islam is our social and political law. It is a complete constitution of social and economic laws and a system of government and justice.
>
> (King Fahd of Saudi Arabia in *International Herald Tribune*, 15 March 1992; in Halliday, 1995, p.138)

In this statement King Fahd is representative of Muslims who argue that the historically and culturally specific origin of human-rights discourse limits the scope of its applicability. Islamic systems are simply different from western ones, they work for Arabs, and so there is no reason to try to impose western systems such as human rights on Arab countries. Such a position may be further supported by arguing that the negative consequences of western freedoms – materialism and sexual immorality, for example – are incompatible with Islam. Aspects of equality between sexes may be challenged on these grounds, arguing that a complementary rather than equal relationship between the sexes – as encoded, for example, in Islamic inheritance laws – is a better model for a just society. Such an argument may be described as *particularist*: it defends the denial of the relevance of human rights discourse in a different cultural setting (Halliday, 1995, p.137).

Halliday dismisses such an argument as an example of the 'fallacy of origin: the fact that a set of ideas were produced in a one particular context says little about their subsequent authenticity' (ibid., p.158). Perhaps a better argument, as we shall suggest at length later in this chapter, is that modern developments such as the globalization impinge on everyone's lives, so that particularism is now only ever a partial defence, for particular cultures always exist in tension with the various global systems that claim to be universal (e.g. human rights).

A second argument maintains that provisions for human rights are already contained in the Qur'an, and these are in themselves sufficient to safeguard human dignity – hence no further supplementation, such as a secular conception of human rights, is needed. Halliday (ibid., p.136) describes such a position as *assimilationist*: the principles of human rights are already respected in Islam, so concerns related to human rights can be assimilated within existing Islamic frameworks. Dalacoura quotes a statement from former Iranian President Rafsanjani, which exemplifies this position:

> That which the international community is trying to draw up nowadays has been under discussion in Islam for a long time, and in the Islamic country of Iran, many of the individual and social rights from which Muslims have benefited also hold good for [religious] minorities; a clear example of this is the presence of deputies representing those minorities in the *Majlis* [representative assembly] with the same rights as deputies of the Islamic *ummah* [community].
> (*Summary of World Broadcasts* (1174 A/6 11 Set 1991); quoted in Dalacoura, 1998, pp.54–5)

The clue to the problem here lies in the word 'many' – religious minorities in Iran do enjoy 'many' rights, including those of political representation referred to, but these are not the same as those enjoyed by Muslims, and therefore they are not equal as citizens, as the UDHR demands. Rather, the position of recognized religious minorities in Iran is a modern version of the traditional Islamic policy towards 'the people of the Book' (Jews and Christians), which provides them with a protected but subordinate status. While this may have been enlightened in comparison with medieval European arrangements, it falls short of standards for modern human rights. Furthermore, it falls far short of religious liberty, for groups which are not recognized have no such protection – for example, members of the **Baba'i** faith, who are persecuted in Iran (Esposito, 1994, p.210).

Another example is the various laws relating to women which we have considered – inheritance and competence as witnesses. At least at a literal level, these laws plainly contradict principles of modern human rights, even if various forms of *istihsan* or *ijtihad* might be able to find a deeper compatibility. Thus such an assimilationist position refuses to recognize differences between modern human rights and traditional Islamic systems.

A related position is *appropriation* (Halliday, 1995, pp.136–7), which can be seen as a more aggressive version of the same position. Here is argued not only that *sharia* provides fully for human rights, but also that its provision is superior to western formulations. This position is represented by the various Islamic declarations of human rights, for example the 1981 Universal Islamic Declaration of Human Rights (UIDHR) and the 1990 Cairo Declaration of Human Rights (see Mumm, 2001). For example, the former, produced by the London-based, Saudi-backed, Islamic Council, states, 'Islam gave to mankind an ideal code of human rights fourteen centuries ago' (quoted in Dalacoura, 1998, p.50), thus suggesting that all other formulations are less than ideal. In this document, all rights specified are described as 'subject to the Law', i.e. *sharia* – for example, 'no one shall be exposed to injury or death, except under the authority of Law' (Article 1, quoted in Dalacoura, 1998, p.50) – thus ignoring any possible conflict between the *hadd* penalties (amputation for theft, flogging for adultery etc.) and international understanding of 'cruel and degrading treatment'.

The Cairo Declaration (CDHR) has greater significance than the UIDHR because it has been endorsed by the foreign ministers of the Organization of the Islamic Conference, to which 'all Muslim countries belong' (Mayer, 1994, p.327). Mayer provides a detailed discussion of this document. Article 1 states:

> Human beings are equal in terms of basic human dignity and basic obligations and responsibilities, without any discrimination on the grounds of race, colour, language, sex, religious belief, political affiliation or social considerations.
>
> (ibid., p.329)

Mayer describes this article as 'typical of the evasiveness in the formulations often seen in Islamic human rights schemes' (ibid.): it looks at first sight like a guarantee of equality, but in fact it substitutes the concept of dignity for one of rights and freedoms, and hence specifies no entitlement, in contrast to the corresponding Article (2) in the UDHR:

> everyone is entitled to all the rights and freedoms set forth in this Declaration, without distinction of any kind.
>
> (ibid., p.330)

Considering the consequences for women – Article 6 of the Cairo document provides that a woman is equal to a man in human dignity, not rights – Mayer argues:

> In a human rights scheme that purports to follow a religious law that, as traditionally interpreted and applied, has reinforced patriarchy and denied women equality, invocations of women's 'dignity' or equality in 'dignity' in lieu of rights are not likely to provide legal grounds for challenging ingrained patterns of discrimination.
>
> (ibid., pp.330–1)

Furthermore, in linking dignity to responsibility without any statement of entitlement, the Declaration undermines a key principle of human rights:[8] as Dalacoura explains, 'it is of crucial importance to the idea of human rights that the right exists independently of and prior to its correlative duty' (Dalacoura, 1998, p.57). In other words, however much politicians may insist on their linkage, in many modern understandings rights *precede* responsibilities. Furthermore, this concept of rights as inviolable is a distinctively modern Western innovation. This is not to say that it is uncontested – even in the West; indeed there is lively philosophical debate on the topic (MacIntyre, 1985, pp.66–70; Gray, 1995, pp. 71–2). But the concepts of the violability of fundamental rights and their priority over duties is central to the legal concept of human rights as embodied in international human rights instruments such as the UNUDHR. And it is this legal concept – rather than popular or philosophical understandings, which are more varied and contested, that confront governments in Muslim countries when they are called up to fulfil their international human rights obligations. Thus it is the failure to come to terms with this concept that Dalacoura sees as the fundamental problem with many Muslim responses to human rights.

The Catholic German Bishops' Conference Research Group on the Universal Tasks of the Church further spell out the distinctiveness of modern concepts of human rights:

> It is the inner connection between the ... claim of universality, emancipatory essence, [and] legal implementation ... which constitutes human rights as a specifically modern phenomenon ... Human rights cannot simply be deduced from Christian and Muslim traditions ... Religious liberty is traditionally unknown to Islam, and it does not belong to the traditional values of Christian churches either.
>
> (Schwartlander and Bielefeldt, 1994, pp.17–21)

---

[8] This remains a controversial point among philosophers. However, in legal understandings of human rights as embodied in the UNUDHR or the ECHR it is clear that at least some rights precede duties, and are considered inviolable.

The bishops were also disappointed by the failure of the Cairo
Declaration to critically address contentious issues such as corporal
punishment, inter-faith marriage and women's rights. Instead, 'the
general tendency is to "harmonize" contradictions rather than
reconcile them critically', a procedure which tends to involve
subordinating differences to *sharia,* as in the case of religious liberty,
where missionary work is specifically prohibited by the CDHR
(Schwartlander and Bielefeldt, 1994, pp.33–4).

However, not all assessments of the Cairo Declaration are so
negative. While admitting the apologetic function and regretting the
lack of critical historical engagement with the text, Islamic reformer
Arkhoun none the less argues:

> The great virtue of this declaration is that it expresses the convictions,
> modes of thought, and demands that contemporary Muslims are
> coming to embrace ... to cloak such precious rights as religious
> freedom, freedom of association, freedom of thought and freedom of
> travel in the full authority of the Islamic tradition is not a negligible
> phenomenon.
>
> (Arkhoun, 1994, p.107)

Thus such documents can be seen as a step on the way towards the
critical integration of Islam and human rights, opening up a process
of intercultural dialogue which has been largely neglected:

> While the UN Universal Declaration of Human Rights and succeeding
> documents built up an important body of universal doctrine, there has
> been a mounting volume of criticism of these norms on the basis that
> they incorporate Western-oriented ideas and that, especially at the
> time of the Universal Declaration, insufficient note was taken of other
> traditions, especially the Islamic ... If [the benefits of the UDHR] ... are
> to be preserved and built upon, more understanding of the Islamic
> legal tradition is important.
>
> (Weeramantry, 1988, p.168)

None the less, this does not alter the fact that such critical integration
remains, as yet, largely absent from such documents. The same is also
true even of the author of this last remark, Sri Lankan scholar
Weeramantry, who tries his best to liberalize the Islamic tradition to
make it compatible with human rights, but fails to engage with the
presence of the fundamental differences between the tradition as
historically construed and modern human rights. It is not really fair to
categorize Weeramantry's position as assimilationist – he does not
insist that Islam already contains everything required to support
human rights. On the other hand, he does tend to harmonize rather
than tackle difference head on. For this reason his position might
be described as a *liberal (harmonizing)*, emphasizing the positive

relationships between Islamic and human rights traditions, but neglecting their differences.

However, other liberal Muslims do seek to face such differences head on. Such Islamic liberals, the 'confrontationalists', openly challenge differences between *sharia* and human rights, arguing that the terms of integration of contemporary society are so different from pre-modern forms – in particular, that the political supremacy of Islam can no longer be presumed – that substantial re-interpretation of the tradition is required. They may also combine support for a secular conception with an argument that this has been too narrowly defined, and hence that distinctive Islamic perspectives – as well as those of other religions and cultures – are necessary for a truly universal conception of human rights. Such arguments complement those of some western critics of a static western conception of human rights (Galtung, 1994).

An example of a *confrontationalist liberal* approach is the work of the Sudanese scholar An-Na'im. Educated in law at Khartoum, Cambridge and Edinburgh universities (Curzmann, 1998 p. 222), An-Na'im was forced to flee Sudan after translating the controversial work of Muhammad Taha, who was executed as an apostate by the Sudanese authorities in 1985 (Dalacoura, 1998, p.61). Controversy over Taha's work centres on the distinction he makes between Meccan and Medinan *surahs*, arguing that those verses revealed post **hijra** (after Muhammad and his followers migrated to Medina, where the first Islamic political community was established) reflect the needs of the early political community, and are not intended as everlasting law. An-Na'im accepts and develops this distinction, and on this basis challenges even commands which are clearly stated in the Qur'an, such as the *hadd* penalties. An-Na'im has been head of Africa Watch, a human rights organization based in Washington DC and currently (2000) he teaches at Emory University. An-Na'im states clearly:

> Unless the basis of modern Islamic law is shifted away from those texts of the Qur'an and *sunnah* of the Medina stage, which constituted the foundations of the construction of the *shari'a*, there is no way of avoiding a drastic and serious violation of universal standards of human rights ... we must prepared to set aside clear and definitive texts of the Qur'an and *sunna* as having served their transitional purpose and implement those texts of the Meccan stage which were previously inappropriate for practical application, but are now the only way to proceed.
>
> (An-Na'im, 1998, p.234)

The significance of setting aside the 'clear and definitive texts of the Qur'an and *sunna*' is that An-Na'im moves manifestly beyond the boundaries of traditional interpretation, including *ijtihad*, which is bound by such texts.

An-Na'im does not insist that his particular methodology – rejecting Medinan in favour of Meccan *surahs*, thus reversing the traditional method of abrogation[9] – is the only way to reform Islamic law. What he does insist on are three points: first, that such drastic reform is necessary because *sharia* can no longer function as the public law of Islam; second, that the cultural legitimization of human rights discourse in Islamic idiom is crucial for human rights implementation (An-Na'im, 1992, p.21), and third, that the rejection of *sharia* does not necessitate the rejection of Islamic public law – hence he does not confine the scope of *sharia* to the private sphere.

Other reformers have suggested alternative methodologies. Merad, for example, suggests a radicalization of the concept of *istihsan*, attempting to discern divine intention beyond the letter of the law:

> We must therefore strive to peer through the contingencies of history in order to discover the very direction in which revelation points, to formulate normative criteria, and to find out what God's intention is. But this is a hazardous route to take.
>
> (in Schwartlander and Bielefeldt, 1994, p.36)

The Tunisian reformer Talbi attempts to draw a line between the Qur'an and *sunna*, disputing the provenance of some of the latter and arguing that although all Muslims are bound by the Qur'an's basic teachings, Muslim traditional theology, for historical reasons, does not always reflect the spirit of the Qur'an (ibid.). The feminist scholar Fatima Mernissi adopts a similar approach (1988 – see also Part Two). Such approaches demonstrate that Muslim scholars are attempting to construct forms of Islamic practice which are compatible with principles of human rights, and that such constructions are not necessarily contradictory. However, Muslim liberals face a difficult task in the contemporary Middle East, given the history of authoritarian government and of Islamist responses to this. We now turn to consider one example of such a struggle in Tunisia, a Middle Eastern Muslim society in which a liberal understanding of Islam has achieved some public influence and stimulated public debate.

---

[9] 'Abrogation' means, in this context, choosing which text to favour, where there is a contradiction between them.

The human rights debate in Tunisia

> Few Middle Easterners I spoke to seem ready to dismiss the idea [of human rights] from their cultural repertoire: they may challenge its foundations, or its provenance, or the content given it by specific groups, but the concept itself has come to constitute a symbol of great power.
>
> (Dwyer, 1991, p.192)

Such is the conclusion of a comparative study of human rights debates in Morocco, Tunisia and Egypt conducted in the 1980s by the American anthropologist Kevin Dwyer. This section focuses specifically on debates over human rights in Tunisia, first placing the Tunisian situation in the broader context of the Muslim-majority Middle East, examining features specific to Tunisia, and then looking in detail at one debate within a Tunisian human rights organization.

In Tunisia, as elsewhere in the Muslim-majority Middle East, human rights discourse is used by all three main groups competing in public space: the state, opposition groups including political Islamist groups, and non-governmental organizations (NGOs) (including human rights organizations (HROs), women's groups, and social Islamist groups).[10] The background against which such mobilization occurs is the state's attempts to control all organizations that seek to operate independently of it, including political parties and HROs. Dwyer explains the process:

> Individuals desiring to form an association submit a formal request to the government, usually to the ministry of the Interior. Upon favorable response the association acquires legal existence. Until then it is not permitted to hold formal meetings or to publish a journal ... in either status, either with the authorization or without it, the association is likely to be under constant observation from the powers that oversee it, and control or harassment from above becomes more onerous the more controversial are the group's aims ... among those highly controversial aims that have motivated people to form associations, to construct 'civil society', in Morocco, Tunisia and Egypt, are the protection of human rights and women's rights.
>
> (Dwyer, 1991, pp.146–7)

HROs, women's organizations and other NGOs, such as Islamist groups, are thus liable to constant government interference and harassment. In this context, mobilization of human rights discourse to challenge human rights violations has occurred primarily in

---

[10] These groups include Islamic welfare organizations, hospitals, clinics and businesses (see Herbert, 2001, pp.176–80, for Egyptian examples).

opposition to government repression rather than to the violence of Islamist groups, although the latter has also had an impact. But what about the use of Islam in public discourse? While most Middle Eastern governments claim some kind of official Islamic legitimacy, and hence cannot accurately be described as secular, their roots lie in secular-oriented independence movements, and their use of Islamic discourse and the introduction of Islamizing measures is best seen as part of a strategy to appease more radical Islamist demands. This reflects a situation in which:

> In the Arab Middle East in the last quarter of the twentieth century, the language of religion has come to dominate discourse about the nature of society, as much as leftist vocabulary dominated the post-independence years.

> (ibid., p.37)

Moreover, both governments and at least the main Islamist opposition groups have embraced human rights discourse. The latter include the Tunisian *Mouvement de la Tendance Islamique* (MTI), renamed **Nahda** ('Renaissance') in 1989. The discourses of Islam and of human rights are therefore both influential and prestigious: so we need to ask, how they are used, and how do they interact with each other? Above, we considered the Cairo Declaration (CDHR), which Tunisian and Egypt governments signed, and which suggests a critical integration between Islam and human rights is lacking at the level of the state. The CDHR adopts an appropriationist stance, asserting the superiority of 'Islamic' human rights while failing to face up to differences between *sharia* as historically practised and modern concepts of human rights. Thus while human rights are recognized by governments as an important discourse to use for international legitimacy, the underlying problems of integrating Islamic culture with the standards of modern human rights are neglected in favour of evasive formulations designed to reinforce governmental authority. As Mayer concludes on a range of such official Islamic human rights schemes, including the CDHR:

> They accord priority to rationalizing government repression, protecting and promoting social cohesion, and perpetuating traditional hierarchies in society, which means discriminatory treatment of women and non-Muslims ... Political authorities are allowed to curb rights and freedoms by reference to vague Islamic criteria, which the authors do not bother to define.

> (Mayer, 1995, p.163)

Islamist adoption of the language of human rights can also be seen as self-interested, in the sense that it has been primarily a response to the experience of state oppression (Dalacoura, 1998, p.167). However, it would be wrong to dismiss all Islamist use of such discourse as purely cynical. As Wickham (1997) argues in relation to Islamist mobilization through the powerful professional associations in Egypt, Islamist groups are capable of organizing on the basis of principles of democratic and human rights: indeed their success owes much to this mode of organization. Excluded from forming a political party, Muslim Brothers have gained influence in these professional bodies (especially those of engineers, lawyers and doctors) through democratic means, promising 'the development of more responsive and egalitarian models of political leadership and community which contrasts sharply with the hierarchical practices of state elites' (ibid., p.130). Once in power, they have maintained their position by implementing democratization measures, specifically:

> By initiating new programs to address the grievances of members, taking a public stand in support of democracy and human rights, and in some associations actively seeking the cooperation of secular opponents, the young Islamist leaders have attempted to portray themselves as representatives of a broad consensus rather than a narrow set of political objectives.
>
> (Wickham, 1997, p.130)

What, though, of Islamists in Tunisia? Although there are similarities between the relationship of Islamist organizations, government and NGOs in Egypt and Tunisia, the situation in Tunisia is rather different, and this has effected the character of the Islamist movement. Dalacoura describes Tunisia as 'the only country in the Middle East which has come close to achieving a harmonious relationship between Islam and human rights and becoming a liberal state without becoming a secular one' (Dalacoura, 1998, p.151). This situation is the result of the conjunction of a number of features.

First, the reform of the Personal Status Code at independence in 1956 led to the creation of laws which approach equality between men and women, but on an Islamic basis. This banned polygamy and male repudiation (divorce without grounds, simply by male declaration), made female consent a prerequisite for marriage, and made divorce a right of both parties (ibid., p.153). However, provisions over inheritance and male guardianship of children remained unreformed. Second, a strong independent trade-union movement. Thus whereas in Egypt the government has been able to co-opt most groups in society except Islamists, other opposition voices have remained effective in Tunisia. Thus the public sphere has more players and is less polarized. Third, the intrusion of the state into society has been hindered, and civil society strengthened, by the relative absence of the military from public life.

Arguably as a result, the Islamist movement itself is more liberal than elsewhere, and has a stronger intellectualist flavour.

However, like HROs, Islamists in Tunisia have experienced government oppression. The *Mouvement de la Tendance Islamique* (MTI) first experienced persecution in 1981 when, politicized in the aftermath of the Iranian revolution and the government's crackdown on trades unions, it applied to become a political party: soon after, the leadership was imprisoned. Bombing of tourist targets of which Islamists were suspected led to a fresh wave of arrests in 1986, by which time President Bourguiba, who had led the country since independence, was becoming obsessed with the Islamist threat (Dalacoura, 1998, p.167). Indeed, his insistence that those acquitted of the bombings be retried led to his removal by the Prime Minister Ben Ali. At this time the MTI (but since 1989 renamed *Nadha*) signed a pact with other political parties which included respect for the Personal Status Code. When they won 17 per cent of the vote in the 1989 elections – with up to 30 per cent in some urban areas – Ben Ali took fright, and further repression began. The MTI's response shows how far they had become assimilated into the opposition mainstream and secular politics. They issued joint statements with the secular opposition and co-operated with Amnesty International to publicize their cause; they entered the trade-union movement and even participated in the LTDH (Tunisian Human Rights League), as we shall see below.

However, their pre-1989 attitude indicates some ambivalence towards human rights: in 1985 they had challenged the Personal Status Code, specifically opposing the right of a woman to marry a non-Muslim, and the right of a Muslim to renounce Islam (ibid., p.168). In an interview in 1985, Ghannouchi, the MTI leader, argued that the head of state and ministers in posts dealing with 'instruction, values and morals must be held by Muslims' (Dwyer, 1991, p.44). More crucially, although they show the effects of liberalization, *Nadha*'s position still reflects an assimilationist or, at best, a liberal harmonizing perspective in terms of the types developed on pages 82–3, rather than one which struggles to reconcile difficulties between *sharia* as historically accumulated – even in the modified form of the Personal Status Code – and human rights. This form of engagement (liberal confrontationalist) is only to be found within a small offshoot of the MTI, the Progressive Islamist Movement:

> The Progressive Islamists are exceptional in accepting that the concept of human rights is not contained in the Koran and the Sunna and that the principles of human rights are part of the universal humanism of our time, which must be incorporated into the Islamic world-view.
>
> (Dalacoura, 1998, p.173)

Figure 2.2 Islamists on trial in Egypt for the murder of 57 foreign tourists and ten Egyptians at Luxor on 17 November 1997. Jamaa Islamiya, a radical Islamist group, claimed responsibility for the incident. IMAX/SIPA Press/ REX Features.

This party has exerted an influence beyond its small numbers by affecting the MTI/*Nadha*, contributing to the further reform of the Personal Status Code in 1992–3 and to the reform of the school curriculum to ensure the presentation of 'an open, tolerant and modernist' version of Islam. Partly through its magazine *15–21*,[11] these Progressive Islamists are seen as making an important contribution to debates on Islamic identity and human rights beyond Tunisia, including Morocco and Egypt (Dwyer, 1991, p.46).

What of HROs in Tunisia? One of the main organizations is the Tunisian Human Rights League (LTDH).[12] Founded in 1977, LTDH has had considerable success in uniting a wide range of groups from across society and the political spectrum (including Islamists, as has been mentioned). Its main focus has been on human rights problems in Tunisia, and it is organized on cross-political lines. However, this has not meant that it has been easy to avoid politicization: indeed, the LTDH experience illustrates one of the main difficulties facing human rights organizations in contexts where opportunities to express political opposition are limited. In the absence of alternative forums,

[11] See the interview with *15/21* editor al-Naffyar in Mumm, 2001 (also in Beinin and Stork, (eds) 1997, pp.370–5).

[12] *La Ligue Tunisienne pour la défense des Droits de l'Homme.*

there is a danger that they become politicized, or that interest groups seek to use them for political ends. As Muhammad Charfi, former president of the League, comments:

> The League in Tunisia isn't at all the equivalent of a human rights league in France or in the United States or Britain. In those countries, political parties fill the political stage, and the human rights organizations are marginal – they busy themselves with particular cases of individuals whose rights have been violated. Here, because our freedoms are so weak, our political parties are weak too. They don't fill the political stage, so the League is called onto this stage too. Now, when the UGTT [trade union movement] is attacked everyone turns to the League ... So, the League is pushed into a role that is much more important than its fundamental role should be.
>
> (quoted in Dwyer, 1991, p.180)

Thus such organizations come under enormous pressures – especially when they are successful. Not only are they subject to intensified government surveillance, but the expectations of a wide and often conflicting range of groups, from secularists to Islamists, falls upon them. The following somewhat dated example (the events discussed took place in 1985), draws mostly on Dwyer's work. It illustrates some of these pressures by demonstrating the role of human rights discourse and of a human rights organization in a situation of contested social transformation in a contemporary Muslim society. Most of the quotations used come from Muhammad Charfi, the president of the LTDH at this time.

During the first few years, the League was concerned mainly with the rights of specific political prisoners in Tunisia – which led to accusations of political bias. Therefore, one of the major projects of the League in the 1980s was to try to build consensus on human rights across society, and to do so they worked on the production of a Charter. This was prompted by two specific events. First, during a meeting of the League a Jewish man was elected to the executive committee. This led to a protest by one member who objected to the election of a Jew, giving as a reason that Palestinian Arabs were being oppressed by Jews in Israel and the occupied territories. A spontaneous outburst against this objection followed; but the incident made the leadership realize that the broadening of the membership base should not be at the expense of clarity of mission, of which a central element is the treatment of people on an individual basis without discrimination as to race, religion or ethnicity. Second, the League had come to public attention because of the success of its campaign to persuade the government not to administer the death penalty to demonstrators convicted after the

Figure 2.3 Military crackdown in Tunis in response to bread riots of 1984, which left more than 20 dead and hundreds injured. Such tensions formed the background to the LTDH's production of a human rights charter for Tunisia. UPI/Popperfoto.

'bread riots' of 1984.[13] This meant that many people from different backgrounds wanted to join, leading to the danger that the focus of the League would be lost in the midst of competing political pressures.

From one perspective, the Charter can be seen as an attempt at 'cultural legitimization'[14] – seeking to make human rights relevant to Tunisian culture (which includes Islam) while at the same time remaining true to the principles of the UDHR on which it is based. In its drafting, three main areas of dispute arose: over the right to change one's religion, the right of a Muslim woman to marry a non-Muslim man, and over the rights of illegitimate children (Dwyer, 1991, pp.172–3). Considering the first will enable us to introduce the other two, since their logic is related in *sharia* law.

The predominant historical Islamic view has been that apostasy (deserting one's faith, *riddah*) is punishable by death. To appreciate the Tunisian case, let us briefly consider the issue of apostasy in this broader historical and contemporary context:

[13] A popular protest against food shortages, which had led to violence (Dwyer, 1991).

[14] For further discussion of this topic see pp.99–101 below.

> Muslim attitudes are still influenced by the pre-modern *shari'a* rule
> that forbade Muslims to convert from Islam. Under the interpretations
> of the medieval jurists, apostates were to be given the opportunity to
> repent and return to Islam, but if they refused, they were to be executed if
> they were male and imprisoned until they changed their minds if they
> were female. Pre-modern *shari'a* rules also provided that apostasy
> constituted civil death, meaning, among other things, that the
> apostate's marriage would be dissolved and they would be incapable
> of inheriting.
>
> (Mayer, 1995, p.141)

For example, this interpretation prevails in modern Egyptian law,
where it is particularly problematic for Coptic Christian men who
often convert to Islam to marry a Muslim woman, because under
sharia women cannot marry non-Muslims. This in turn is related to
the patrilineal concept found in *sharia,* according to which children
take the religion of their father. For similar reasons, illegitimate
children do not have inheritance rights under *sharia.* However, in the
case of the Coptic Christian convert, if the marriage breaks up, the
man often wants to convert back in order to rejoin the Coptic
community, but is prevented from doing so under the law on
apostasy. Although the death penalty has not been enforced since the
re-introduction of the apostasy law in the 1980s, such men may face
imprisonment and dispossession.

As the above quotation makes clear, this view is inherited from
medieval jurists, and reformers have challenged it using the kinds of
methods discussed on pp.73–6, beginning by going back to re-
examine the Qur'anic evidence. Thus we find the Qur'an declares
that 'There is no compulsion in religion' (2:256), and indicates
punishment in the afterlife rather than the present life for those who
turn back from faith (2:217; 16:106). On the other hand, a series of
severe penalties, including death, are prescribed where apostasy is
accompanied by fighting against the Islamic community (5:36–7).
Thus, some have concluded that two kinds of apostasy are envisaged:

> a quiet desertion of personal Islamic duties is not a sufficient reason
> for inflicting death on a person. Only when the individual's desertion
> of Islam is used as a political tool for instigating a state disorder, or
> revolting against the law of Islam, can the individual apostate then be
> put to death as a just punishment for his act of treason and betrayal of
> the Muslim community.
>
> (Ally, 1990, pp.25–6)

The harsh penalty therefore reflects the context of the early Muslim
community struggling for its existence in the post-*hijra* phase, and
should not be applied where no such threat to civil order is

consequent on apostasy. As we have seen, liberal (confrontationalist) reformers such as An-Na'im argue that all post-*hijra* passages in the Qur'an should be reviewed in this way. However, this remains very much a minority position. Therefore, the traditional position remains influential, and so it proved in the Tunisian situation.

Muhammad Charfi (Dwyer, 1991, p.172) recalls that in their initial draft the League's committee opted to strengthen Article 18 from the UDHR on freedom to change religion, adopting the following wording (the original UDHR Article 18 is given first for ease of comparison):

> Everyone has the right to freedom of thought, conscience and religion: this includes freedom to change his religion or belief, either alone or in community with others, to manifest his belief in teaching, practice, worship and observance.
>
> (UDHR, quoted in Dwyer, 1991, p.236)

> Everyone has the right to freedom of thought, conscience and religion; this includes the right to change one's religion or belief or his interpretation [*ijtihad*] of it, and the freedom to express this by teaching or practice, and to publicize and to observe it, either alone or in community with others, upon the condition of respecting the rights of others.
>
> (LTDH draft, ibid.)

Three main changes are made. First, the right to individual interpretation is made explicit, so that individuals expressing unorthodox opinions cannot find themselves accused of apostasy. Second, the right to publicize such changed beliefs is made explicit, to safeguard freedom of speech. Third, a condition is added: respect for the rights of others, so that controversial opinions should not be stated in a provocative or insulting manner. Such conditions might help to make the new freedoms more palatable to conservative opinion in Tunisia, but may also be seen encouraging an ethos of responsibility in an open and free public sphere.[15] Let us consider the first of these modifications in a little more detail. Charfi explains:

> You know, here in Tunisia we are very attached to the notion of interpretation or *ijtihad*. We have introduced important new *ijtihads* here in Tunisia as when, for example, we abolished polygamy. And

[15] It is perhaps worth considering whether a charter like this might have prevented the controversy over Salman Rushdie's novel *The Satanic Verses* in Britain and elsewhere in 1988–9. The initial request of British Muslim leaders, concerned at the representation of the Prophet, was for the novel to be reissued with an explanation that the book is a work of fiction that does not accurately portray early Islamic history (Samad, 1992, p.514).

> logically, in order to guarantee freedom of *ijtihad* you have to, in effect, suppress punishment for apostasy. Why? Because if you suggest an *ijtihad* that goes against establishment thinking, and if your right to express and argue for your *ijtihad* isn't guaranteed, you may be accused of apostasy.

> (quoted in Dwyer, 1991, p.176)

In particular, the execution of Muhammad Taha for apostasy in Sudan in January 1985 was uppermost in the minds of the charter writers (ibid., p.177). (As mentioned earlier, Taha was An-Na'im's teacher in Sudan, and it was for translation of Taha's work that An-Na'im was forced to leave the Sudan.)

As regards the other controversial issues, the draft charter retained Article 16 paragraphs 1 and 2 of the UDHR on freedom to marry a partner of choice, which states:

> Men and women of full age, without any limitation due to race, nationality or religion, have the right to marry and found a family. They are entitled to equal rights as to marriage, during marriage and at its dissolution. Marriage shall be entered into only with the free and full consent of intending spouses.

> (ibid., p.236)

It also weakened slightly Article 25 paragraph 2 of the UDHR on the rights of illegitimate children. The change in the latter was as follows:

> UDHR: 'All children, whether born in or out of wedlock, shall enjoy the same social protection.'

> LTDH draft: 'All children should benefit equally from care and social protection.'

> (ibid., p.237)

The point of the change is that the former may be taken to imply equal inheritance rights, which would be seen as an attack on family values: 'encouraging free love' as Charfi puts it. The latter does not challenge inheritance laws, but is designed to ensure that the illegitimate child is supported by society. Charfi argues:

> Society must take illegitimate children in charge so they have access to society's material advantages ... But that doesn't mean the child should be integrated into the family – that would be to harm the legitimate family.

> (quoted in Dwyer, 1991, p.173)

When the draft charter went out for consultation with the various sections that comprise the membership of the League, it was the articles on freedom of religion (Article 9) and freedom to marry regardless of religion (Article 8) that proved most controversial. In particular, Islamists outside the group were putting pressure on Islamists within it to force changes, using a press campaign accusing the Charter of being 'imported' and 'non-Islamic' (ibid., p.174). In response, when the National Council met to agree the charter on 28 July 1985 amendments to Articles 8 and 9 were discussed, including a new preface which recognized the contribution of 'Arab Muslim civilization' to the development of human rights. We shall consider each of these issues in turn, first looking at the amendments proposed, their fate, and further amendments in the following months, and then at the issue of the preface.

First, Charfi sets the scene at the meeting:

> Among the fifty of us, there was about one-tenth on the extreme left who were adamant against any changes, and were even against the new preamble; about a tenth were Islamists who supported the preamble but wanted to make it stronger, and who were also for the radical reformulation of articles 8 and 9; and then the remaining eight-tenths who were people who I believe are really true partisans of human rights, who believe sincerely in the principles of the UDHR. But even in this group views were divided. Some were saying, 'We should go into battle, because even if there is a battle, we will win it'. Others were saying, 'No, this does too much offence to the feelings of people, all we have to do is change the formulation a bit and it will get through'. So, although these groups may have agreed on the principles, they disagreed on how to get them agreed in our society.
>
> (quoted in Dwyer, 1991, p.175)

The Council voted on two amendments to the draft: to change Article 8 on marriage from 'without discrimination on the basis of race, colour or religion' to the more universal but less specific 'without any discrimination whatsoever', and to change Article 9 from 'freedom to *change* one's religion' to 'freedom to *choose* one's religion', considered less provocative on the apostasy issue. By narrow margins, the first amendment was rejected (24 to 23), and the second passed (25 to 22) (ibid., p.176). However, while the 'choose/change' feature of Article 9 arguably meant that it was weakened, the *ijtihad* and right to publicize modifications of the UDHR were retained, arguably making the article more relevant to the Tunisian context, and hence more useful in practice.

Further controversy followed the LTDH National Council's agreement of the Charter: in particular, pressure against it from the press intensified (ibid., p.178). However, this pressure seems to have had the effect of making the different factions pull together, with the result that when the Council next met on 22 September it confirmed the Charter with one modification, provided some additional clarification to strengthen its position, and agreed not to alter the wording again until at least the next Congress in 1989.[16] The modification served to strengthen the position on the right to marry irrespective of the religion; it reads:

> Men and women, upon attaining legal majority, have the right to freely choose their spouse and begin a family on the basis of their own personal convictions and consciences.

(ibid., p.178)

The League further strengthened and contextualized its position by affirming the Personal Status Code, which, as we have seen, considerably strengthened the rights of women, but had in 1985 come under attack by Islamist groups. They also sought to rebut Islamic accusations of western bias by arguing that the UDHR does not represent only western views, but rather reflects 'a compromise between the world's great civilizations' (Charfi, quoted in Dwyer, 1991, p.178).

This brings us to the issue of the contribution of the 'Arab Muslim civilization' which had been adopted in the preamble. On the one had this point may be readily substantiated by facts such as that Islam gave inheritance rights to women fourteen centuries before Christian Europe, specified rights for widows and orphans, and recognized the rights of Christian and Jewish communities which went further than anything in Europe prior to the emancipation of the Jews (eighteenth to nineteenth centuries). On the other hand, problems arise when, as we have seen with assimilationist, appropriationist and liberal (harmonizing) positions above, this kind of argument is used to mask real differences between pre-modern understandings of *sharia* and modern human rights. In particular, these rights in *sharia* are not premised on equality between sexes and different religious groups, but rather on the subordination of women to men and of non-Muslims to Muslims. As Charfi comments in relation to the Islamist position in the Charter debate:

> On the question of freedom of religion, the Islamists take the orthodox view – freedom of religion means the freedom of each person to practise his own religion – not to interpret it, but to practise it. When one talks of freedom of religion in Islam, the point of reference is the context of the conquering Islamic armies that crossed Egypt and Africa starting in the seventh century and that, contrary to the behaviour of other invading armies, did not destroy churches and synagogues but allowed Christians and Jews to continue to practise their religions.

[16] In fact, the Charter was little discussed then, and has remained unaltered (Dwyer, 1991, p.237, n.9).

> That's the Islamic meaning of religious freedom: we, the Muslim
> rulers, allow the Jew or Christian to freely practise his religion.
>
> (quoted in Dwyer, 1991, p.177)

However, while this may have been a benign arrangement in the
medieval period, it fails to come to terms with the structural
transformation of societies during the modernization process,
specifically the change in the ordering principle of societies from
one of stratification to one of social differentiation. The increased
social mobility of individuals and groups under the principle of
differentiation – including the fact that one person can adopt many
different social roles – means that the resolution of difference by
social stratification is no longer tenable. Hence the need to accord
rights primarily on an individual basis, although for those groups
lacking the social capital to mobilize as individuals, group rights
remain an important means of achieving equity (Galtung, 1994, p.16).

To return to the charter, its achievement may be seen partly in its
combination of a recognition of the social role of Islam with the social
principle of differentiation, for example, by upholding the distinction,
in a civil context, between legal and theological competence. Thus:

> Let's say a Muslim woman wants to marry a non-Muslim man. And
> here, on one side, is a great theologian who says that Islam prohibits
> such marriages. But on the other side there is Fatima or Leila, daughter
> of Muhammad, who indeed wants to marry a particular non-Muslim
> man. Well, I believe the great theologian has the right to say that such
> an act is a sin, has a right to go and preach to young women and advise
> them against these marriages. But he has no right to prohibit these
> marriages; the tribunal and civil officials *must* accept her choice, not
> the voice of the theologian. This is the proper distinction between law
> and religion. We at the League never wanted to change Islam, but we
> wanted to affirm that the rule of law coexists with religion, side by side
> with religion, not against religion. Each norm must be given its proper
> sphere of application.
>
> (Charfi, quoted in Dwyer, 1991, p.179)

More generally, the charter sought to clarify the relationship between
human rights and Islam in a Muslim majority society, to avoid the
dismissal of human rights as a western import and to present it as a
non-partisan discourse relevant to the needs of Tunisian society. As
Charfi summarizes its achievements:

> Before, you know, there was a lot of confusion, and that's why the
> charter was necessary. Now things are clear: we are not anti-Islam, we
> are not against Islamic civilization, we are not pro-West. We may have
> a way of looking at things that is not the way of the majority, I don't

know. But in spite of that, we're willing to co-operate with everyone,
and we're accepted with our differences.

(ibid., p.181)

This Tunisian example thus shows the difficulties and dangers of
using human rights discourse in a Middle Eastern context, but also
how, given sufficient political freedom and determination, a HRO can
convey the meaning of modern human rights in the public sphere of
a Muslim majority society. Furthermore, the LTDH did so in a way that
articulates with Islam, both affirming, challenging and recognizing
the reciprocal challenge of Islamic culture, and drawing both Islamist
and secularist groups together into the debate.

   We have now considered (i) aspects of the tensions between the
primary sources of Islam (Qur'an and *sunna*, and *sharia* discerned
on the basis of both of these) and human rights (UDHR, ECHR, etc.),
(ii) different Muslim interpretations of *sharia* and the different
responses to human rights to which they lead, and (iii) the actual uses
and effects of human rights discourse in a particular Muslim society.
In the last, we have seen what the relationship between human rights
and culture can mean in practice in one situation at one time. In the
final section we shall also consider the relationship between human
rights and culture, but in an ethical or philosophical rather than
descriptive sense. What ought this relationship to be? Are advocates
of human rights correct to insist on their universality? Or are Muslim
particularists, however repugnant their arguments might be to
western sensibilities, justified in their rejection of human rights on
the grounds of cultural specificity?

Human rights, culture and modernization

The human rights activist and Islamic scholar An-Na'im makes the
following observation on the question of whether the Qur'anic
prescription of amputation as a penalty for theft is a case of 'cruel,
inhuman or degrading treatment or punishment':[17]

> From a secular or humanist point of view inflicting such a severe
> permanent punishment for any offence, especially for theft, is
> obviously cruel and inhuman, and probably degrading. This may
> well be the private intuitive reaction of many educated modernized
> Muslims. However, to the vast majority of Muslims, the matter is settled

---

[17] From Article 7 of the International Covenant on Civil and Political Rights
(An-Na'im, 1992, p.30).

by the categorical will of God as expressed in the Qur'an and, as such, is not open to question by human beings...

Thus, in all Muslim societies, the possibility of human judgement regarding the appropriateness or cruelty of a punishment is simply out of the question. Furthermore, this belief is supported by what Muslims accept as rational arguments. From the religious point of view, human life does not end at death... In the next, *eternal* life, every human being will stand judgement and suffer the consequences of his or her actions in this life. A religiously sanctioned punishment, however, will absolve an offender from punishment in the next life because God will not punish twice for the same offence... To people who hold this belief, however severe the Qur'anic punishment may appear to be, it is in fact extremely lenient and merciful in comparison to what the offender will suffer in the next life should the religious punishment not be enforced in this life.

(An-Na'im, 1992, p.35)

This passage raises in acute form the issue of the role of culture in relation to human rights: according to An-Na'im, the majority of Muslims simply perceive the human condition differently from their secular counterparts, and therefore their understanding of what constitutes 'cruel, inhuman or degrading treatment or punishment' is different. Both Muslim and secular reactions, however, are equally rational responses to reality as differently perceived. In an increasingly interconnected world, how might we respond to such continuing cultural differences?

Two issues are central to the relationship between rights and culture. First, the role of culture in the implementation of rights. Irrespective of how rights are derived, how important is culture to their implementation? Second, what is the role of culture in the origination of rights? Are rights something which exist in some universal sense above or beyond culture, or are rights the product of culture?

Culture and the implementation of rights

To those who would argue that human rights are alien to their culture, the liberal would retort that so is the model of the modern state and its mechanisms of control – against which human rights are the only possible protection for the individual.

(Dalacoura, 1998, p.204)

In the modern world the enforcement of law is primarily the role of the state: indeed, the state claims a monopoly on violence (Giddens, 1987, p.121). However, in the case of human rights violations it is the state – with its police and military – that is the main perpetrator: this is certainly the case in the Muslim societies of the Middle East (Middle East Watch, 1992; Amnesty International, 1994, 1997; Egyptian Organization for Human Rights, 1997). Hence the importance of human rights as a standard whose legitimacy claims to reach beyond the borders of the state to protect people from abuse by the state under whose jurisdiction they live. This, as we shall argue later, is one of the strongest arguments for the universal *need* for human rights (as distinct from their universal *existence*).

However, without the powers of the state it is very difficult for other agents – other nations, or international actors, such as the United Nations – to enforce the implementation of human rights. International law[18] has historically proved notoriously difficult to enforce effectively, and this is particularly so in the case of human rights law. This contributes to what might be called the 'vulnerability' of human rights law, and is a further reason why it is important that local cultures support human rights laws if these are to be effectively implemented.

There are also further reasons why international law (and hence human rights law) has proved difficult to enforce. One is the domination of foreign policy by national self-interest - in spite of recent developments in 'ethical' foreign policy - such as tying aid to human rights. Another is the problem that retaliation in kind in the sphere of human rights is self-contradictory, whereas if other infringements of international agreements occur, in trade or military activity for example, retaliation in kind is in principle possible. But to retaliate against the persecution of a particular group by persecuting another would undermine the very principle of human rights that one is setting out to defend.

Even the European Convention on Human Rights (ECHR), the most comprehensive regional system, has only the relatively crude sanction of refusal of entry to or expulsion from the Council of Europe available to it as an instrument of enforcement. As Russia's entry to the Council in 1997 in spite of a highly critical inspector's report illustrates, political considerations may supersede legal or humanitarian ones even here (Janis, 1997, p 93). Furthermore, human rights violations often concern minorities within a society, which creates the further problem of convincing majorities to defend minorities. Enforcement of human rights legislation, then, is particularly difficult.

---

[18] Human rights law is sometimes incorporated into national law (as in many European countries, including the UK since 1998, but this is not the case outside the Council of Europe area), but in most cases it remains a branch of international law.

In these circumstances, what might be termed the 'cultural legitimacy' of human rights is particularly important to their implementation. 'Legitimacy' here means the authority, of a person, institution or idea. 'Cultural legitimacy' in particular means respect for and acceptance of the concept of human rights within a cultural system. Unless the concept of human rights is regarded as valid within a particular cultural setting, it has little chance of being implemented. And in the Muslim majority Middle East, where one of the unexpected consequences of the latest phase of modernization has been the increasing importance of religion in the social system, cultural legitimacy means legitimacy within Islamic discourse (Stark, 1999; Herbert, 2001). Hence, here, as in many other parts of the contemporary world:

> To believe one can deal with issues of rights while neglecting religion is to lose power to deal with most human beings. To believe one can deal with them from some supposed neutral point above the religious fray, for example in the name of some secular Enlightened republicanism, is to show unawareness that the religions of the world regard Enlightenment reasoners to be one more set of competitors on the religious scene.
>
> (Marty, quoted in Witte and van der Vyver, 1996, p.15)

This brings us on to the second issue in the relationship between rights and culture: the contested role of culture in the genesis of rights.

Are human rights universal? Culture and the genesis of rights

This is obviously a very large and important question, of which only a brief discussion is possible here.[19] None the less it is crucial to consider, because the answer one gives to it shapes the spirit in which the whole issue of Islam and human rights is approached. For if human rights can be shown to be universally valid, then culture-based opposition to them, however understandable, is simply wrong, and the appropriate response to it is one of refusal and re-education, however tactful. If, on the other hand, no universal basis for human rights can be demonstrated, disagreements between their advocates and opponents are placed in a different light. In situations where advocates and opponents come face to face, as they increasingly do in a globalizing world, the only alternative to unjustifiable coercion becomes an attempt to construct some kind of dialogue, aimed at

---

[19] For further discussion see Galtung, 1994, especially pp.1–25; Fortin, 1996, especially pp.19–28; Stout, 1988, especially pp.60–81.

finding a practical response to the management of shared spaces and of individuals within them. We will argue that while philosophical justifications of the universality of human rights on a priori grounds have so far proved elusive, an argument deriving from the experience of globalization, together with a biologically based argument for basic human needs, does support the universality of human rights, or at least a universal basis from which the articulation of rights in particular situations can proceed.

We shall begin by considering arguments for the universality of human rights in the western legal and philosophical traditions. These approaches to justifying human rights have tended to downplay or deny the role of culture. Before considering particular arguments that do this, we shall ask why in general this has been case. One important reason is that conceding that culture plays a role in the genesis of rights has tended to be seen as the path to moral relativism, the view that there are no moral absolutes, and hence any moral stance is as good (or bad) as any other. If moral relativism is accepted, it is argued, on what grounds can cruelty or tyranny be opposed? In the Muslim world, such opposition can be made in the name of God, but in the West there has been a tendency to divorce religion from the justification of public morality. Thus although religions may contribute to supporting public morality, the latter must, it is argued, rest on another basis. This is partly because the prevalence of religious plurality, agnosticism and atheism mean that there is no shared basis of religion from which such an understanding could derive, and partly because of the history of involvement of religion in social conflict in the West.

Liberal thought[20] in general, from which the modern concept of human rights developed, first emerged in seventeenth-century early modern Europe – a context in which the rival truth claims of Protestant and Catholic Christian groups appeared to be threatening

---

[20] In attempting to define 'liberalism', political philosopher John Gray (1986) argues that 'Whereas liberalism has no single unchanging nature or essence, its origins lie in a definite cultural and political circumstance and its background in the context of European individualism in the early modern period' (p.ix). Gray finds a common, modern conception of humanity and society in all variants of liberal tradition, a conception which he describes as (i) individualist, (ii) egalitarian, (iii) universalist and (iv) meliorist (1986, p.x). Gray sees these as moral claims, (i) asserting the moral right of the individual against the collective, (ii) conferring equal moral status on all people, at least in the negative form of denying the relevance of moral worth to legal and political order, (iii) asserting the moral unity of the human species and the secondary significance of sources of difference, and (iv) insisting on the possibility of change and improvement in society's arrangements. The tension between liberalism's particular origins and its claims to universal validity are a source of tension in an Islamic cultural context, which can be seen in the debates over Islam and human rights.

to tear the fabric of society apart, as the Thirty Years War (1618–48) and the English Civil War (1642–51) illustrate. Hence the need to found public order independently of religion, which had provided the legitimizing ideology of medieval Europe (otherwise known as Christendom). As various liberal theorists have argued, this context led to forms of politics which excluded religion from public life, instituted a secular basis for citizenship and a public principle of religious toleration, and asserted the rights of the individual against the state (Galston, 1991, pp.259–63; Stout, 1988, p.222).

Of course, the exclusion of religion from public life in Europe was not total, and religion remains an important factor in public life in some European contexts, as Chapter 1 has shown. None the less, by contrast, Muslim majority countries have not experienced wars of religion in the medieval or modern periods, and hence (in part at least) have not sought to separate religion from public life in the same ways. As we have seen, there are ways in which religion and state were in fact separated from one another from an early stage in Islamic history – for example, in the differing jurisdictions of caliphal and *sharia* courts, but the distinctive modern forms of separation only arrived in the Muslim world in the colonial period, an association which, as we have seen, remains problematic. Thus there are historical, political and philosophical reasons why the western philosophical tradition has tended to downplay the role of religion and culture in supporting human rights and why Muslims tend to be critical of this position.

Now we shall consider some particular arguments that have been made to support the universality of human rights. Broadly, there are two influential streams of such arguments: 'positivism' and 'naturalism'. The former is typical of legal approaches, the latter of philosophical ones. Their main features are:

> The positivists consider the content of human rights to be determined by texts agreed upon by states and embodied in valid treaties, or determined by obligatory state practice attaining the status of binding international custom. The naturalists, on the other hand, regard the content of human rights as principally based upon immutable values that endow standards and norms with a universal validity. In neither ... instance does culture enter into the deliberative process of interpreting the meaning (or) justifying the applicability ... of human rights.
>
> (Falk, 1992, p.44)

The positivist argument has some merit in enabling governments and non-state agencies to draw attention to the obligations that governments have already undertaken to observe. But they tell us nothing about the ethical validity or authority of human rights concepts, only that these have been approved by proper legal procedures. Hence when, as in the Muslim Middle East, the validity of human rights discourse is called into question on the grounds of its historical origins or cultural specificity, the positivist argument provides no counter argument in kind. Which leaves us with the naturalist argument.

Within the West, naturalist arguments have been called in to question in recent years. The philosopher Alasdair MacInytre has summarized some of the counter-arguments. First, an empirical one derived from the observation of history: if human rights are universal, one might expect to find some evidence of their recognition in different times and cultures. Yet:

> ... there is no expression in any ancient or medieval language correctly translated by our expression 'a right' until near the close of the middle ages: the concept lacks any means of expression in Hebrew, Greek, Latin *or Arabic*, classical or medieval, before about 1400, let alone in old English, or in Japanese until as late as the mid nineteenth century.
>
> (MacIntyre, 1985, p.69, my emphasis)

However, while the absence of rights thinking prior to the modern period may give us pause for thought, it is not decisive. For rights could still be seen as having always existed, only waiting to be discovered. Thus the fact that bacteria went unrecognized until their discovery in the mid nineteenth century, does not mean that they didn't exist until Pasteur discovered them under his microscope. None the less, the historical and cultural fact that no evidence of a concept of human rights is to be found in most times and places does make it difficult to argue that such rights are self-evident or intuitive. Yet, unfortunately for the naturalist case, most arguments presented in its favour have tended to appeal to precisely these concepts (ibid., pp.69–70). In the contemporary context, it seems sufficient for opponents simply to deny that they have such intuitions or find the concept of rights self-evident, for this kind of naturalist case to fall apart. And if the concept of human rights is not already articulated in particular cultural systems, it seems unreasonable to expect its immediate implementation.

However, it will be argued here that the weakness of these particular naturalist arguments does not imply that the concept of human rights as universal must be abandoned, nor even that the naturalist case is entirely without merit. First, something of the naturalist argument can be rescued by considering the basic, biological needs of human beings. Differing metaphysical frames might challenge the priority accorded these needs, for example, whether amputation constitutes 'cruel or inhuman treatment' in rival (in this case) Islamic and secular worldviews. But the satisfaction of many such needs (for food and shelter, and freedom from arbitrary attack and experience of pain) may be agreed across cultures, and may be articulated in terms of rights (the right to food, shelter, etc.). However, this 'bottom up' biological approach does not get us very far: while rights that relate to basic human needs (e.g. food, shelter) can be argued for on biological grounds, rights that relate to more complex social systems (e.g. civil and political rights) cannot, but are essential to modern concepts of human rights.

A further possible development of the 'naturalist' approach is to extend it into the social sphere. For if human beings are by nature a social species, then their sociality is just as much a 'fact of nature' as any physical property. And if the social formations humans produce have common elements, then these can form the basis of an argument for human rights.

Thus rights may be thought of as deriving from the properties of social systems, which require development to be expressed as rights in the modern sense, but can none the less be regarded as implicit.[21] Thus the mutual recognition accorded to individuals in cultures x, y and z may be articulated in terms of rights: of wives to material support from their husbands, of children to support from their parents (and vice versa later in the lifecycle), of strangers to hospitality from the community, etc.

It should be noted, however, that such an argument has at least one important limitation. Because rights are derived 'bottom-up', from observations of the properties of social systems, they are not universal in some transcendental sense, but only as widespread as features of reciprocity in cultures. It may be argued that all cultures actually observed exhibit forms of reciprocity, but this does not prove that all cultures must do so.

Furthermore, such networks of mutual obligation differ from modern systems of rights in important ways. First, they are generally two-way, so that giving or receiving entails entitlements and obligations. In contrast, although the connection between rights and responsibilities is often stressed, an innovative and controversial but influential characteristic of some modern understandings of human rights is that individuals are entitled to at least some of them

---

[21] The philosopher and social theorist Jürgen Habermas (1987) has argued that there are mutual moral obligations implicit in the basic structure of human communication. However, as a universal basis for modern human rights this falls prey to the same weakness as the simpler argument presented here: that is, two specific features of modern rights systems – equal rights for all and the idea that rights precede obligations – cannot be justified on either basis (Bauman, 1993, pp.220–1, n. 30).

Figure 2.4 Girls' literacy project in the Delta region, Egypt. Sean Sprague/
Panos Pictures.

regardless of whether they have honoured their responsibilities or
not: in this sense, they are held to be 'inviolable', as we discussed
earlier (p.81). Second, they are often not equal obligations, but rather
reciprocal obligations based on different roles in the social system.
Thus masters owe certain dues to slaves, husbands to wives, and
elders to children, and vice versa, but these dues are not the same.
Reciprocal rights are compatible with a stratified society (as most pre-
modern societies were), whereas equal rights are not, using 'equal' in
the sense of all individuals being entitled to the same treatment from
others, in relevant specified ways. Thus the idea of equality which is
so prominent in modern concepts of human rights is absent from
traditional cultural formations. One way of thinking about this
difference is to think of traditional rights and duties as 'vertically
oriented': people are tied to each other in chains of obligation which
are reciprocal but not equal. In contrast, rights and duties between
individuals in modern Western societies may be imaged as horizonal,
with people as individuals located at the same level of citizen, and
hence bound by equal rights and responsibilities. None the less, it may
still be argued that the networks of mutual obligation of traditional
societies have the germ of the idea of human rights, and hence, given
appropriate educational or developmental opportunities, provide a
basis for the development of a rights-supportive culture.

   This proposal raises an important question: why should participants in a range of non-western cultures, where the modern Western

concept of human rights remains potential rather than actual, wish to have this potential developed, wish to be educated in the western ways that have brought so much destruction to their cultures? The answer to this lies in their very incorporation into the world-system. We have argued above that the state is the main threat to human rights in most Muslim societies, and more generally that the modern state has brought a whole new set of threats to individuals. Human rights are a moral language particularly adapted to cope with this threat, reaching out beyond the state to an international sense of obligation which transcends the tyranny of state boundaries.

Furthermore, the discourse of human rights responds not only to the emergence of the state system, but also to the unprecedented interaction between peoples brought about by international migration, urbanization and communication, which has created a world of strangers in which traditional, communally based and culturally specific systems of mutual obligation struggle to retain their binding force. However, it is also possible that developments in cheap and accessible communication technologies may serve to preserve these bonds more than was once thought possible. Yet this is turn provides a further argument for rights – to defend dissenting individuals and groups from resurgent forms of communal identity, such as the more radical forms of Islamism.

So perhaps the strongest case for rights is not grounded on whether they exist as a universal property independent of culture, but rather a consequentialist one grounded on the effects of their use, specifically their emergence as a way of protecting the individual from the growing powers of the state in early modern Europe, and later in response to the other moral threats of modernization, including the resurgence of collectivist and politicized forms of religion. From this perspective, the language of rights is a useful, indeed vital, invention for the prevention of cruelty and suffering in modern contexts. Civil and political rights play a crucial role in defending the interests of individuals against the incursions of states and of trans-state actors ranging from multinational corporations to radical Islamist groups. Human rights discourse thus becomes universally applicable by virtue of the empirical universality of the modern nation state and the modern world system. Note that there is a change in the sense of 'universality' here, from *absolute* to *what is in fact found everywhere, but being based on observation, this is only as good as the consistency of observation.* This parallels the shift at an earlier stage in the argument from universal in the sense of *a priori* individual rights to universal in the sense of reciprocal obligations observed across a range of cultures.

Do these arguments help us to decide whether human rights are in some sense always already universally present, or whether, on the contrary, they are invented? I think they show that it is very difficult to demonstrate the existence of a universal concept of human rights apart from particular cultures. Appeals to self-evidence, intuition, and so on are deeply unimpressive in the context of the historical and cultural diversity of patterns of socially sanctioned human interaction. Minimal biological needs may be specified and translated into the language of rights, but these do not tell us very much about more complex human rights which are central to the modern notion: civil and political rights, for example.

However, the inability of philosophers and others to come up with arguments which prove the existence of human rights does not imply that human rights discourse is a bad way to mobilize and to protect people from cruel and inhumane treatment, or that what constitutes cruel and inhumane treatment is merely a matter of opinion (moral relativism). Rather, it has been argued that some basis for the universality of human rights can be rescued by building on commonalities of biological need, and from existing patterns of cultural interaction. Furthermore, the specific form of modern rights (equal, inviolable) may be justified by reference to specific features of modernization made universal through globalization, for example the breakdown of social stratification and the rise of the power of the state. Equally, however, the universality of the modern concept of human rights may be challenged thorough the examination of non-western cultural formations. Such comparison reveals, for example, an individualist bias which discriminates against some groups whose best chance of political mobilization is on a group basis, especially indigenous groups, but also in some cases, religious groups.

Yet while the effects of global social transformations – for example the increasing presence of the state – may be felt everywhere in the modern world, states are associated with very different cultural systems. Indeed, it may be argued that while economic and political systems have become more interconnected and convergent, cultural systems have become more fragmented and divergent (Tibi, 1998, pp.82–113). This may in fact be a reaction to the convergence of other systems, as culture becomes the only way to articulate difference in the modern world system. In these circumstances, the need to articulate rights through culture becomes, as we have seen, both imperative and intensely problematic: that is, imperative to defend the rights of individuals against the problematic products of the world system, including incursions of the state and of culturally based communal groups such as radical Islamists.

Figure 2.5 Tradition and modernity, or two routes to modernization? Two women cross a road, one in hijab and the other in Western-style clothes. Mahdia, Tunisia. © TRIP/H. Rogers.

Conclusion

The relationship between Islam and human rights is a complex and emotive one, and it has not been possible here to do justice to all perspectives on it, or to all its ramifications. In particular, issues of women and religion require further development, and these take centre stage both in the next chapter and in the texts associated with this chapter in Part Two of this book. None the less, we have introduced some of the complex debates that social transformations have triggered in contemporary Muslims societies. It has been argued that culture plays a crucial role both in the legitimization and genesis of human rights, arguments supported by reference to biological, cultural and global conditions. This central role of culture in the mediation of human rights means that where religion is socially influential it becomes an important factor in debates about human rights. Hence the importance of inter-cultural dialogue between Muslims and others in Muslim majority societies in search of formulations of human rights that reflect authentically the local cultural conditions.

Of the five types of Muslim response to human rights which we considered (particularist, assimilationist, appropriationalist, liberal-harmonizing and liberal-confrontationalist), only the last position is

Figure 2.6 Government oppression continues in Tunisia: Najet Zoghlami, sister of Tunisian journalist Taoufik Ben Brik, stands in front of the Tunisian Tourist Office in Paris on 3 May 2000, during a protest organized by the press freedom watchdog Reporters Sans Frontiere. Taoufik Ben Brik (pictured in the photographs at the rear) is on hunger strike in Tunisia for the release of their brother Jalal who was imprisoned after criticizing the Tunisian authorities. Naegelen/Reuters/Popperfoto.

fully receptive to such dialogue, and such a position is very much a minority one in the contemporary Muslim Middle East. Authoritarian governments stifle the development of a civil society within which such debates can take place. However, as the case of the Tunisian Progressive Islamists in the late 1980s illustrates, such a position can become influential, even in a Muslim majority society with an authoritarian government. Furthermore the genesis of the LTDH's Charter shows that wide participation in public debate about human rights discourse is possible, debate that faces up to the differences between the dominant formulations of modern human rights and Islamic tradition, without the debate becoming polarized into mutual rejection.

Glossary

Baha'i A religious movement that grew from an Islamic sect (the *Babi*) in late nineteenth-century Iran. They recognize Mirza Husayn Ali as a prophet (and hence are seen as apostate by orthodox Sunni and Shi'ite Muslims). Ali preached the unity of God, humanity and the eventual unification of all faiths.

fiqh Islamic legal theory (or jurisprudence), which developed to interpret *sharia* (God's way or path) after the death of the Prophet.

hadd penalties specified in the Qur'an, given for theft (amputation of the hand), adultery and false accusations of adultery (flogging), armed robbery (death), wine drinking (flogging) and apostasy (death).

hadith 'traditions', about the actions and words of Muhammad and his early followers. In Sunni Islam, only those about Muhammad himself (*sunna*) constitute a source of *sharia* law.

hijra 'exodus', of Muhammad from Mecca to found the first Islamic political community Medina in 622 CE. The Islamic calendar dates from this event.

ijtihad 'struggle' – referring to intellectual struggle to discern Islamic law. Comes to refer to new interpretations.

Islamist person or group who supports an increasing role for Islam in society, not just in private life. This often includes the ideas of 'implementing *sharia*', and of an Islamic government or state.

istihsan 'to approve, or deem something preferable'. Refers to the process of discerning a fundamental intention within a law which may override its literal interpretation.

Nadha 'Renaissance' – name of the Tunisian Islamist Party (LTDH) since 1989.

qadi judge who implements Islamic law.

qiyas reasoning by analogy, as a principle in interpreting Islamic law.

sharia there are two main senses of this term. First, in the Qur'an, this literally means a 'way' or 'path' to a watering hole, referring to God's guidance. However, since the Qur'an specifies relatively few laws, the legal tradition has been expanded greatly over the years through the development of traditions of legal theory (*fiqh*). This gives rise to the second sense of *sharia* as the outcome of this process of development.

shubha doubt, as a principle in interpreting Islamic law, which may be used to prevent the implementation of severe penalty.

Surah chapter in the Qur'an.

ulama Islamic scholars, specializing in *fiqh*, the interpretation of *sharia* law.

References

Ahmed, A. (1992) *Postmodernism and Islam*, London: Routledge.

Al-Azmeh, A. (1993) *Islams and Modernities*, London: Verso.

Ally, M. (1990) 'Second introductory paper', in Commission for Racial Equality, *Law, Blasphemy and the Multi-faith Society*, London: Commission for Racial Equality, pp.21–9.

Amnesty International (1994) *Tunisia: Rhetoric Versus Reality: The Failure of a Human Rights Bureaucracy*, January, London: Amnesty International.

Amnesty International (1997) *Tunisia: A Widening Circle of Repression*, June, London: Amnesty International.

An-Na'im, A.A. (1992) 'Cultural foundations for international protection of human rights', in A.A. An-Na'im (ed.) *Human Rights in Cross-cultural Perspectives*, University Park, PA: University of Pennsylvania Press, pp.19–43.

An-Na'im, A. A. (1998) '*Shari'a* and basic human rights concerns', in C. Curzmann (ed.) *Liberal Islam: A Sourcebook* Oxford: Oxford University Press, pp.222–38.

Arkhoun, M. (1994) *Rethinking Islam: Common Questions, Uncommon Answers*, translated and edited by R. Lee, Oxford: Westview.

Ayubi, N. (1991) *Political Islam*, London: Routledge.

Banman, Z. (1993) *Postmodern Ethics*, Oxford, Blackwell.

Beinin, J. and Stork, J. (eds) (1997) *Political Islam*, Berkeley, Calif.: University of California Press.

Curzmann, C. (ed.) (1998) *Liberal Islam: A Sourcebook*, Oxford: Oxford University Press.

Dalacoura, K. (1998) *Islam, Liberalism and Human Rights*, London: IB Tauris.

Dwyer, K. (1991) *Arab Voices: the Human Rights Debate in the Middle East*, London: Routledge.

Egyptian Organization for Human Rights (EOHR) (1997) *Torture Inside Police Stations Must Be Stopped*, Cairo: EOHR.

Eminov, A. (1997) *Turkish and Other Muslim Minorities of Bulgaria*, London: Hurst.

Esposito, J. (1994) *Islam: The Straight Path*, 2nd edn, Oxford: Oxford University Press.

Falk, R. (1992) 'Cultural foundations for international human rights protection rights' in A.A. An-Na'im (ed.) *Human Rights in Cross-cultural Perspectives*, University Park, PA: University of Pennsylvania Press, pp.44–64.

Fortin, E. (1996) *Human Rights, Virtue and the Common Good: Untimely Meditations on Religion and Politics*, London: Rowman and Littlefield.

Galtung, J. (1994) *Human Rights in Another Key*, Cambridge: Polity.

Galston, W.A. (1991) *Liberal Purposes: Goods, Virtues and Diversity in the Liberal State*, Cambridge: Cambridge University Press.

Giddens, A. (1987) *The Nation State and Violence*, Berkeley: University of California Press.

Gray, J. (1986) *Liberalism*, Milton Keynes, Open University Press.

Habermas, J. (1987) *The Theory of Communicative Action*, vol. 2, Cambridge: Polity.

Habermas, J. (1996) *Between Facts and Norms*, Cambridge: Polity.

Halliday, F. (1995) *Islam and the Myth of Confrontation: Religion and Politics in the Middle East*, London: IB Tauris.

Herbert, D. (2000) 'Virtue ethics, justice and religion in multicultural societies', in K. Flanagan and P. Jupp (eds) *Virtue Ethics and Sociology: Issues of Religion and Modernity*, London: Palgrave.

Herbert, D. (2002) *Religion and Civil Society: Rethinking Public Religion*, Basingstoke: Ashgate.

Herbert, D. (2001) 'Representing Islam: the "Islamization" of Egyptian society 1970–2000', in G. Beckerlegge (ed.) *From Sacred Text to Internet*, Aldershot: Ashgate with The Open University, pp.161–218.

Huntingdon, S. (1993) 'The clash of civilizations?', in *Foreign Affairs*, vol. 72, no. 2, pp.22–50.

Janis, M. (1997) 'Russia and the 'legality' of Strasbourg law', *European Journal of International Law*, vol. 1, pp.93–9.

Kamali, M.H. (1991) *Principles of Islamic Jurisprudence*, Cambridge: Islamic Texts Society.

Kymlicka, W. (ed.) (1995) *The Rights of Minority Cultures*, Oxford: Oxford University Press.

Lapidus, I. (1992) 'The Golden Age: the political concepts of Islam', *Annals of the American Academy*, no. 524, November, pp.00–0.

MacInytre, A. (1985) *After Virtue*, 2nd edn, London: Duckworth.

Makdisi, J. (1985) 'Legal logic and equity in islamic law', *American Journal of Comparative Law*, vol. 32, pp.63–92.

Marty, M. (1996) 'Religious dimensions of human rights' in J. Witte and J. van der Vyver (eds.) *Religious Human Rights in Global Perspective*, Netherlands: Kluwer Law International, pp.1–16.

Mayer, A. (1994) 'Universal versus Islamic human rights: clash of cultures or a clash with a construct?', *Michigan Journal of International Law*, 15, pp.307–402.

Mayer, A. (1995) *Islam and Human Rights: Tradition and Politics*, London: Pinter.

Mernissi, F. (1988) *Women and Islam*, Oxford: Blackwell.

Mernissi, F. (1993) *Islam and Democracy*, Virago: London.

Middle East Watch (1992) *Behind Closed Doors: Torture and Detention in Egypt*, New York: Human Rights Watch.

Mumm, S. (ed.) (2001) *Religion Today: A Reader*, Aldershot: Ashgate.

Rahman, A. (1984) *Shari'ah: The Islamic Law*, London: Ta-Ha.

Rosen, L. (1987) *The Anthropology of Justice*, Cambridge: Cambridge University Press.

Ruthven, M. (1991) *Islam in the World*, 2nd edn, London: Penguin.

Samad, Y. (1992) 'Book burning and race relations: political mobilization of Bradford Muslims', *New Community*, vol. 18, no. 4, pp.507–19.

Schwartlander, J. and Bielefeldt, H. (1994) *Christians and Muslims Facing the Challenge of Human Rights*, Bonn: Deutsche Kommission Justitia et Pax.

Stark, R. (1999) 'Secularization R.I.P.', *Sociology of Religion*, vol. 60, no. 3, pp.249–73.

Stout, J. (1988) *Ethics After Babel*, Cambridge, Mass.: James Clarke and Co.

Tibi, B. (1998) *The Challenge of Fundamentalism: Political Islam and the New World Disorder*, Berkeley: University of California Press.

Weeramantry, C. (1988) *Islamic Jurisprudence: an International Perspective*, Basingstoke and London: Macmillan.

Wickham, C. (1997) 'Islamic mobilization and political change: the Islamist trend in Egypt's Political Associations', in J. Stork and J. Benin (eds) *Political Islam: Essays from Middle East Report*, London: IB Tauris, pp.120–35.

Wilson, B. (1992) 'Reflections on a many-sided controversy', in S. Bruce and R. Wallis (eds), *Religion and Modernization: Sociologists and Historians Debate the Secularization Thesis*, Oxford: Clarendon Press, pp.195–210.

Witte, J. and van der Vyver, J. (eds.) (1996) *Religious Human Rights in Global Perspective*, Netherlands: Kluwer Law International.

CHAPTER 3

What it meant and what it means: feminism, religion and interpretation

SUSAN MUMM

'Better ... or worse? ... Better, or worse?' Anyone who has ever had their eyes tested will be familiar with the ritual chant of the optician, as lenses of various strengths are tried out against the eye, in an attempt to improve the perception of the world. This is precisely the goal of this chapter. In it the reader will be invited to try out a number of feminist, anti-feminist, and post-feminist perspectives, in an attempt to see if the world of religion can be perceived more vividly, more fully, more accurately, more clearly, through a different lens. Our goal is to see the world of religions differently – and even if only for a moment – to see it as others see it.

If one were to compare the world of religion today with that of the 1940s, perhaps the most visible shift in the religious landscape has been the position of women. In the 1940s Simone de Beauvoir posed her key question, 'What is a woman?': 'She is defined and differentiated with reference to man and not he with reference to her; she is the incidental, the inessential as opposed to the essential. He is the Subject, he is the Absolute – she is the Other' (de Beauvoir, 1949, p.xix) (Figure 3.1). But what does this classic feminist insight have to do with religion? My starting place is John Phillips's claim that 'feminism is the truly revolutionary movement of the twentieth century, because it cannot be reconciled with Western religion' (Phillips, 1984, p.174). The purpose of this chapter is to examine some aspects of how feminism has related to religions and how it has changed them, and in the process of doing so to consider the validity of Phillips's bold claim.

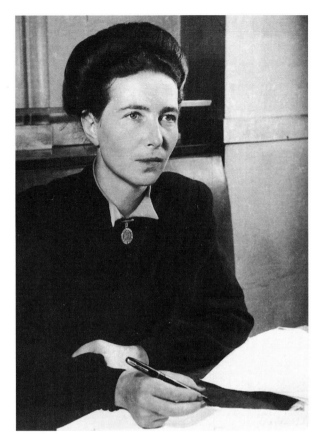

Figure 3.1 Simone de Beauvoir. Hulton Getty.

Until relatively recently, the role, status, and place of women within the historic world religions has been fairly noncontroversial. This is despite the fact that women, as half of the world's population, make up considerably more than half of the devotees in most major religions. The point at which women's place becomes an issue depends on the religion and, even more, on the culture within which the religion is operating. For the first few generations of a new religious tradition, while it is settling down and establishing and codifying its norms, women play quite a prominent part: think, for example of the Prophet's wives and daughter in Islam and the preaching women in early Methodism and Quakerism. Once the early burst of innovation is over, when conservatism and consolidation take the place of innovation and charisma, women tend to be relegated to the role of followers only. Typically, this is accompanied by an ideology which argues that women are fundamentally different from men, and part of this difference is their inherent inability to lead in the religious sphere. This relegation remains generally uncontested until the wider society begins to regard women as having equal rights with men. For most world religions, this creates immediate and obvious tensions, as this is not how sacred texts and accrued traditions relating to women are understood.

Even in the most male-dominated traditions, the role and nature of women has come up for debate in the last half century in a newly insistent and persistent way. Another important change that accompanies, and indeed created, this paradigm shift is that women have again become active participants in the conversation: they are not passive subjects of discourse. They have agency even in the most apparently oppressive religions. So how do we study women in religions? Is it enough simply to add on a section that deals with women's roles and position? This is the traditional view. Feminists argue that this is not enough, that women need a change from the heart of the tradition, and as the study of religion becomes **androgynous**, our ideas of what is important or distinctive about the tradition may change - Public ritual? Domestic worship? Private vows and fasts of Hindu women? Temple rituals conducted by men? Increasingly, anthropologists and religious studies specialists are arguing that lived religious experience is what requires more and closer study, and this is an area where women are full participants.

Thus, when seeking to understand the relationship between religion and social transformation, it seems essential to examine the way women relate to religion and religions relate to women. As Rita Gross reminds us, both feminism and religion are academic subjects, taught in universities world-wide. But they are also subjects that create strong emotional responses in most people, and they are 'belief systems that directly affect people's lives' (Gross, 1996, p.5). It is important to stress that there are no 'right' answers to the questions posed in this chapter, and I hold no brief for a 'true' interpretation of women's place within religions: my purpose here is to introduce the emerging arguments. As a result of my own cultural background and academic training, the religion foregrounded in this discussion will be Christianity; other traditions, especially the other monotheistic traditions, will be discussed, but relatively briefly. Some readers may be dismayed by the proliferation of different models of feminist response to religion. Feminism is not a monolith. It is variable, contested, and continues to evolve. Western feminism is quite different, in many respects, from the feminisms evolving in other parts of the world. Thus the flowering of models may be a useful reminder that over-generalization is a real intellectual danger in discussions of feminism internationally, but that attempting to find structural similarities may help us to understand the range of positions currently available. Often, the differences between the models discussed in this chapter are minimal, and largely the result of the model-maker's own perspective.

Feminism claims equality for women but does not always claim that women and men are similar in essence. Obvious biological differences between the sexes aside, feminism has paid most attention to how cultural socialization, specifically gender acculturation (that is, the accentuation of gender differences through cultural training and expectations), has accentuated and exaggerated the differences between men and women. Nancy Chodorow's research has led her to claim that women are encouraged to empathize with others, while men are encouraged to distance themselves from others. Carol Gilligan's research into language and moral dilemmas argues that women and men, as a result of gender acculturation, have different ideas of morality. Men (encouraged to be individual and separate) advocate an ethic of justice; women develop an ethic of care. In Gilligan's eyes, women's morality centres around what she calls *emphasis* (a stress on the value of the act), *consequence* (calculating the effect of an act on others), and *context* (assessing the social circumstances surrounding the action). Gilligan's research led her to conclude that men and women understand moral dilemmas and make moral decisions differently. She challenges older theories of ethical maturation, especially those of Erikson and Kohlberg, where maturity is equated with stereotypically 'masculine' qualities: separation, independence, and distance from others. Such differences in the moral worldviews of men and women, if they exist, have obvious implications for how the genders experience religion.

Definitions of feminism are as various as writings on feminism. Some postulate an absolute equality of mind, ability and spirit between the genders; others suggest that women have intrinsic qualities that could be seen as superior to those attributed to men; others argue that the struggle for women's status and a wider political, social and economic struggle are inseparable (sometimes called 'feminist advocacy'). Feminism in India or Africa may well identify an almost entirely different set of oppressions to fight, but will share the underlying belief of Western feminism that the equal dignity of men and women should be reflected in social and religious practice. In this analysis, I shall adopt Gross's simple formulation; 'the conviction that women really do inhabit the human realm and are not "other", not a separate species'.[1] She goes on to point out the implications of this:

[1] Much of the following argument is based on Gross's *Feminism and Religion: An Introduction* (1996).

> A more accurate mode of humanity would compel recognition that humans come in two sexes and that both sexes are human. It would also recognize that in virtually every religion, culture, or society, gender roles and stereotypes intensify biological sexual differences. As a result, men's and women's lives are more separate and different from each other's than is biologically dictated. An accurate model of humanity would also forbid placing one gender in the centre and the other on the periphery.
>
> (Gross, 1996, p.20)

What is it that feminism wishes to eliminate? Some writers term it patriarchy: more recently, it has also been called **androcentrism**. It has three central characteristics. 'First, the male norm and the human norm are collapsed and seen as identical.' Androcentrism fails to acknowledge that being male is only one side of human experience. Secondly, androcentrism assumes that the generic masculine automatically includes the feminine, meaning that there is little need to study women's experience: 'we study males, and think we are studying all humanity'. Thirdly (and according to Gross, most problematically), is 'its attempt to deal with the fact that, since men and women are taught to be different in all cultures, the generic masculine simply does not cover the feminine. The generic masculine would work only in religions and cultures that had no sex roles, but no such culture exists' (Gross, 1996, pp.18–9).

Why has there been such a strong reaction against the patriarchal elements of religion? Patriarchy, or 'rule by fathers', includes both a power relationship and a social structure that subordinates women to men. 'First-wave' feminism, which emerged in the United States and Britain in the middle of the nineteenth century, was a development of women's involvement in the anti-slavery movement. Women who had become politicized through their opposition to the slave trade, began to see their own situation as containing elements of oppression, especially after female activists were barred from attending an American anti-slavery convention, solely on the basis of their gender. In Britain, Josephine Butler began to use her Christian beliefs as a basis for a radical rethinking of women's roles, whereas secular feminists agitated for political representation and equal access to education. In the United States, two nineteenth-century suffragettes published important works on religion (Figure 3.2): Cady Stanton produced *The Women's Bible* (1895), an early attempt to reinterpret the scriptures dealing with women from a feminine point of view, and Matilda Gage wrote *Woman, Church and State* (1893), a pioneering study of religion as a patriarchal system, which attempted to argue for the existence of prehistoric, matriarchal religions. Thus, Stanton and Gage are early representatives of important tendencies in

Figure 3.2 American suffragettes Elizabeth Cady Stanton (1815–1902), holding the Women's Bible, and Susan Brownell Anthony (1820–1906) at the twenty-eighth Annual Convention of the National American Woman Suffrage Association. Hulton Getty.

feminist analysis of religion today (Figure 3.3). Many biblical scholars, primarily in Europe, had been arguing for the better part of a century that the scriptures should be seen as documents of their time and culture, containing divine truth, but also evidencing culturally limited views, which should no longer be held as binding in the modern world. After the First World War and the achievement of the vote for at least some women in most of the English-speaking world, the western feminist movement fell into quiescence, to be reawakened in the 1960s and '70s: this is sometimes called 'second-wave' feminism.

But before we turn to the varieties of feminist approaches to the 'problem' of male-dominated religions, we must briefly survey the range of traditional responses to the 'problem' of women. First, we cannot unpick religions from the societies in which they develop and

Figure 3.3 Elizabeth
Cady Stanton
(1815-1902).
American suffrage
activist and author of
The Women's Bible,
Hulton Getty.

in which they take root. Gender is reflected in both social structures
and religious understanding, and it can be very difficult to determine
where the boundary is. Is patriarchy the poisoned fruit of a religious
tree, or is the denigration of women in religions the tainted flowering
of a patriarchal culture? Certainly, it is true that culturally defined
sexual distinctions determine men's and women's economic, political, social and spatial places in a society. Religious ideologies solidify
these functions, and participate in creating them, through their claim
that such roles are divinely mandated. They also promote gender
identities that can criticize and redefine previously acceptable sex
roles. The extremes of this dynamic relationship can be found in
societies that have reconstructed rigid sex roles as a response to the
tensions of the contemporary world (for example, some Muslim
societies and groups on the American religious right, such as the
Promise Keepers[2]). Of course, all religions claim that they treat
women in the proper, divinely ordained fashion, and that women are

[2] The Promise Keepers attained prominence in the 1990s; they emphasized
restoring family relationships by reclaiming their God-given authority as husbands
and fathers within the family.

treated best in their tradition. There is a strong tendency to criticize the treatment of women in other traditions, and to seek out examples of how women are worse off in other religions. Thus women can become little more than ammunition in the faith/culture wars.

A tripolar model is sometimes used to explain the near-universal subordination of women in the world religions. Many, but by no means all, societies share a conceptual framework in which culture and nature are seen as diametrically opposed, and where culture supersedes and is seen as being superior to nature. Women, it is assumed, are closer to nature, while men represent and create culture. This is linked to a sexual division of labour where women's labour (typically childbearing and caring) is viewed as subservient to, and less important than, men's labour in terms of production and control of power. The third aspect of the model focuses on men's control of the dominant public domain, with women restricted in large part, to the private sphere.

Although there is, in theory, an unlimited range of possible interactions between women and religion, many follow the nature/culture divide. This idea sees women in all religions as being associated with nature which is 'lower' – with birth, fertility, the body and 'darkness' (Colour Plates 7 and 8). Men are linked to culture – to improvement, to intellect and the mind, to striving and to the 'light'. Nature is assumed to be inferior to culture overall, and is required to be kept in subordination to culture, and to be controlled by it.[3] Historically, the nature/culture divide has also been pressed into the service of racism: 'one of the legacies of slavery is that black women, even more than white, have been cast as the body and nature' (Thistlewaite, 1990, p.85).

While Gerami and other writers on the nature/culture dichotomy agree that societies with this conceptual framework all perceive culture to be superior, this may be coming into question at the beginning of the twenty-first century. Newer perspectives, such as that of the green movement, have begun to challenge this assumption, depicting uncontrolled culture as being ultimately destructive of all life in its exploitation of nature. Increasing concerns about genetic manipulation also reverse the traditional status of culture and nature. However, instead of trying to achieve a nature/culture equilibrium, some movements, such as ecofeminism and deep

---

[3] Much of the discussion of the nature/culture dichotomy is derived from Shahin Gerami (1996), and from the work of Barbara Stowasser (1994).

environmentalism,[4] have simply nature's being inferior to culture: they redefine culture as destruction of the natural world; an inversion of the former hierarchy.

It has been argued that many traditions have buttressed the nature/culture dichotomy with a deep-seated hostility to female sexuality, as well as to the female sex. Christianity, especially in its Catholic and Orthodox manifestations, has denigrated sexuality and celebrated virginity (which it often assumes to be asexual), from the virginity of the mother of Jesus through to the life-long celibacy of nuns in the Catholic and Anglican traditions. Traditional Judaism and Protestant Christianity seek to contain sexuality firmly within a heterosexual family structure, making it very difficult for Jews, in particular, to choose life without marriage. Many Hindus see in the teachings of Manu a rationale for confining women entirely to the domestic sphere.[5] Middle Eastern Islam has seen female sexuality as destructive and thus advocates seclusion. While post-war modernism has relaxed sex segregation in some Muslim countries, the rise of Islamic movements has resurrected (or introduced) spatial segregation of women and men as central to a godly society. In the largely Protestant USA, the tension is expressed as conflict between family obligations and economic aspirations: the mother in the home is still often portrayed as the ideal role for women, but economic realities mean that few women of child-bearing age can afford to remain out of the workplace.

There are some broad areas of agreement when trying to organize and understand the role of women in religions, although different sociologists of religion and theologians call them by different names. In this discussion I will use both the terminology of Shahin Gerami and Daphne Hampson.

Gerami, focusing primarily on Islam, sees three streams of thought.

The *modernists* make a distinction between the perfect model from the past, such as early Islam or apostolic Christianity, and later corruptions and damaging acculturation. Modernists practice *ijtihad* (individual interpretation of scripture) and, in Islamic countries,

---

[4] 'Ecofeminism' is synonymous with 'green feminism', a movement which links feminist and environmental issues. 'Deep environmentalism' sees the earth itself as a deity, rather than having been created by one. It is environmentalism with a strongly spiritual, often neo-pagan, dimension.

[5] Some of Manu's strictures regarding women are discussed in the Gupta text in Part Two of this book. The best known ones are probably: 'In childhood a female must be subject to her father, in youth to her husband, when her lord is dead to her sons: a woman must never be independent'; and 'Though destitute of virtue or seeking pleasure [elsewhere] or devoid of good qualities, [yet] a husband must be constantly worshipped as a god by a faithful wife' (quoted in Gross, 1996, p.84).

demand legal reforms. In Christian countries, they may favour the ordination of women or align themselves with similar reform movements.

The *conservative traditionalists* view their religion as an inherited system of faith balanced by scripture and tradition on the one hand, and by community consensus on the other. Islamic conservatives often see modernity as equivalent to westernization, colonialism, or cultural contamination.[6] Christian conservatives view cultural modernity as equally undesirable, being equivalent to secular humanism or, again, cultural contamination. Regardless of the tradition in which conservatives are found, they emphasize preserving stable structures for the religion and for the society based on past tradition. Except for a marginal minority, conservatives of most traditions have largely abandoned the assumption of inherent inequality between the sexes, although many have replaced it with a doctrine of complementarity which may function little differently.

Gerami's third category is the *fundamentalists*. These can perhaps be described most accurately as scriptural activists: they tend to stress the literal interpretation of scripture, and they attempt to translate the sacred text directly into contemporary thought and action. They ignore or reject traditional theological accretion and customary interpretation in their emphasis on acting out the scripture today. Fundamentalists often see themselves as the 'conscience' of the religion and its associated way of life, and putting women back into their God-mandated places is a key objective in their struggle to re-Islamicize or re-Christianize society. The contemporary Middle East, the USA and, to a lesser extent, Europe can each offer a number of examples of such groups from across the religious spectrum.

Hampson, a post-Christian theologian who left Anglicanism after campaigning for women priests, and then decided that Christianity itself was fundamentally hostile to women, also categorizes responses to the dilemma posed by feminism for the historically-based religions. She identifies four streams of thought, one of which is conservative, with the other three departing from tradition to some extent.

The *conservative* response allows 'what is essentially normative for the religion to reside in the past' (Hampson, 1990, p.12). In other words, conservatives look to the past for the blueprint for how the divine wants life to be lived. In the Christian tradition, they often argue that Jesus was not limited by the cultural boundaries of the time in which he lived - if he had no female disciples, it was not because

---

[6] Few reject structural modernity (i.e. literacy); but cultural modernity (of which feminism is a part) is much more problematic.

these would have been unacceptable and scandalous in first-century Palestine; it was because Jesus did not want female disciples.[7] Conservatives also argue that God has continued to guide the church, and that, for instance, its history of subordinating women is clearly what God intended. (ibid., p.13).

Hampson identifies three types of *bridgebuilders* – schools of thought which attempt to 'throw a bridge between past and present'. The *kairos* approach sees the past as essentially normative but also sees and respects development over time because it suggests that the divine will for the religion may itself change as time passes. The *golden thread* approach, 'where a leading motif is lifted out of the past and applied in another situation' (ibid., p.22), describes those who see in their tradition one key moral lesson which is of transcendent value. For example, the golden thread approach might include those who see the overall religious message as one of liberation, or as one of the redemptive value of suffering. This group may emphasize certain texts, which they see as containing the golden thread, over others which seem to contradict it. The last group holds what Hampson terms the '*a priori ethical*' position, where most authority is found in the present, but the past is not seen to be completely alienating. For many in this group, lived experience is authoritative.

Of course, there are many other ways of understanding the issues, and we are not limited to the categories suggested above. Some analyses of religion claim that the essential divide in the treatment of women is between monotheistic and polytheistic traditions, where monotheistic religions are perceived as more oppressive of women religiously, while both traditions are oppressive socially. This argument is based in part on the evidence of the importance of female deities in polytheism, although even within these traditions the female deities are ordinarily subordinated to the male, and there is not necessarily a positive relationship between the high status of female deities and the standing of women. However, it might be salutary to pause before accepting this line of analysis uncritically. What about traditions that cannot be described as either monotheistic or polytheistic? How does this argument operate in religions that see their female (and male) deities as multiple manifestations of a single, unseen and unseeable deity? In addition, Gross warns us against the 'deeply entrenched tendency in Western thinking to turn differences

---

[7] It is important to remember that the situation of a religion accommodating a practice, such as slavery or patriarchy, which is already in the culture, isn't necessarily the same as the religion requiring such practices. Others may feel that this is a 'chicken-and-egg' type of argument.

into a hierarchy', deciding that some traditions are 'better' than others because of how they view women, or that some approaches to religion are 'better' than others, and deserving of more respect. 'If we are different, then one of us must be better – the classic scripts of patriarchy, monotheism, and Western thought in general assume this' (Gross, 1996, p.51). Dividing religions' treatment of women along the lines of monotheism and polytheism may ultimately be yet another instance of false hierarchy building.

At this juncture, some readers may be feeling impatient. If most world religions contain within them a wide range of alternative views of the social roles, religious roles, and correct treatment of women, why then is there a need for feminist analysis at all? Surely women will simply align themselves with that strand of their religion with which they feel most comfortable? I would argue that this is an unsustainable position because women's religious choices are constrained for several reasons. First, many women in the world today do not have a choice of religious allegiance. They are born not only into a tradition, but into a subgroup of customs within that tradition. Some of these subgroups are liberal, and allow for female freedom of conscience and action, but some do not, being instead prescriptive and authoritarian. The religious choices women make are not made in isolation: they are bound up with their social, cultural, and economic situations. An example of this is to be found in Judy Brink's study of Sunni Muslim women in rural Egypt. In the village where Brink did her fieldwork in 1983–4, there were no Islamic fundamentalists resident, and the village women were amused by the whole-body veiling of an urban visitor. When Brink returned in 1990, many of the younger women were wearing the *higaab* and *niqaab* (waist-length head coverings and face veils – see Colour Plate 6).

> When I asked *muhaggabat* [women who wear religious dress] in Sadeeq why they wore the veil, they never spoke of a personal moral decision but always referred to the wishes of a male relative. Women said they veiled because their brother or husband was 'sunni' (fundamentalist). The long religious *higaab* or the *niqaab* was a symbol of the husband's or brother's religious conviction, not that of the woman.
>
> (Brink, 1997, p.201)

Brink goes on to argue that this decision is a supremely pragmatic one: if a woman's husband mistreats her, she can only run away to her father's or brother's house. If she accedes to a relative's wishes to become *muhaggabat*, she retains his goodwill and his protection in case of need. In urban Egypt, women tend to see veiling as a more positive statement, often in relation to an anti-colonialist or anti-western position, although male demands still make it a constrained choice for many (McLeod, 1991, pp.142–63). Some women find considerable social and emotional support in fundamentalism, while in Latin America fundamentalism gives women the opportunity to renegotiate family relationships in ways beneficial to them.[8]

I would suggest a modified model; one that finds four dominant modes of positioning women within the world religions. Historically, all religions have portrayed themselves as defenders of women, and have argued that only in ... [name any religion here] are women accorded their proper place.

Traditionalists proclaim that the faith has raised the position of women to a height of respect and dignity beyond that found in any other religious tradition. However, they teach that this does not imply role equality: women's roles are complementary to those of men, but ultimately subordinate to male authority.

Egalitarians argue that there are historical reasons for seeing religion as the first attempt to establish the equality of the sexes in terms of roles as well as dignity; on this view a priesthood composed of both sexes is appropriate and necessary.

More recently, *radicals* argue that religion by its very nature perpetuates the permanent subjection of women, likening the movement for the ordination of women as equivalent to American blacks petitioning to join the Ku Klux Klan.[9] This, ironically enough, constructs a continuum which places those egalitarians who argue for the ordination of women squarely in the middle of the spectrum, both theologically and ideologically.

Also active in the debate are *revisionists* who seek to purify, modify, perhaps even reinvent their tradition, striving to create theologies, rituals and liturgies that do not legitimate patriarchy.

At the extremes of this model are two antagonistic groups who paradoxically share some theological ground: traditionalists who argue that women cannot usurp male authority within the church, and post-religion feminists who agree, but for a very different reason: that women cannot stay within the traditions at all, contaminated as they are by their sexist origins and structure.

---

[8] See, for example, Elizabeth Brusco, 'The Peace that passes all understanding: violence, the family and fundamentalist knowledge in Columbia', pp.11–24 and Nancy L. Eiesland, 'A Strange Road Home: adult female converts to classical Pentecostalism', pp.91–116; both in Brink and Mencher (1997).

[9] The remark was originally made by Mary Daly, quoted in Maitland, 1983, p.119.

Few if any religions are egalitarian, with all aspects of religious life being equally open to all.[10] In Christianity and Judaism, the issue which ignited controversy has been the question of women's right to ordination or rabbinical status. The virulence of these debates has forced a re-examination of the entire question of women's place within religion; debates which usefully map out the range of ideological and theological positions that have emerged around the issue of how women can be faithful to religions which seem to regard them as less central than men at best, inferior to men at worst.

Reforming feminism

Most of the reformers work within the monotheistic religions, especially Christianity and Judaism, and focus on the historical continuity between the religion in its past and present forms. They see the problems as falling into three main categories. First, women are excluded from the full practice of the religion because of the male-oriented language of the tradition. Secondly, images of the divine (where used) are male. Thirdly, there is male monopoly of ritual and of public roles. When reformers look at their religions, they see traditions which exclude, limit, or forbid women.

> I saw that the rhetoric of Reform [Judaism], while it held out the hope of equality, masked the reality of women's exclusion from religious leadership. I also know that the educational opportunities available to friends in the Conservative movement had similarly conveyed contradictory messages: for example, while a girl could be bat mitzvah, this event marked the end, rather than the beginning, of her participation in congregational life.
>
> (Plaskow, 1991, p.xi)

The importance of ritual (praxis), while downplayed by those that Mary Daly, a pioneer in feminist theology, categorizes as 'spiritual-ists',[11] is historically important in the development of feminist theology. In Judaism and Christianity, it was the exclusion from leadership roles and ritual practice that pushed women to re-examine their theology.

A similar pattern can be seen in the Hindu tradition, where reformers urge a return to a 'true' ancient pattern of religion; these are sometimes called 'revivalists', because they claim that a return to the core teachings of Hinduism will give women an improved role in the

[10] Some, like Sikhism and the Society of Friends (Quakers) approximate it.

[11] 'Spiritualists' argue that exclusion from ritual roles is irrelevant, since both the included and the excluded can be equally pure of heart.

religion and in Indian society (Robinson, 1999, pp.48–9). Sarojini Nadu (1879–1949), reformer, poet and president of the Indian National Congress, saw this return as her birthright: 'We ask for nothing that is foreign to our ideals, rather we ask for a restoration of those rights, those rights that are the immortal treasures [of Hinduism]'. A good example of this restoration is Rosen's edited collection of essays examining how women within the Vaisnava traditions (saints, goddesses and ordinary women) can be seen to be 'liberated'. It is important to remember, though, that anthropologists and religious studies specialists have claimed that the real conditions of women within this strand of Hinduism differ very little from those in others, calling into question how important the symbolism has been for women's and low castes' lived experience.

Very recently, there has been some change to Judaism and Christianity, most dramatically with respect to the right of women to officiate in the rituals of the traditions. In 1976, the American Episcopalian Church sanctioned the ordination of women, reversing a decision reaffirmed in 1973. (The first women had been ordained, illegally but validly, in 1974, and these ordinations were retroactively recognized two years later.) The first woman bishop was consecrated in 1989 (Figure 3.4). In 1992, the Church of England voted to ordain women; the debate over women bishops continues, although most commentators agree that it is only a matter of time. Today, most mainstream Protestant Christian churches ordain women, as do Reform and Conservative Jews (Figure 3.5). The largest groups within Judaism and Christianity to continue to refuse women to serve in this role in public ritual are the Roman Catholic and Orthodox churches and orthodox Jewry. Many women involved in the demand for full female participation in religious ritual have been influenced by one of the basic tenets of **process theology**: 'We do not think ourselves into new ways of acting; we act ourselves into new ways of thinking' (quoted in Maitland, 1983, p.191). This means that while they may share the serious concerns about liturgical language and so on, they believe it is of primary importance for women *to be seen* to be active in the faith, and this can be done only through women taking leadership roles (Figure 3.6).

The other major focus of the reformers has been the reform of liturgical practice and language. The goal here has been to make language inclusive, not to challenge the tradition's mainstream theology, although some claim that this may be the inevitable consequence of changing the language. A key question for feminist interrogations of religions is the representation of the deity. How is it represented? Is there a female form or forms? How can women identify with a male deity? The three major monotheistic religions

Figure 3.4 Barbara Clementine Harris, self-educated theologian and advocate for the dispossessed, consecrated first woman bishop in the Anglican Communion in 1989. The Church Times.

portray their god in very male terms (the monotheistic god in Sikhism is linguistically neuter; it takes on gender only when translated into languages such as English); most polytheistic religions offer alterna-tive versions or incarnations of the deity, some of which will be female. Some inclusive language campaigners are content to replace male-oriented language with more general terms when the text refers to humankind (for example, 'for us men and for our salvation' in the Anglican liturgy has been reformulated to remove the gender reference). The majority argue that the terminology for the divine, as well as for the worshipper, must be reformulated to be gender-inclusive. Linguistic reformers of both types, in Adrienne Rich's famous phrase, share 'the dream of a common language', in an attempt to increase the sense of connection between women and men, as well as between humankind and the divine.

Like the involvement of women in ritual, the demand for inclusive language has provoked strong reactions from traditionalists. Op-ponents of the inclusive language movement argue that prescriptive attempts to change a language are doomed to failure, as they doubt whether people's attitudes can be changed by changing their language. Others argue that the demand for the elimination of sexist language may be a 'passing fad', and fear that it may alienate

Figure 3.5 Deacons ascending the steps of St Paul's Cathedral en route to their ordination ceremony, 17 April 1994. Brenda Price/Format.

Figure 3.6 Ruby Lee Blanche, a Methodist minister, preaching in Bentonia, Mississippi. Val Wilmer/Format.

traditionalists without attracting or retaining new congregations. Additionally, the movement is argued against by those who say that changing language is a superficial change - treating symptoms rather than the disease – and that the tradition may itself suffer: 'The finest hymnody and devotion will be damaged if anarthrous [without any article] man is not used' (Liturgical Commission, 1989, pp.13–4). In the eyes of conservatives, the most serious criticism is that the impetus for change is seen as coming from secular feminism, and may result in the substantial reconstruction of the religion itself (ibid.).[12] One laywoman summarized the hostility she had experienced, and what she believed to be the unconscious core of that antagonism and resistance to change: 'the minute you try and offer alternative feminine symbols for the divine, you're met with accusations of heresy ... Men are little Gods. God is a big man' (Miles, 1994, p.6).

Mary Daly, in an early and important book in the feminist re-evaluation of the Christian tradition, responded to these and similar objections (Daly, 1985, pp.5–6). She divided the arguments resorted to into four types (Daly's counter-arguments are in parentheses).

Trivialization, which argues that the oppression of women is less serious than the evils of racism, environmental destruction and war. (Sexism and other abuses of power are connected: to attack one is to weaken all.)

Particularization, which sees the sexism in Christianity as a uniquely Catholic problem, and is slow to see signs of patriarchy elsewhere: an example would be 'Get rid of Paul and all will be well'.[13] (The patriarchal element within Christianity was so close to the core that all Christian sects participated in it, although some did so to a greater extent than others.)

Spiritualization, which responds to feminist criticism by emphasizing that women should focus on the spiritual benefits of religion, and acquiesce in the cultural oppression that accompanied it. (This was a refusal to look at 'concrete oppressive facts'.)

Universalization, which argues that the real need is for human liberation. (This is true, but it is not useful to avoid one problem because others exist.)

[12] There are many publications on this subject of the challenge offered to the 'way things are' by feminist ideas; some even argue for preconcerted conspiracy! See, for example, Michael Gilchrist, (1991).

[13] The key texts that limit women's roles in the church are found in the writings attributed to Paul: especially 1 Timothy 2:9–15, and 1 Corinthians 14:34–5.

It would be a mistake, however, to assume that reformers approach their tradition timidly, or with naive optimism. Judith Plaskow's situation within Judaism is typical.

> I am not a Jew in the synagogue and a feminist in the world. I am a Jewish feminist and a feminist Jew in *every moment of my life*. I have increasingly come to realize that in setting up Judaism and feminism as conflicting ideologies and communities, I was handing over to a supposedly monolithic Jewish tradition the power and the right to define Judaism for the past and for the future. 'Judaism' was not a given that I could fit myself into or decide to reject. It was a complex and pluralistic tradition involved in a continual process of adaptation and change – a process to which I and other feminist Jews could contribute. Like the wicked child of the Passover Seder, I was handing over Judaism to *them*, denying my own power as a Jew to help share what Judaism becomes ... For me, the move toward embracing a whole Jewish/feminist identity did not grow out of my conviction that Judaism is 'redeemable', but out of my sense that sundering Judaism and feminism would mean sundering my being. Certainly, I did not become a feminist Jew by adding up columns of sexist and nonsexist passages in the Bible and deciding the nonsexist side had won. Judaism is ... a deeply patriarchal tradition. To change it will require a revolution as great as the transition from biblical to rabbinic Judaism precipitated by the destruction of the Second Temple. I do not believe there is some nonsexist 'essence' of Judaism in the name of which I struggle, nor do I believe that success is assured.
>
> (Plaskow, 1991, pp.xi–xiii)

The dividing line between 'reformer' and 'revolutionary' is a vague one. Many reformers have begun, while retaining loyalties to their tradition, to draw on sources beyond its traditional teachings and texts. An example of this in the Church of England is the St Hilda's Community, and in American Catholicism, WomenChurch. Both these groups practise explicitly feminist forms of Christianity, and both have experimented extensively with liturgy. As time has past, they have begun, however cautiously, to incorporate symbols and rituals from beyond Christianity into their worship.[14]

But feminist approaches to religion have come under attack, not only from its traditionalist voices, but by women of colour, non-western women and lesbians, who point out that just as white heterosexual women's experience was ignored by androcentric religions, their experiences were equally subsumed in feminist spirituality, which sometimes talked about 'women's experience' as if

[14] Both have published inclusive-language and woman-oriented liturgies, and both exist as worshipping communities as well, where liturgical innovation is developed and practised.

it were universal and uniform. For example, American Hispanic women within this stream of thought call themselves *mujerista*: their emphasis is not the liberation of the individual woman, but of the self as part of the community. Chung Hyun Kyung, an important Korean theologian educated in Britain and America, reflects on her experience:

> Throughout my eleven years of theological training, I have written countless term papers and theological essays for highly educated people who were my teachers. The style and content of my speaking and writing have been shaped in such a way that persons like my mothers[she is referring to her birth and adoptive mothers] could never understand what I was saying. The more I become a 'good', 'professional' theologian, as defined by European and American theological scholarship, the more I become alienated from my mothers and people like them. Now it has become clear to me that I no longer want to write so-called 'comprehensive' theology seeking to answer questions of privileged Europeans. I want to do theology in solidarity with and in love for my mother so as to resurrect crucified persons – like her – who are located on the 'underside of the underside of history' in a white, capitalist, male-dominated world.
>
> To choose the despised women of Asia as the primary context for my theology means to do theology that is accountable to their experience. Theological languages, paradigms, and questions that come from the life experiences of Western male intellectuals, who are the brains of the cultural hegemony which reduced poor Asian women to the status of non-persons, cannot serve as a source of Asian women's theology. The resources for Asian women's liberation theology must come from the life experiences of Asian women themselves. Only when we Asian women start to consider our everyday concrete life experiences as the most important source for building the religious meaning structures for ourselves shall we be free from all imposed religious authority.
>
> (Chung, 1991, p.5)

Marianne Katopo of Indonesia, is another theologian who claims Asian women need to free themselves from both western and men's control. Again, it is important to remember that *all* theologies are coloured by the cultural contexts: in the case of much of Asia, the women and men studying religion work within a recent and lived history of colonization, neo-colonialism, poverty, militarism, dictatorship, and racism as well as the experience of deeply patriarchal societies[15] (ibid., p.24). **Liberation theology**, theology from beneath,

---

[15] It would be a mistake to dismiss the concerns of Asian theologians as a minority issue: Asia contains 58 per cent of the world's population; Asian women are a quarter of the world's humanity. One could more rationally argue that western preoccupations are marginal.

urges us to 'read the Bible with the eyes of the poor'. Feminist theologians are beginning to question whether this is possible:

> [W]e have to try to read with our eyes in fact – the eyes of dominant people who are intensely aware of the poor and of our relationship to them. When we do not learn this, we get caught in the trap of criticizing others, without changing ourselves, in spite of all our structural analyses.
>
> (Eck, 1986, p.179)

This is an important point that I will be returning to later in this chapter.

Revolutionary feminism

The 'revolutionaries', many of whom, like Daly, started out in the reformist camp, see the traditions differently. In their view, even the core teachings of the traditions are so contaminated by sexism and patriarchy that they cannot be cleansed; to eradicate patriarchy from the world religions would be to dismantle the religions themselves. Their solution is to leave the tradition, sometimes for a post-religious life without faith or religious practice (such as Daphne Hampson) or for a form of spirituality inspired by paganism, which Gross describes as 'an umbrella term for a wide variety of pre- and nonbiblical traditions, that often include female images of the divine' (Gross, 1996, p.44). Sometimes called the *feminist spirituality movement,* or feminist witchcraft, it began its period of rapid growth in the 1970s, with the early prominence of WomanSpirit.

These feminist theologians see Christianity and Judaism as too broken to be fixed. Mary Daly is perhaps the best known post-Christian feminist in the tradition. She began her career as a conventional student of Catholic theology, developed a critique of the sexism within Christianity, and eventually moved beyond Christianity altogether, finding patriarchy too hopelessly embedded in Christianity.[16] For Daly, Christianity did not contain patriarchy; it *was* patriarchy. Unlike reformers, who continue to see a liberating core in the religions, the post-tradition feminists see inextricable patriarchy at the heart of the world religions. This progression can also be traced (from a Protestant/Anglican perspective) in the writings of the theologian Daphne Hampson. Hampson begins her book by asserting that feminism is a revolution: 'It is not in essence a demand that women should be allowed to join the male world on

---

[16] Mary Daly is probably best-known for describing Mary, the mother of Jesus, as a rape victim (Daly, 1978, p.85).

equal terms. It is a different view of the world' (Hampson, 1990, p.1). She argues that feminism may be the death of Christianity as an important religion, while reasserting its continuing cultural import-ance in the West.

This does not mean that post-religion feminists embrace an entirely secular worldview. On the contrary, both Daly and Carol P. Christ have become prominent in different elements of the alternative spirituality movement. While Daly left Christianity because of its history of oppressing women, Christ lost her belief in Christianity because of her concern over the effects of its core religious symbolism and language on consciousness. In one of the essays published in *Laughter of Aphrodite* (1988), she tells the story of acting as the godmother to a friend's baby girl.

> Evelyn was the only child being baptized, and the ... minister ... spoke only of the Christian and 'his' baptism into the 'fellowship' of Christian 'men'. I had expected to hear God referred to only as Father, but I had not been prepared to hear this young girl's identity stolen from her by a man whose words were saying that she could not at one and the same time be a woman and a Christian.
>
> (Christ, 1988, p.28)

For Christ, this was one small example of an overwhelming deluge of imagery that was inevitably psychologically damaging to women.

The prepatriarchal hypothesis

Are there religions that do not display patriarchy? Some nominate prepatriarchal religions for this role. This prepatriarchal hypothesis[17] is very controversial, adopted by some, but by no means all, of those I have termed revolutionaries, seeks to demonstrate that perhaps religions were not patriarchal at the time of their foundation. As Gross points out, 'determining that patriarchy is a relatively recent historical development means that patriarchy is not inevitable and that male dominance is not somehow written into our genes' (Gross, 1996, p.151). The argument continues that very early societies could not have survived without full female participation, including the use of female skills and intelligence. Thus, foraging and early agricultural societies may not have been strongly male dominated: defenders of the patriarchal hypothesis reinforce their arguments with examples from the surviving foraging societies, which tend to be egalitarian, with an emphasis on gender complementarity. Advocates of this hypothesis claim that patriarchy requires a level of social stratification

---

[17] This section is based closely on Gross, 1996, pp.151–72.

and cultural complexity that can only be achieved by societies when they reach a certain population density, a kind of 'critical mass' of people living close together.

It is important to remember that the prepatriarchal hypothesis does not assume *matriarchy*, as some critics of the perspective have assumed: some may have been *egalitarian*, **matrifocal** or **patrifocal**. Neither does evidence of goddess worship prove that women were highly regarded in daily life, although some have assumed that this would be the case. Another problematical aspect of the hypothesis is that it accounts for the collapse of these cultures, and their religions, by their invasion and conquest by violent marauders from patriarchal societies. This assumes an *essentialist* view of human nature, that is, one in which women are seen as inherently peaceful and egalitarian, and men as tending toward violence and authoritarian behaviour. This, as Gross and others have pointed out, is 'as biologically determinist as any patriarchal religion's insistence that women's lives be bounded by their reproductive responsibilities' (ibid., p.162). Latin-Americans also claim a prepatriarchal religion, based on 'balanced opposition between the sexes', where the male god Ometacuhtli and female god Omecihuatl were worshipped, which was destroyed by the arrival of the Aztecs.

Other views of the prepatriarchal hypothesis see not a violent end to matrifocal societies, but a gradual decline in the power and status of goddesses, which may either have reflected or have encouraged a corresponding decline in the status of women in the society. However, ancient Israel was the only religion-founding tribe to end by absolutely rejecting goddesses in all their forms, although the logic of monotheism meant that female aspects of divinity had to be subsumed into male forms, along with the worship of all 'foreign' deities. Some argue that these aspects re-emerged in Christianity in the Catholic view of the Virgin Mary, and in the (posited) femininity of the third member of the Trinity, the Holy Spirit.[18]

Introducing feminist hermeneutics

In the above discussion, it will have become apparent that the interpretation of sacred texts is central to a feminist analysis of religion, unless one is to reject revealed religion altogether. Hermeneutics (broadly, text interpretation) is a very old activity, which for centuries confined itself to trying to determine which was

[18] This is not a new idea: the concept of the femininity of the Holy Ghost was a commonplace in medieval theological speculation.

the most authentic and accurate reading of a text. However, it should be remembered that alongside the search for the most accurate reading of a text, runs a parallel history of interpreting texts in terms of myth and symbol, with a devotional goal: Christianity, Judaism and Islam all have a long tradition of symbolic interpretation. The Semitic religions have generally relied on religious authorities to establish and maintain hermeneutic boundaries: those interpreting texts in ways unsanctioned by authorities were commonly classed as heretics. One of the profoundest changes of the modern period is that with the rise in literacy and the development of cheap, mass-printed books, sacred texts have become widely available, and are thus subject to the individual interpretation of believer and sceptic alike. With technological and social change came new ideas, centrally that cultures produce the religions and values that buttress their survival. This makes religious and moral values relative to the cultures that produced them.[19]

But surely a text, religious or not, means what it says? The key conceptual contribution of modern hermeneutics is that there is more to text interpretation than that. As a starting point, I would like to suggest that hermeneutics can be understood as 'what it meant and what it means'. In its simplest form, hermeneutics reminds us that texts were written in a specific culture and historical period. Thus, texts are artefacts: created by people, for human reasons, and in a particular context. As one Christian commentator describes the problem:

> Whereas the exegesis of a text is concerned with a relatively fixed point in the past – what the author meant and how the original readers are likely to have understood it – its application moves us into an area of uncomfortable flexibility. The question is not now what the text meant, but what it means to me in my situation and to you in yours as well as to Christians of many different races and ages in many different parts of the world. The only thing these various points of application are likely to have in common is that each of them is far removed from the specific context and situation for which the biblical book was written.

(France, 1995, pp.24–5)

The writers had a readership in mind, but not the reader of today, who is inevitably almost unimaginably distant from the original scriptural context. So time transforms that which appears on the surface to be immutable. For example, within the Christian tradition, both the old and new testaments refer to, and unquestioningly

[19] Strictly it would depend on what the causes were. For example, if they were biological, then they may be relative to some biological conditions.

accept, slavery, and for centuries this practice was justified by a simple appeal to the surface of the biblical text.[20] When the British, and later the American, anti-slavery movements began, just as secular commentators accumulated arguments on both sides, so theologians turned again to scripture for arguments either to buttress or to attack slavery. But as cultural ideas about moral behaviour increasingly found slavery unacceptable, theologians began to find their readings of scripture coming down ever more solidly on the side of liberty. There are other instances, such as the resumption of the veil by Muslim women in some societies, where scriptural reading seems to have predated cultural change.

The 'father' of modern hermeneutics is Friedrich Schliermacher (1768–1834), who added a philosophical dimension to hermeneutics and established its basic principles: these are summarized below as expressed by Walter Jeanrond:

1 We cannot assume that understanding is automatic; even in everyday life we often misunderstand words and speech. We are even more likely to misunderstand when reading ancient documents. Understanding is an art; but the personal (subjective) understanding must be accompanied by a proper respect for the object to be understood (an objective dimension).

   'All understanding presupposes language; in language we think and through language we communicate. There is no understanding without language ...' (Jeanrond, 1994, p.45). A grammatical understanding of language must be accompanied by a psychological interpretation of the same language.

2 The two dimensions of interpretation (grammatical and psychological) are equally important in every act of text-understanding.

---

[20] Paul's epistle to Philemon was delivered by a runaway slave whom Paul was returning to his master and to servitude; the text of Galatians 3:28 was interpreted for centuries as being a statement about the equal value of all human souls, rather than as a condemnation of slavery, sexism or racism in this life.

3   A text can never be understood totally; we aim at approximation rather than a total grasp of the text. But interpretation must be guided by rules. The aims of 'these rules, then, are to help the interpreter to acknowledge both the relationship between the text and the linguistic system out of which the text has emerged, and the text's own particular impact on this linguistic tradition' (ibid., p.46).

4   Central to 'the rules' is the concept of the Hermeneutical Circle: the whole can be understood only from the parts, the parts from the whole.

Two 'moves' are essential in this circle:

- The first is an examination of a 'text's internal structure, i.e. how we appropriate the overall sense from its parts and how we learn about the parts from a comparison of the linguistic devices in the text'.

- The second is a consideration of 'the text's relationship with the whole of similar linguistic productions, i.e. how we can grasp a text's sense in the light of similar texts'. (ibid., pp.47– 8)

Take, for example, the person reading a novel. She has read other novels before; she understands the novelistic format and conventions. However, in this case she is reading a novel for the second time. She will probably be reading it for different reasons, and may get very different meanings and ideas from it. The same book, the same words on the same pages in the same order, is being read by the same person, yet the meanings may have shifted. Why? Time has passed: the perspective has changed. This experience teaches us that understanding is 'not an automatic and unproblematic exercise in deciphering a set of consistently identical signs on paper in front of us. Rather text-understanding always demands our active participation in recreating the text in question. It demands that we lend of our reality to the text so that it can become real for us' (ibid., p.1).

Hermeneutics claims that we cannot read neutrally; we read as individuals with unique understandings and interpret uniquely: thus there is no single 'true' reading of a religious text. As the liberation theologian James Cone writes in *God of the Oppressed* (1977), 'Theology is not universal language; *it is interested language* and thus is always a reflection of the goals and aspirations of a particular people in a definite social setting' (Cone, 1977, p.39, my emphasis on 'language'). Hermeneutics gives us an alternative to the literalism that demands that we believe that God guided the hand of the writer of scripture, as if he were an automaton, ensuring that every word, every nuance of syntax, and every piece of punctuation precisely conveyed the divine meaning. (Some also claim that the same spirit that inspired the writing of scripture inspires the reader too, so that the 'true' meaning is guaranteed from both directions.) Hermeneutics can help us to navigate the relationship between two realms, the realm of the text (or non-textual source such as a work of art) on the one hand, and the people who wish to understand it on the other.

Because hermeneutics is the art of interpretation, it has obvious relevance to the interpretation of religious texts, symbols, images and liturgy. The word itself is derived from Hermes, the messenger of the gods in Greek mythology, whose function was to explain the decisions and plans of the gods to people. This is precisely how some see the role of the interpretation of the sacred text in several world religions. Many religions view their sacred texts as a form of sacred law. In the secular realm, legal experts continually reinterpret the law in light of changing conditions. No law can anticipate all the situations to which it might apply; thus it must be interpreted and reinterpreted. Often religious authorities sanction hermeneutics in this limited role of interpreter, while remaining reluctant to allow the activity full play. Modern theological hermeneutics has a wider focus; not only does it try to understand the text, 'it tries to see how the text adds to understanding of the divine presence in the world, and of its wishes for us' (Jeanrond, 1994, p.8). This means that hermeneutics often takes text interpretation further than religious authorities are comfortable with.

Theological interpretations and reinterpretations have direct social consequences, since texts are seen as telling us how to live in accordance with the religion. They are thus of considerable interest to feminist theologians, who often struggle to find in ancient texts images of women and models of women that portray them in a positive light. Feminism, with its roots in modernity, finds that the male and female roles ascribed by religions a millennium or two ago are no longer fully applicable or appealing to people in the twenty-first century regardless of their nationality or tradition. These roles must be reinterpreted by people of today for the lives of today. Thus, feminist hermeneutics is typically considered to be one of the most important developments of modern religious thinking. Feminist theologians take seriously Martin Heidegger's claim that a 'faith that does not perpetually expose itself to the possibility of unfaith is no faith but merely a convenience: the believer simply makes up his mind to adhere to the traditional doctrine. This is neither faith nor questioning, but ... indifference ...' (Heidegger, 1959, p.9).

However, it is essential to stress that many believers, regardless of tradition, remain entirely unconvinced by the newer ideas derived from hermeneutics. For this group, the text is supernatural in origin, and unchanging in its absolute authority.

Varieties of feminist hermeneutics

In *The Color Purple*, two of Alice Walker's characters discuss the problem of imaging God in a way that is meaningful not just to women, but to black women. It summarizes several of the major themes to be explored in the remainder of this chapter: images of deity, scripture as a human artefact, women's experience as a religious source, and race.

> '... God wrote the bible, white folks had nothing to do with it.'

> 'How come he look just like them, then?' she say. 'Only bigger? And a heap more hair. How come the bible just like everything else they make, all about them doing one thing and another, and all the coloured folks doing is getting cursed?... Ain't no way to read the bible and not think God white, she say. Then she sigh. When I found out I thought God was white, and a man, I lost interest.'

> (Walker, 1983, p.166)

Jacqueline Grant, an African-American 'womanist'[21] theologian, has made a helpful distinction between three strands of feminist hermeneutical thinking, which also highlights issues of authority. While writing specifically about Christianity, her model can be utilized when thinking about other religions that also consider their scriptures the key to understanding the divine revelation.

At one end of the spectrum are the *biblical feminists*. In this school of interpretation, the sacred text is more important than woman's experience, so it critiques women's lived experience. 'Though the Bible is read in the light of women's experience, it [the Bible] holds primary authority.' This strand focuses on correct understanding of the sacred text or time-hallowed practice. 'Reinterpretation is the mechanism par excellence of religious change. Paradoxically, it actually promotes change and renders it possible by means of the fascinating mechanism of ostensibly denying the obvious process. Reinterpretation poses as a return to the original, correct, interpretation' (Biderman and Scharfstein, 1992, p.5). Of course, this approach (or any of the others) is not confined to people working in the Jewish

---

[21] The term 'womanist' is derived from Alice Walker, who wrote that 'Womanist is to feminist as purple is to lavender' cited in Gross, 1996, p.54. Many black feminists describe themselves as womanist.

or Christian traditions. Sartaz Asiz, an Islamic scholar from Bangladesh, turned to feminist hermeneutics after the horrifying consequences of the 1971 invasion, when at least one million Bangladeshi were killed and over two hundred thousand women sexually abused, by a foreign army claiming to be restoring the purity of Islam. She never considered repudiating Islam, but instead turned

> in the most radical way to the roots of Muslim experience ... to separate from it everything that was patriarchal. Patriarchy is the great enemy of everything that is good in spirituality and religion because it teaches that nations and individual persons can only define themselves by dominating others ...
>
> (quoted in Mollenkott, 1992, p.42)

With an approach identical to that of biblical feminists, she claims that 'all the misogynist interpretations and practices were accretions added later, after Muhammad's time, by ambitious and sexist males' (ibid.). In the Part Two of this book, there is an essay by Lina Gupta on traditional and feminist understandings of the goddess Kali, which argues that a reinterpretation of Kali's meanings can help Hindus find the 'true' meaning of Manu's apparently anti-woman passages.

Liberation feminists tend to disagree on the issue of where ultimate religious authority is located, with some taking the position of biblical feminists. The Victorian reformer Josephine Butler was typical of this strand (Figure 3.7). For other liberation feminists, women's

Figure 3.7 Josephine Butler (1828–1906), social reformer and Christian feminist, in 1905. Mary Evans Picture Library/The Women's Library.

experiences are more authoritative than scriptural texts. Probably the majority of recent hermeneutical studies by feminist theologians follow the second strand, in which priority is given to experience. Experience is necessarily concrete, immediate and particular. This passage from a discussion of Asian feminist hermeneutics is typical in its range of sources and approaches. It argues strongly for women liberating the text, rather than being liberated by the text.

> According to the new methodology ... the most important source of theologizing is lived-world experience. This is women's specific experience, which cannot be universalized the way some traditional, bourgeois European male theologians have standardized common human experience. The specific historical experience of Asian women is manifested in their struggle as victims and agents of liberation as women. Asian women also use their religious-cultural and socio-political traditions for theologizing. They claim their identity as both Asian and Christian. They take themselves seriously. Asian women have begun to appropriate life-giving living traditions into their theology while rejecting male-defined or imperialist traditions which hinder Asian women's growth to full humanity.
>
> Recently Asian women theologians have started to look into Asian myth, folktales, songs, poems, proverbs and religious teachings from Hinduism, Buddhism, Islam, Taoism, shamanism, tribal religions, Confucianism, and Christianity for their theological resources. They also have begun to discover the work of women revolutionaries, freedom fighters, and radical thinkers from our historical past. Asian women are inspired by their foremothers' courage, wisdom, political ideologies, and alternative vision for a new society. This process has helped Asian women theologians see how patriarchal traditions inherited to them from so-called normative theological sources are inadequate and oppressive.
>
> Asian women theologians also accept scripture as a theological source. They use the Old and New Testaments along with other teachings from Asian traditional religions. They selectively choose liberating messages from the text in light of their *hyun jang*. They also expose patriarchal evil by illustrating the oppressive messages from the texts. Asian women theologians learn from texts but go beyond them to meet the community. In this sense they liberate the texts.
>
> (Chung, 1991, pp.108–9)

For *rejectionist feminists*, 'women's experience critiques the Bible, therefore women's experience and not the Bible is solely authoritative. Because the Bible has been used primarily against women, it is used as a negative source by rejectionists' (Grant, 1989, p.177). Theologians in this camp see the founders of the world religions, at best, as 'model breakers', in that they rejected oppressive structures and pointed to the divine in new ways. 'As a model-breaker, Jesus enables us to break our idolatrous relationships not only with him, but with other Christian symbols as well' (ibid., p.187). Grant's remark is a useful reminder that hermeneutics' broadening out in the last century has meant that its insights are applied to art, ritual, and other forms of representation, as well as to texts.

Some figures are difficult to classify. Elisabeth Schussler Fiorenza, a theologian working out of the Catholic tradition, sees the task of feminist hermeneutics as being based in the experience of women today, but without turning its back on either the positive or the negative aspects of scripture as historically understood.

> Feminist theology begins with the experience of women, of women-church. In our struggle for self-identity, survival, and liberation in a patriarchal society and church, Christian women have found that the Bible has been used as a weapon against us but at the same time it has been a resource for courage, hope, and commitment in this struggle. Therefore, it cannot be the task of feminist interpretation to defend the Bible against its feminist critics but to understand and interpret it in such a way that its oppressive and liberating power is clearly recognized ... A feminist critical theology of liberation, therefore, must reject all religious texts and traditions that contribute to 'our unfreedom'.
>
> (Schussler Fiorenza, 1990, pp.x, xvi)

Schussler Fiorenza suggests that in order to make religious texts useable for women today, it is necessary to develop what she terms a 'hermeneutics of suspicion', a 'hermeneutics of proclamation', a 'hermeneutics of remembrance and historical reconstruction', and a 'hermeneutics of ritualization and celebration'.

Briefly, a hermeneutics of suspicion involves the recognition that the sacred text was formulated in androcentric and patriarchal societies, and in the context of historical social structures that accepted a domination-subjugation view of the world. A hermeneutics of proclamation is to be preferred to a hermeneutics committed solely to historical fact, because scriptures are still relevant to communities today. Thus texts which demean women should not be part of worship, but those 'identified as transcending their patriarchal contexts and as articulating a liberating vision of human freedom and wholeness' should be (ibid., p.19). The hermeneutics of remembrance moves from accounts of women in the sacred texts to a rediscovery of women's history and the lives of ordinary women. And the hermeneutics of celebration (sometimes called *creative actualization*) retells sacred stories from the point of view of the women on the margins of them, and incorporates dance, poetry, music and art in ritual, seeking for new symbols which can more fully express the relationship of the limited human to the unlimited divine (ibid., pp.15–22).

Language for god

A key issue of contemporary feminist hermeneutics has been obliquely touched upon in the pages above, but deserves closer examination. For many women involved in feminist retellings of religion, the starting point was a sense of alienation from, and revulsion at, the scriptural language and metaphors for god. The way in which the divine is imaged is usually predictable: imagery of a male, warrior, ruling-class god-king. Feminists argue that this has little to offer women looking for ways to connect with religion, who find the imagery alienating and excluding. Once the divine is identified as male, even subconsciously, women become less divine than men, and 'for Christianity that also meant less human' (Maitland, 1983, p.8). This insistence on the maleness of god,[22] simply reiterates the old heresy of dualism, which attempts to divide the world into good and bad, inferior and superior. Some, like the gay-identified feminist theologian Virginia Mollenkott, who see the sacred texts as being inspired in a supernatural way, emphasize the hidden, almost forgotten, female imagery for god in the texts. To Mollenkott, as to the most conservative of theologians, 'God is no more literally Father than Mother, no more literally male than female', but she argues that the way that god is envisioned does matter, because of the limitations of human nature and human imagination. In other words, the male usage subsumes the generic usage of words such as 'man'. A feedback loop is in operation, where changes in the divine image can produce social and psychological change (Mollenkott, 1992, pp.92, 94). Mary Daly, one of the earliest writers to identify the problem, agrees, writing in *Beyond God the Father* that the idea of a male-identified supreme being controlling the world is a patriarchal concept that is in decline, due to historical changes that have liberated people from aristocratic or royal subjection in many parts of the world:

> The sustaining power of the social structure has been eroded by a number of developments in recent history, including the general trend toward democratization of society and the emergence of technology. However, it is the women's movement which appears destined to play

---

[22] God in the Christian tradition is spirit, neither male nor female. But hermeneutics says that the language of the texts matters, and the metaphors for god are almost always male.

the key role in the overthrow of such oppressive elements in
traditional theism, precisely because it strikes at the source of the
societal dualism that is reflected in traditional beliefs. It presents a
growing threat to the plausibility of the inadequate popular 'God' not
so much by attacking 'him' as by leaving 'him' behind ...

(Daly, 1985, p.18)

Feminist theologians do not seek to write men and men's experience
out of their hermeneutics: instead, their stated goal is to create a
holistic and inclusive theology, which embraces and challenges men
as well as women. For example, the WomanChurch movement,
originating in American Catholicism and an important source of
liturgical innovation, is not woman-only. Men who sympathize with
the group's aims have always been welcome to participate as equal
partners in corporate worship.

As mentioned earlier in this chapter, women of colour often
articulate a distinctive feminist voice when writing about religion,
feeling that white, western, feminist theologians cannot fully express
their experience. Given the key importance given to women's lived
experience in feminist theology of all stripes, this position is an
important one. Just how fully can the experience of an American
descendant of slaves or a woman living in desperate poverty in Asia
or Africa[23] be assumed to be identical to that of theologians who in
everything but gender, belong to the dominant power group?

Jacqueline Grant shares the position of many other practitioners of
feminist hermeneutics in giving women's experience an authority
equivalent to, or greater than, that of the sacred text. She describes
the project thus:

> Feminist theology is a recent discipline in theology which is an
> articulation of the significance of the gospel as read in the context of
> women's experience. It is an attempt to take seriously women's
> experience as the primary source and context for understanding the
> nature of God and God's Word to humanity. In considering the nature
> of God, feminist theologians have uncovered a direct relationship
> between exclusive male imagery of God and the structural oppression
> of women ... . [I]n my adulthood, not only did I recognize the sexual
> politics in theology in a patriarchal society, but also the racial politics
> in theology in a racist society...

[23] For an overview of the current state of African feminist theology, see Phiri
(1997). The first organization on that continent established to research women's
experiences in religion, The Institute of African Women in Religion and Culture,
was founded in 1989.

The analytical principle for determining the adequacy or inadequacy of White feminist Christology[24] is twofold: (1) Because a single issue analysis has proven inadequate to eliminate oppression, a multi-issue analysis must be constructed. The race/sex/class analysis must be embraced as a representative corporate analysis for the destruction of oppressive structures; and (2) because Jesus located the Christ with the outcast, the least, Christology must emerge out of the condition of the least. The representative corporate analysis of race/sex/class is one such situation of the least. Indeed, Black women's tradition is where these three contradictions intersect.

(Grant, 1989, pp.ix, x and 6)

Liberation theology, which rejects universalist theologizing in favour of seeing the divine in the particular experience of the poorest and most oppressed, feeds naturally into feminist and womanist hermeneutics:

Liberation theologians including Christian feminists, charge that the experience out of which Christian theology has emerged is not universal experience but the experience of the dominant culture. It is a kind of shaking of this foundation of theology that is called for by proponents of the theology of liberation. Recognizing inherent problems in the universalist approach to the doing of theology, liberationists therefore, propose that theology must emerge of particular experiences of the oppressed people of God.

(ibid., p.10)

Liberation theology argues that the male-female partnership model advocated by most feminist theologians is inadequate, since it does not interrogate issues of class and race.

[T]he language of partnership lends itself easily to White women who, for the most part, have been part of the oppressing class and additionally who are victimized primarily by one form of oppression. Since White women and men share the same racial identity, Black women perceive White women as being more oppressor than victims. From a Black woman's vantage point then, the language of partnership is merely a rewording of the language of 'reconciliation', which proves to be empty rhetoric unless it is preceded by liberation.

(ibid., p.191)

Chung Hyun Kyung, whose work has already been quoted at some length earlier in this chapter, argues in *Struggle to be the Sun Again*,

---

[24] Christology is a key issue for feminist analysis of Christianity, because Jesus was physically male and he is seen by some as uniquely redemptive for all believers. Thus the male god-bearer must be made relevant for women through the construction of adequate christological models.

that claims that nationalism or class struggle must come before women's liberation are just reinforcing the patriarchal status quo.

> It is obvious that the term *feminism* originated from the capitalist West. But Asian women none the less rightly contend that the liberative core of feminism cannot be automatically despised merely because of geographical origin ... Asian women define what feminism is for themselves and in their own concrete historical situation. If people can accept the fact that Christianity in Asia still has some liberative power in spite of its Western, missionary, and colonial background because Asian Christians rediscovered its liberative core, then they should be able to accept the liberative core of feminism rediscovered by Asian women... Asian women are not mere imitators of white women from the West. They have minds of their own. Some Asian men who claim that Asian feminists are brainwashed by white women presuppose the intellectual inferiority of Asian women in relation to white women. This illustrates that those Asian men are the ones who have internalized Western colonialism ... Asian men learned how to despise their own people of colour (especially women) by imitating the values of their white masters. If white women can think for themselves, why not Asian women? Asian women do not fight for their liberation as women because they have been brainwashed like childish little girls by white women. Asian women fight for their rights because they experience the evil of patriarchy in their own family, church, and community, and they are determined to destroy it.
>
> (Chung, 1991, p.25)

In recent years, western feminists have begun to recognize that feminism and its insights cannot be given or bequeathed to women in other cultures. Instead, feminism, whether applied to theology or to the workplace, must be of indigenous growth in order to be authentic. It needs to grow out of a specific historical situation and a particular set of cultural opportunities and limitations. Increasingly, this is happening world-wide, although some women, especially in Islamic cultures reject the name 'feminism' while arguing that female independence, equality and male-female partnership is an Islamic concept.[25]

Conclusion

This chapter has introduced two issues: first, the impact of feminist ideas on the world religions and the chicken-and-egg relationship

---

[25] See, for example, Sandra Hale, 'Ideology and identity: Islamism, gender, and the state in Sudan', in Brink and Mencher, 1997, pp.117–42. Hale's informants repeatedly insisted that Islam was liberative for women; the problem was the attitude of Arab men.

between religion, feminism and social transformation. In the second part, we have looked at examples of feminist hermeneutical principles, in order to determine how feminism has changed and challenged religion in recent times. Through the variety of competing models introduced, it has argued that feminism is not a monolith, but is instead a flexible, changing set of ideas which share certain key values about the equality of women and men and the importance of liberation from oppression. I believe it has provided evidence for Phillips's claim that feminism has had a revolutionary impact on religion today: whether religion can survive that challenge unchanged is less clear. While this statement is true, it is also true that for many women and men, the revolutionary tendency of contemporary hermeneutics has been absolutely and firmly rejected, in favour of what is often depicted as the 'traditional interpretation'.

But for those groups that have accepted the idea of interpretative change over time, Chung identifies four tendencies for the future of feminist theology, and the reader may find them useful when looking at other examples in this book and beyond it. First, 'we are the text' (ibid., p.111) – the authority of scriptures and of religious institutions is coming under increasing scrutiny, and it is not likely that they will regain their dominance in framing people's religious worldviews. For many, experience has become the yardstick by which to evaluate the text, rather than trying to make one's life conform to the ancient patterns of the sacred documents.

Secondly, the focus of feminist religion is increasingly shifting towards the study of popular religiosity among women and men, rather than studying institutions, which are increasingly seen as irrelevant, irresponsive, or even complicit. Religion from the underside is the religion which is increasingly of interest to scholars, as well as to practitioners.

Thirdly, single causal interpretations of traditional religions' oppressive power are becoming rare, as more theologians come to appreciate the complexity of the relationships between gender, class and race. 'Religious solidarity and revolutionary praxis' are the goals which feminist theology now seems to be working towards, regardless of the nationality or politics of the scholar involved.

Finally, doctrinal purity of whatever stripe is becoming less important and less valued by the pioneers of feminist theology. Orthodoxy and its enforcement are increasingly seen as male preoccupations, where some theologians still 'talk as if [religious] identity is an unchangeable property which they own' (ibid., p.113). Feminist theology and hermeneutics are increasingly reconciliatory, as scholars search for texts, symbols and metaphors with the potential for empowerment across an ever wider range of sources. Others find

Colour Plate 1 Crowds greet Pope John Paul II in Poland, 1979. Bruno Barbey/Magnum.

Colour Plate 2 A confessional scene. Bruno Barbey/Magnum.

Colour Plate 3 Priests with ciboria about to distribute Holy Communion. Bruno Barbey/Magnum.

Colour Plate 4 A demonstration in Karl Marx Platz, Leipzig, 16 October 1989. Ullstein/ADN Zentralbild.

Colour Plate 5 The Berlin Wall, 11 November 1989. Brauchli-Reuter/Popperfoto.

Colour Plate 6 Veiled women swimming at Beach Park, Dubai, United Arab Emirates. © *TRIP/H. Rogers.*

Colour Plate 7 Paul Gauguin, The Birth of Christ (1896), oil on canvas, 96 × 131 cm. Neue Pinakothek, Munich/Interfoto/Bridgeman Art Library, London.

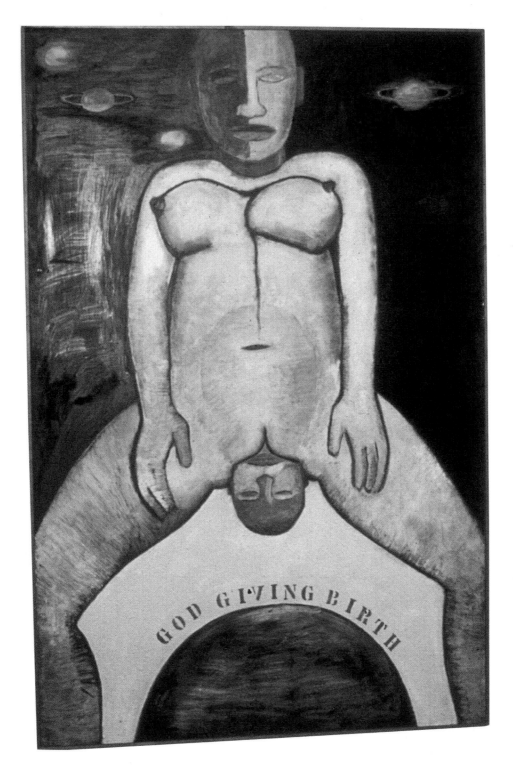

Colour Plate 8 Monica Sjoo, God Giving Birth. *Courtesy of the artist.*

Colour Plate 9 A Buddhist monk and children planting tree seedlings they have grown themselves. This will reforest the hills surrounding their village deforested by their parents. Mark Edwards/Still Pictures.

Colour Plate 10 Buddhist monks encircle a threatened forest in Thailand. Boonsiri–UNEP/Still Pictures.

that theology moves them out of the traditions altogether, or pushes them to examine alternatives to the 'world religions'.[26] New ways of seeing, and new things to see, are being offered to us by scholars of all nations, all religions and both genders, and our understanding of religion is being enriched by their vision, whether we share it or not.

Glossary

androcentrism to have man, or the male, at the centre - the view of the world that sees the male experience as normative.

androgynous a two-gender model of human experience, combining the physical, mental and cultural characteristics of both sexes.

egalitarian asserting the social equality of all human beings.

hyun jang a Korean phrase meaning the place where historical events are happening.

liberation theology a theology which originated amongst Roman Catholics in Latin America, which sees social, political and economic liberation from oppression as necessarily linked to the gospel.

matrifocal mother-centred.

mujerista a word coined by Hispanic feminist theologians to describe Hispanic women's concern with communal rather than individual liberation (Gross, 1996, p.55).

patrifocal father-centred.

process theology Process theology emphasizes becoming rather than being, change rather than certainty. It borrows from the philosophical thought of the philosopher A.N. Whitehead (1861–1947).

References

Bait-al-Hikmat (Academy of Rationalism), (1983) *National Seminar on the Status of Women in Islam*, New Delhi.

Biderman, S. and Scharfstein, B.A. (1992) *Interpretation in Religion*, Leiden: Brill.

Brink, J. (1997) 'Lost rituals: Sunni Muslim women in rural Egypt', in Brink and Mencher, 1997, pp.199–208.

Brink, J. and Mencher, J. (eds) (1997) *Mixed Blessings: Gender and Religious Fundamentalism Cross Culturally*, London: Routledge.

Christ, C.P. (1988) *Laughter of Aphrodite: Reflections on a Journey to the Goddess*, San Francisco: HarperCollins.

---

[26] See, for example, Pearson (2001).

Chung, H.K. (1991) *Struggle to be the Sun again: introducing Asian Women's Theology*, London: SCM Press.

Cone, J.H. (1986) *A Black Theology of Liberation*, New York: Orbis.

Cone, J.H. (1977) *God of the Oppressed*, London: SPCK.

Daly, M. (1978) *Gyn/Ecology*, Boston: Beacon.

Daly, M. (1985) *Beyond God the Father: Toward a Philosophy of Women's Liberation*, London: Women's Press.

de Beauvoir, S. (1949) *The Second Sex*, trans. H.M. Parshley, New York: Random House, 1974.

Eck, D.L. and Davaki Jain, (1986) *Speaking of Faith: Cross Cultural Perspectives on Women, Religion, and Social Change*, New Delhi: Kali for Women.

France, R.T. (1995) *Women in the Church's Ministry: a Test Case for Biblical Hermeneutics*, Carlisle: Paternoster Press.

Gerami, S. (1996) *Women and Fundamentalism: Islam and Christianity*, New York: Garland.

Gilchrist, M. (1991) *The Destabilization of the Anglican Church: Women Priests and the Feminist Campaign to replace Christianity*, Melbourne: AD2000 Publications.

Goldenberg, N.R. (1979) *Changing of the Gods: Feminism and the End of Traditional Religions*, Beacon Press: Boston.

Grant, J. (1989) *White Women's Christ and Black Women's Jesus: Feminist Christology and Womanist Response*, Atlanta: Scholars Press.

Gross, R. (1996) *Feminism and Religion: an Introduction*, Boston: Beacon.

Hampson, D. (1990) *Theology and Feminism*, Oxford: Blackwell.

Heidegger, M. (1959) *An Introduction to Metaphysics*, trans. R. Manhiem, New Haven: Yale University Press.

Jeanrond, W.G. (1994) *Theological Hermeneutics*, London: SCM.

Liturgical Commission of the General Synod of the Church of England (1989) *Making Women Visible: the Use of Inclusive Language with the ASB* [Alternative Service Book], London: Church House.

Maitland, S. (1983) *A Map of the New Country: Women and Christianity*, London: Routledge and Kegan Paul.

McFague, S. (1987) *Models of God: Theology for an Ecological, Nuclear Age*, London: SCM Press.

McLeod, A.E. (1991) *Accommodating Protest: Working Women, the New Veiling, and Change in Cairo*, Oxford: Columbia University Press.

Miles, R. (1994) *Not in Our Name: Voices of Women who have left the Church*, Nottingham: Southwell Diocesan Social Responsibility Group.

Mollenkott, V. (1992) *Sensuous Spirituality: Out from Fundamentalism*, New York: Crossroad.

Pearson, J. (ed.) (2001) *Belief Beyond Boundaries*, Aldershot: Ashgate with The Open University.

Phillips, J.A. (1984) *Eve: the History of an Idea*, San Francisco: Harper & Row.

Phiri, I.A. (1997) 'Doing theology as African women', in J. Parratt (ed.) *A Reader in African Theology*, rev. edn, London: SPCK, pp.45–56.

Plaskow, J. (1991) *Standing Again at Sinai: Judaism from a Feminist Perspective*, San Francisco: HarperCollins.

Robinson, C.A. (1999) *Tradition and Liberation: the Hindu Tradition in the Indian Women's Movement*, Richmond: Curzon.

Rosen, S.J. (ed.) (1996) *Vaisnavi: Women and the Worship of Krishna*, Delhi: Motilal Banarsidass.

Schussler Fiorenza, E. (1990) *Bread not Stone: the Challenge of Feminist Biblical Interpretation*, London: T. & T. Clark.

Stowasser, B.F. (1994) *Women in the Qur'an: Traditions and Interpretations*, New York: Oxford University Press.

Thistlewaite, S. (1990) *Sex, Race and God: Christian Feminism in Black and White*, London: Geoffrey Chapman.

Walker, A. (1983) *The Color Purple*, London: Women's Press.

CHAPTER 4

Buddhist Responses to Environmental Crisis

HELEN WATERHOUSE

The unintended and the unforeseen are... indicators of both the necessity and the reality of the transcendent. Religion gives them meaning and promises the power to overcome them. The nature of environmental crisis is therefore just the sort of problem religion addresses: it is virtually religious.

(Beyer, in Part Two, p.274–5)

Modern environmental consciousness can be seen as a new, quasi-religious doctrine of the western type. The 'religion' of environmentalism emphasizes the wonder of creation, contrasts this with the alienation and folly of humans which urgently need to be replaced by reconciliation and wisdom, and looks forward either to a 'saved' (ecologically balanced) world or to the hell of an environmental armageddon if we do not repent our ways.

(Bocking, 1994, p.163)

These two quotations set the scene for a chapter which is about the ways in which Buddhists have responded to the challenge of the ecological or environmental 'crisis'. The nature and extent of the crisis is not at issue here and neither is the question of whether it is indeed a reality. The United Nations World Charter for Nature, reproduced in the appendix to this chapter, outlines prevailing perceptions about our world and the actions which ought to be taken to preserve it. I am concerned here instead with how representatives of a religious tradition – the Buddhist tradition – understand the response which ought, and can, be made to this late twentieth and early twenty-first century challenge.

Concern for the welfare of the planet and its continuing ability to sustain varieties of life is one among the major ethical issues which we face. As a major area of concern it is perhaps surprisingly recent. So much so that in spite of the fact that it is one of the most pressing social concerns of the day, the founding fathers of sociology, writing from the nineteenth to the early twentieth centuries, saw no need to address it as a central issue of modern life. Prominent sociologist Anthony Giddens writes that, 'Ecological concerns do not brook large in the traditions of thought incorporated into sociology' and argues therefore that 'it is not surprising that sociologists today find it hard to develop a systematic appraisal of them' (Giddens, 1990, p.8). The same issues are equally challenging for adherents of religions. Although historically religions have usually expressed a view of the place of nature within the world, it was not until the late 1960s that religious environmentalism first appeared. By 'religious environmentalism' I mean an engagement by religious groups with what had previously been regarded as a non-religious issue, or indeed not even as an issue of general concern at all.

Concern about environmental degradation was first evident within the counter-culture of the 1960s (Campbell, 1999, p.37; White, 1967; Eckel, 1997, p.328). Friends of the Earth and Greenpeace, two international organizations based on ecological concerns, were founded in the 1970s and ecological awareness became broadly popular in the late 1980s (Campbell, 1999, p.38). This was the time when the Green Party took 14.5 per cent of the vote in the 1989 election for the European Parliament (ibid.). In the same year Pope John Paul II issued a papal statement devoted to ecological awareness; the first of its kind (ibid., p.39).

A common and enduring stereotype holds that eastern religions promote harmony between nature and humanity, while western religious forms promote division through notions of dominion and control (White, 1967; Eckel, 1997). Responsibility for the subjugation of nature by humanity is laid squarely at the door of the western monotheistic traditions. The historian Keith Thomas illustrates this when he writes that:

> Man's task in the words of Genesis (1:28), was to 'replenish the earth and subdue it': to level the woods, till the soil, drive off the predators, kill the vermin, plough up the bracken, drain the fens. Agriculture stood to land as did cooking to raw meat. It converted nature into culture.
>
> (Thomas, 1984, pp.14–15)[1]

In keeping with this stereotypical classification, sociologist Colin Campbell sees the development of environmental concern within western cultures as a part of what he calls the 'Easternization of the West'. 'Western' values, he argues, have been based, for the most part, on the idea that natural and spiritual, body and spirit, god and

---

[1] While this view is widely shared it is not of course the only possible view of the relationship between Christianity and the wider environment.

humanity are separate, whereas 'eastern' worldviews tend not to set up dualisms such as humanity and nature, spiritual and physical, mind and body.[2] The radical change in the western perspective which came about, according to Campbell, as a result of influence from the East has become so thoroughly disseminated that it is now hard to imagine a time when such ideas were not part of ideological currency within western culture, whether or not one accepts them as true. The major world religions have all added to the debate about the degradation of the planet. Indeed representatives of the maligned western traditions now argue that Christianity can offer everything required for an environmental ethic (e.g. Haught, 1996). Members of every religious tradition, while often joining the inter-religious initiatives led by liberal Christians among others, have tended to suggest that its own tradition has the answers.[3]

Religions are not static entities the ideologies of which are forever determined at a moment in time and preserved intact for future generations. It is always necessary for people to evaluate the truths that a religion teaches and apply those truths in new situations. Religious people are sometimes reluctant to admit this is the case, preferring instead the idea that religions teach essential truths that endure over time and space and that there is no need for further interpretation. Religions are, however, inevitably embedded in social and cultural structures. Though they may act as containers and portrayers of truth, they also change in response to the conditions in which they find themselves. Within any given religious tradition there are a multiplicity of responses to the important issues of the day; environmentalism is no exception.

In the introduction to a book which directly addresses a range of contemporary ethical issues in Buddhism Damien Keown writes:

> The task that faces students of Buddhist ethics today... is to generate a response to new problems that is consistent with the spirit of Buddhist values and in harmony with its extensive scriptural tradition. This is no easy task since there are very few signposts or landmarks in this new terrain. After all, the earliest Buddhist canonical literature is well over two thousand years old, and many problems we face today are the result of modern social, economic and technological developments which could scarcely have been imagined in ancient times.
>
> (Keown, 2000, p.1)

---

[2] Like all broad generalizations of this type, this one has its exceptions. Just as not all western traditions promote dualism, not all eastern traditions promote non-duality. Such oversimplifications are, however, useful in making the overall point.

[3] This, of course, applies equally to all the other questions to which religions claim to provide answers.

With just a few changes to names and dates this same paragraph could have been written about any other of the major religious traditions which operate in the contemporary world. From the outset one of the central concerns of these traditions was with teaching their followers about right ways to live. These teachings about how to act within the world were naturally informed by the social conditions in which they lived, not by the pressing concerns of our own age. The challenge to scholars and practitioners of religion therefore is to construct ways through which to understand contemporary ethical challenges, and social transformations in the light of ancient texts and developed tradition. The environmental debate poses very particular problems. Can religions cope with these problems and what tools do they posses with which to attempt this?

Peter Beyer, the author of the quotation with which this chapter opens, is a sociologist of religion. He argues that the environmental crisis is exactly the kind of problem that religions deal with. The reason for this, he claims, is that the ecological problems we face are transcendent in nature. That is that they are in some sense beyond our everyday experience and out of our personal control. Over-population, the 'greenhouse effect', radioactive contamination, and so on, result from wider forces than simply our own personal actions. They stem from the effects of global industrial, technological and financial systems which have created unintended problems that they have not solved.

The author of the second opening quotation, Brian Bocking, is a scholar of Japanese religion. In an introduction to Japanese attitudes to nature he takes a rather different perspective. Instead of presenting the environmental debate as a problem for religions, he suggests that activity designed to promote ecological awareness and to take action to solve problems which have already arisen, has become virtually a religion in its own right.

These two quotations perhaps indicate the nature of the relationship between religion and environmental ethics. Ecological crisis is either an issue for religions to deal with as part of a wider transcendental task or it is a pressing concern of contemporary humankind which is not simply a religious issue but a religion in itself; that is, it either operates alongside them or takes precedence over traditional religious structures. Many of the approaches to ecological questions which are proposed by religionists wrestle to find a balance between the two positions. This chapter is about some elements of that struggle.

Before we move on, however, is Beyer right when he claims that the ecological crisis is a transcendent problem rather than an immanent problem. Is it a problem which goes beyond the universe and the range of normal human experience rather than one which pervades the universe and is inherent within it? And if he is right where does the solution to the problem lie – in religious practices or in political, economic and scientific action? Where does the power of ultimate resolution lie? While, as we have seen, Beyer accepts that environmental problems are exactly the kind of problems that religions deal with, he also argues that:

> Religion cannot do anything direct about environmental problems. To be sure, various individuals may convert to a thorough going environmental ethic, perhaps on the basis of their own traditions, perhaps in switching allegiance to another. But these are likely to be a minority. As with peace and justice issues, many religious people and organizations will become deeply involved in the problems, but the proffered solutions are going to be political, educational, scientific, economic, and medical... Put slightly differently, as with other negative effects of the global system, religion can offer significant organizational, ideological, and motivational resources which primarily religious, but also non-religious, people can use to conceptualize 'residual' problems and mobilize to deal with them.
>
> (Beyer, in Part Two, p.280–1)

Here Beyer claims that the role of religion in ecological activity is to provide an organizational, ideological and motivational basis for action. In declaring that religion can do nothing directly about environmental problems he seems to be arguing that religious practices aimed at religious goals which are not embedded in social action (such as, perhaps, prayer, meditation or worship) can have no impact on environmental problems. On the other hand, social justice initiatives, which may or may not be embedded in religious ideology and institutions can do so. We might call this a **liberal** approach because it downplays what traditionalists might see as the critical ontological differences between religions: the contrasting explanations they provide to questions of ultimate meaning. It is also a reductionist approach – it reduces religions to social structures, because it effectively denies certain core religious practices their claims for transformatory power. Indeed, Beyer's implication that there is a difference between what religions can do directly and what they can do via peace and justice initiatives is itself pertinent to this chapter. Part of what we shall go on to examine is the fluidity of the boundary which lies between 'religious' and 'non-religious' practices.

Faced with a potential environmental catastrophe in which the survival of the earth is threatened, each religion has an interest in showing how it is well fitted, if not best fitted, to provide an ideological basis for preventative or even restorative action. Beyer describes environmentalism as an example of 'public-influence-oriented liberal religion in a global context' (Beyer, 1994, p.218). He argues (ibid., p.219) that environmentalism is predominantly a liberal phenomenon because, in order to have a chance of success, environmental effort needs cooperation and in order for there to be cooperation across religious divides there needs to be an acceptance of pluralism.

In contrast, the following quotation from an essay by a western Buddhist scholar and practitioner, reverses the order:

> The only true solution to the problem, in a Buddhist analysis, will be neither technological nor legal. It must be **soteriological**. It must involve the evolution of a significant number of us human beings to a higher level of awareness, to a higher ethical sensibility. This is not to say that efforts-both technological and legal-to safeguard the environment are pointless, only that they are at best a stop-gap measure, and not an ultimate solution.
>
> (Sponberg, accessed June 2001)

In this essay, Alan Sponberg explains how only through a right understanding of self – the right understanding provided by a Buddhist analysis – can ecological problems be ultimately solved. He acknowledges the role of technological and legal efforts but claims that such efforts can only *assist* in the process of saving the earth. Any real salvation, he argues, will ultimately come from the kind of individual development that Buddhism offers. This perspective attributes the ultimate value and the corrective practices to a particular kind of religion rather than to science or social transformations. The solution, Sponberg argues, will come from right understanding rather than from restorative action by scientists or others who do not understand the basis of the problem. This view represents just one contemporary Buddhist approach. It is a deeply *illiberal* perspective because by focusing on the mystical transformation of individuals, Sponberg claims that if it is to be truly effective, environmental activity cannot be a common pursuit. While Sponberg advocates inter-faith and cross-cultural dialogue he is clear that such dialogue, can only usefully take place if Buddhist representatives contribute a correct presentation of the Buddhist understanding of the truth.[4] Sponberg's contribution to this debate promotes the view that Buddhism has the answers to solve the problem in the long term.

---

[4] This is problematic since there are many contrasting presentations of Buddhist truth and no one with the authority to check that the perspective offered in dialogue is 'correct'. See Waterhouse, 2001. In addition to being a scholar, Alan Sponberg, who is also known as Saramati, is an order member in the Friends of the Western Buddhist Order. The position he presents here is broadly in keeping with the FWBO perspective.

In the course of this chapter we shall encounter a number of tensions, such as the opposing perspectives Beyer and Sponberg represent, but we begin with a further investigation of Beyer's perspective before turning to the contrasting ways in which Buddhists understand the relationship between Buddhism and environmentalism.

Beyer's three-fold typology

Beyer outlines three religious approaches to environmentalism: eco-spirituality, eco-justice and eco-traditionalism. According to Beyer, eco-spirituality easily crosses religious boundaries because its ideology, or indeed its theology,[5] stresses the holistic and interconnected nature of life. This type of religiosity developed largely on the North American west coast and therefore because of, in Campbell's terms, the 'Easternization of the West' it emerged out of western cultural assumptions and norms. It is embraced by confessing Christians usually of a liberal inclination but, because it operates independently of the formal institutional structures of any religion, it can also be embraced by adherents of other religions, including Buddhists or by secularists. It resonates with Bocking's remarks about environmentalism *as religion*. Beyer argues that:

> secular environmentalists adapt religious language to conceptualize their concerns, while representatives of various religions highlight or even refashion those elements of their traditions that seem to resonate with secular environmental concern.
>
> (Beyer, in Part Two, p.275)

Eco-spirituality is a burgeoning form of religious expression. What it may lack in philosophical rigour is countered, for many, by its direct appeal and because it embraces the idea that, 'humankind loses its privileged position to become a feature in a larger organic and cosmic whole' (Beyer, 1994, p.217). Buddhist examples of eco-spirituality feature later in this chapter.

Eco-justice is an ethical approach to environmental problems which is rooted within wider social and political concerns. Environmental ethics is one element within a broader ethical agenda which includes egalitarianism and social inclusivity. This ethical agenda operates as an integrated package (within, for example, the World Council of Churches) in which environmentalism is seen as one

---

[5] Within Buddhism there is no notion of an all powerful and eternal, creator god. Buddhism does, however, have systematic ideologies which act as equivalents to theology within theistic traditions.

among a number of agenda items which must be addressed in order
to end inequality and the marginalization of groups of human beings.
It is therefore different from eco-spirituality in that human beings are
of primary importance and not regarded, as in eco-spirituality, as
merely part of an organic whole. Eco-justice has an important
practical side: it is concerned with strategies for action rather more
than with developing a structured theology. In other words any
understanding of god (or any other formulation of ultimate truth) and
the role of that in the world must be reconciled with the given values
of **environmental ethics**. There are eco-justice initiatives within the
Buddhist countries of Thailand and Sri Lanka which fit into this
category.

Beyer's third type, eco-traditionalism, he explains mainly in terms
of the Christian notion of stewardship of the earth. In other words,
the idea that God has charged human beings with the task of caring
for the world – of acting as his stewards. Writers of this type usually
represent more conservative religious groups or traditions. They
advocate the liberalizing of these traditions to the extent that they 'call
for the revitalization of traditional religion in the light of ecological
crisis' (Beyer, 1994, p.218). They do not, however, envisage a need to
develop new religious truths, but promote the rearticulation of old
ones. They argue that the activities of humankind, having caused
problems for the earth, must be changed for alternatives which are
not damaging to it, but they maintain that we are in this mess because
we have strayed from the original message, which, they claim,
contains all the necessary answers. We shall meet this type also within
the account of Buddhism which follows.

Like all typologies, Beyer's does not claim that these three
approaches are mutually exclusive: it is simply intended as a useful
tool with which to understand contemporary religious responses to a
comparatively new but pressing problem.

Buddhist responses to environmentalism

We turn now to Buddhist responses to this issue. Buddhism is an
interesting case of an Asian religion which has become popular in the
West during roughly the same period in which environmentalism has
become a matter of popular concern. Much of the debate about
Buddhism's relationship with environmental concern and activity is
being enacted in the West among Buddhist converts and scholars of
Buddhism. The problem they face is that Buddhism, like other
religious traditions, was initially formulated at a time when there was
no particular concern for the environment, for example, because

there was no overpopulation, no large-scale industry, no threat from nuclear war, etc. None the less, if Buddhists wish to respond to the environmental crisis while remaining Buddhists, they must find a way to do that which does not contradict their Buddhist identity. Otherwise that response is not a Buddhist response but begins to resemble a more general eco-spirituality.

Buddhists have been writing about environmentalism since the 1980s. Some western scholar/practitioners have taken up the cause and promote ecological awareness. As a result there are now well-established Buddhist communities, for example, in California, which are run on ecological lines where organic methods of production have replaced the use of pesticides and trees are planted to replace those destroyed by cattle grazing (Kaza, 1997, p.229). One Zen Buddhist centre even offers a programme of environmental education (Yamauchi, 1997, pp.259–63). Under pressure from western concerns and activity, and from the severity of the problem, some prominent Asian Buddhists have been unable to remain silent. As we shall see later, fitting environmentalism together with Buddhist doctrine is not necessarily a straightforward process but rather one which raises controversy. Depending upon how they are presented, Buddhist doctrines can support or even hinder an environmentalist ethic. The same could be said for Christian doctrines (Haught, 1996; Harris, 1994, p.8). The literature on Buddhist approaches to environmentalism is not yet as extensive as it is for the Christian traditions, for example, but there are now sufficient published accounts to identify contrasting approaches. Ian Harris, a scholar of Buddhism and a prominent writer on Buddhist environmentalism mainly from the perspective of Buddhist canonical writing, has recognized that Buddhist writings on environmentalism fall into a number of categories. He has proposed a five-fold typology which can be used to understand the contrasting characteristics of that material (Harris, 1995). He is at pains to indicate that this typology is provisional – this is a comparatively new area and the literature is bound to increase, so new categories may emerge. Although there are points at which the types may appear to merge into one another, each distinct category in the typology is described below and illustrated using examples, some of which are cited by Harris himself.

The Harris typology

The first category in the Harris typology is 'Straightforward endorsement of Buddhist environmental ethics by traditional guardians of doxic truth' (ibid., p.3). (Harris uses the word 'doxic' here as a synonym for orthodox.) Such endorsement is based on factors which are non-controversial and which are not necessarily exclusively Buddhist in their orientation. Harris suggests that the present (fourteenth) Dalai Lama, Tensin Gyatso is the most important representative of this category.

In his Nobel Peace Prize lecture, delivered in Oslo on 11 December 1989, the Dalai Lama argued that 'we must develop a sense of universal responsibility not only in the geographic sense but in respect to the different issues that confront our planet' (Dalai Lama, 1992, p.112). In the same lecture he claimed that though everyone must take responsibility 'for each other and for the natural environment', whether individuals do so through religious practice or through non-religious practice is unimportant. It is clear that when the Dalai Lama and others write in this way they are not attempting to promote an exclusively Buddhist view. Though representing the Tibetan Buddhist tradition much of what the Dalai Lama writes on ecology would be equally acceptable to a person, with the same orientation to ecology, operating from, for example, an avowedly Christian background. Though he does discuss specifically Buddhist doctrines in such writings, and makes links between Buddhist doctrines and the need for environmental action, his writings are generally expressed in inclusive, liberal language. Much of the purpose of this kind of writing appears to be to facilitate initiatives which cross traditional cultural and religious boundaries. These kinds of initiative support the preservation of global resources but at the same time they support the preservation of natural resources in local situations. Tibetan Buddhism in its Asian context employed strategies to deal with the relationship between human activities and the natural environment in which such activities took place (Samuel, 1998, pp.130–3),[6] but it was not a consciously environmentally aware religion in the terms in which we now understand environmental awareness; it did not have to be. Since this is the case, in order to make a positive expression about environmentalism using contemporary language, it is a great deal easier not to use Buddhist concepts when in dialogue with non-Buddhists with no specialist knowledge of Buddhism.

This first of Harris's categories has much in common with the style of religious environmentalism described by Peter Beyer as eco-spirituality. In taking an eco-spiritual approach in his public writings, the Dalai Lama speaks to a broad audience. As possibly the most

---

[6] For example, Tibetans carry out ritual practices focused on regional or local deities associated with geographical features such as mountains and lakes.

prominent Buddhist of his day,[7] the Dalai Lama chooses to present Buddhist ethical teachings in such a way that they can support eco-spirituality. He leaves aside more specialized Buddhist cosmological and soteriological teachings. This approach is by no means at odds with the primary ethical teachings of Buddhism which we might abbreviate using a popular verse:

> Not to do any evil,
> To cultivate what is wholesome,
> To purify one's mind:
> This is the teaching of the Buddhas.

> (*Dhammapada*, 183, trans. in Harvey, 2000, p.42)

The advantage of the Dalai Lama's approach is that it facilitates inter-religious and cultural dialogue among the liberally minded rather than embedding a Buddhist approach in a complex and specialist Buddhist way of looking at the world. As the foremost representative of the Tibetan people in exile, the Dalai Lama has much to gain from this approach. He has articulated a dream in which 'the entire Tibetan plateau should become a free refuge where humanity and nature can live in peace and in harmonious balance'(Dalai Lama, 1992, p.112). He calls this new Tibet a 'Zone of Non-violence' and likens it to 'a natural park or biosphere'. It may very well be that such a strategy would be of benefit to the planet; it would certainly be of benefit to the Tibetan people, since if reclassified in this way Tibet could no longer sustain large Chinese populations. In advocating this strategy therefore, the Dalai Lama is serving several interests which are likely to gain ideological support, at least, from liberal and anti-communist factions in society.

The second category of writings in the Harris typology he describes in the following terms:

> Equally positive treatments by predominantly Japanese and North American scholar/activists premised on an assumption that Buddhism is blessed with the resources necessary to address current environmental issues. Generally the material limits itself to finding the most appropriate Buddhist doctrinal bases from which an environmental ethic could proceed, e.g. the doctrines of **interpenetration**, ***tathagatagarbha***, etc.

> (Harris, 1994, p.1)

---

[7] Moral and spiritual leadership is problematic for Buddhism partly because it is so diverse. The Dalai Lama does not represent all Buddhists nor even all Tibetan Buddhists. He is none the less probably the most high profile Buddhist in world terms.

This category is in some ways similar to the first in that the treatments are positive. The assumption is that Buddhism supports an environmental ethic: Buddhism is good, environmentalism is good and therefore the two must be compatible. However, unlike those in the first category these writings are more self-consciously based on an appeal to Buddhist doctrine. This is partly because these writings are not authored by people with traditional claims to represent the Buddhist tradition. I observed above that the Dalai Lama does refer to Buddhist concepts in his writings,[8] however, these references are not always prominent and tend not to be grounded in authoritative Buddhist scriptures. Instead he relies on his own traditional status and his apparent personal qualities. Many of those whose writings fall into this second category, however, are western converts to Buddhism and/or scholars of Buddhism, others are Japanese Buddhists but none of them carries the broad appeal of the Dalai Lama.

A prominent writer in this category is the American scholar and Buddhist practitioner Joanna Macy, who argues for an authentic environmental ethic based, she believes, in early Buddhist texts. Prominent within her viewpoint is the claim that the final goal of Buddhists, **nirvana**, does not represent a rejection of the world or escape from it but instead a world-affirming attitude.

> Far from the nihilism and escapism that is often imputed to the Buddhist path, this liberation, this awakening puts one *into* the world with a livelier, more caring sense of social engagement.
>
> (Macy, 1990, p.61)

As is typical for writers in this category, Macy bases her analysis in support of an environmental ethic on carefully selected Buddhist doctrines. Her understanding of nirvana as expressed above, for example, though not particularly unusual is not shared right across the traditional Buddhist world. Many Buddhists *do* understand *nirvana* in terms of escape from the round of birth, death and rebirth in the world. Other doctrines used by her are, *not-self* or *emptiness* and *dependent origination* and the doctrine of interpenetration. The emptiness or not-self doctrine teaches that beings have no eternal, unchanging selves which have always existed and which live on from day-to-day and life-to-life. All phenomena – trees, whales and human beings equally – have no abiding self or self nature which stays the same and is not subject to change. Change,

---

[8] For example in a published version of an interfaith dialogue he draws on the Buddhist notion that all conditioned phenomena are 'empty', that is, that all things both physical and mental have no abiding essence and are therefore subject to change. Conditioned phenomena are explained below.

decay and death as much as birth, growth and becoming are an inevitable part of all life and nothing is exempt from this process.

The second Buddhist teaching central to Macy's arguments is that all these fleeting empty phenomena are dependent on causes which bring them into being. This is a logical extension of the idea that phenomena have no intrinsic unchanging essence for if they had they would exist of themselves, eternal and unchanging. Since, according to Buddhism, all phenomena are devoid of an eternal unchanging substance, they are subject to causes to start them off or, more technically to 'bring them into being'. They are therefore said to be conditioned by other phenomena which are equally lacking in a permanent self or nature. These conditioned phenomena are themselves conditioned by other conditioned phenomena and each acts as a cause for the starting up or bringing into being of other phenomena in their own turn. So it goes on in a cycle or chain: phenomena arise and decay and in their turn act as a condition for other phenomena to arise. This central Buddhist doctrine is known as 'dependent co-production' or 'dependent origination'. It explains how impermanent, insubstantial phenomena (i.e. all phenomena) come into being. This explanation is accepted, so far as I know, by all Buddhist schools.

When Buddhism arrived in China the doctrine of dependent origination was the subject of development particularly within one influential school (the *Hua Yen* school). This doctrine holds that rather than there being a causal relationship in the chain between just some things – the specific causes which bring a phenomena into being – instead, all things are interpenetrated by all other things so that everything is interconnected and nothing is separate from any other thing. The possibility for this doctrine to be brought into the service of an environmental ethic is clear. If a species dies out or a piece of land is poisoned then that has an effect on everything else. Macy and others argue therefore that an ecological ethic is built into Buddhism, based on this understanding. A metaphor to explain this idea is the jewelled net of Indra. The god Indra's net is hung about with innumerable jewels each of which reflect, in their mirrored surfaces, all the other jewels in the net. What is more all the jewels in the net also reflect all the reflections. Based on this understanding, Macy argues that a rainforest tree is a part of my body or yours – they are our external lungs which allow the earth to breathe. Because everything is connected, the tree is as much a part of our bodies as our own legs (ibid., p.62.).

Writings within this category are largely based on doctrines which have been prevalent within Chinese and Japanese forms of Buddhism but which do not necessarily feature strongly in doctrinal accounts of

Buddhism which emanate from elsewhere in the Buddhist world. The buddha-nature (*tathagatagarbha*) doctrine holds that the pure, undefiled nature which characterizes Buddhas is present in all beings. The difference between Buddhas and ordinary beings (including animals) and all other phenomena, is that in ordinary, unenlightened beings that pure nature is hidden by impurities. A simile often used to explain this teaching likens ordinary beings to an image of a Buddha which has been wrapped up in old rags and therefore cannot be detected. Once the rags have been removed the Buddha image is visible. In just the same way, it is argued, once the impurities which obscure the buddha-nature have been removed by Buddhist practices, the true nature of all beings can be revealed. Since all things share in this pure buddha-nature, all things are inextricably related. There is ultimately only one nature and all things partake in that. Logically therefore, this teaching argues, all phenomena are part of the same thing and though at one level distinct, ultimately interpenetrate each other and are not separate since they are all part of a whole.

Buddhist environmentalist writers in this second category of the Harris typology argue that since this is the case human beings ought to care for life in its entirety. One writer presents Buddhism as follows:

> It advocates an urgent challenge that humanity free itself from a distorted arrogance and recognize itself as originated in dependence upon a reality more than itself, that it is conditioned by and coexists in dynamic interdependence with all things. Such a cosmology, grounded in universal Emptiness, would reinvigorate the human in an ethic of reflection upon and care for life in its entirety, as the species which can identify the integrity of the whole in the richness of its diverse particularities.

> (Brown, 1993, p.136)

This argument for a Buddhist environmental ethic based on interpenetration is not without its problems. The fact that it is based on a predominantly east Asian account – one which is not accepted across the Buddhist world – is one of them. There also remains the logical problem that if everything is interconnected then nuclear waste is just as interconnected as the rainforest tree (Harris, 2000, p.125). But regardless of any problems with analysis of this type, it is this positive promotion of a version of a Buddhist environmental ethic which tends to form part of the general perception of Buddhism. For example, it is a positive Buddhist environmental ethic which is implied when Buddhism is brought into service to add weight to what has been labelled 'eco-protest'

(Letcher, 1999, p.2). Eco-protesters are individuals or groups who take direct action, for example, to prevent road-building projects across the countryside. While not all protesters involved in such activity perceive a need for a 'spiritual' motivation, where they do Buddhism is the only one of the major world religions likely to feature in the list of positive 'spiritual' influences. It takes its place there alongside religious paradigms such as Wicca, Druidry and 'New Age' thinking.[9]

The third category of writings about Buddhism and environmentalism in the Harris typology is accounts of environmental activity among Asian Buddhists. According to Harris, activities such as those undertaken by Buddhist writers in his third category are 'accorded authenticity merely by virtue of the fact that they are performed by high profile Buddhists' (Harris, 1995, p.3). Many of these accounts emanate from Thailand where the need for such activity arises from ecologically damaging practices which have taken place in traditionally Buddhist nation states, often as a result of the impact of western consumerist values (Harvey, 2000, p.178). For example, it is claimed that Thailand's forest cover was depleted by almost 80 per cent between 1945 and 1989 to satisfy demand for tropical hardwoods and to enable large scale food and tobacco production (ibid.). Logging was banned completely in 1989 but, in response, the logging companies moved their activities into the neighbouring states of Burma, Laos and Cambodia, other areas where Buddhism has represented the dominant traditional religion (ibid., p.181).

The large scale operations of the logging companies and highly productive agribusinesses opened up areas of the forest so that after the large trees had been removed the smaller trees were also taken by locals for furniture and charcoal production (Scott & Pasanno, 1996, p.10). Other areas were cleared for cultivation. This has proved to be particularly problematic in northern Thailand where hill-tribes practising traditional slash-and-burn agricultural methods (partly in order to grow opium), have now destroyed further areas of forest and have been partially responsible for disrupting the flow of streams to the lowland areas (Harvey, 2000, p.181). In response to this destruction, some Buddhist monks have taken action to protect, initially on a local scale, the land and the creatures which live on it. Harvey (2000, p.182) cites the case of Ajahn[10] Pongsak Tejadhammo, a Buddhist monk who initiated a self-help cooperative that already

---

[9] Wicca, Druidry and New Age are the subjects of essays in Pearson, 2001.

[10] '*Ajahn*' is the title given to a teacher in Thai Buddhism.

involves over 1000 villages and 97,000 people (Swearer, 1995, p.128). The cooperative has replanted many acres of forest, using trees grown in its own nurseries. It has also terraced eroded hillsides. Ajahn Pongsak is of the opinion that since Buddhist wisdom and ethical action are mutually complementary, wisdom can only arise where Buddhists take:

> responsibility for themselves and for society. It is the regular discipline of doing our duty that establishes ethical principles in our daily lives and in the general life of society.
>
> (quoted in Batchelor and Brown, 1992, p.98)

The Ajahn's activities are among a number of initiatives which have attracted support from international agencies, but this activity has not been without controversy. For example, Ajahn Pongsak has been involved in disagreements with the Thai government and with the monastic establishment about appropriate policies with regard to the Hmong hill-tribes. He would prefer that the hill-tribes were brought down to the lowlands and given land where their opium cash-crop could not grow. However, the government continues to allow them to live in their traditional areas and has encouraged them to grow cash-crop cabbages (Harvey, 2000, p.182).

In 1986, Wildlife Fund Thailand (WFT) initiated a project called 'Thailand: Buddhism and Nature Conservation', which aims to coordinate such localized activities. The main objective of the project is 'to provide channels of communication between "active" Buddhists, and to promote their work as models for teaching Buddhist conservation throughout Thailand' (www.panda.org/resources/inthefield/lop/lop_th.htm). In their account of the project, WFT claim not only that Thai Buddhists (who make up 94 per cent of the population) 'have a poor understanding of the modern concept of conservation' but also that they,

> lack, to a large degree, the many teachings that stem from Gautama Buddha, which advocate the careful use and preservation of natural resources. Some guidance is therefore needed to educate people on the Buddhist way of conservation and sustainable development.
>
> ...
>
> As part of the project, monks are encouraged to act 'as community leaders and model conservationists'.
>
> (ibid.)

This account of the WFT project illustrates some of the issues which are raised when traditional Buddhism encounters late twentieth and early twenty-first century notions of conservation. It is understandable that

Thai villagers and urban dwellers lack knowledge of modern conservation, because effective initiatives have not been in place to provide education in such areas. What is less clear is why, when they are immersed in a Buddhist culture, Thai people should lack knowledge of the teachings of the Buddha on this subject. The reason for this is probably not that Thai Buddhists do not know about their own religion, as the WFT suggest. It is much more likely that in order for Buddhist teachings to be presented as pertinent to the conservationist agenda, they need to be applied in new ways. Though the basis of a textual justification for what is referred to by the WFT as 'the Buddhist way of conservation and sustainable development' can be discerned, some of the teachings which may provide this basis are aimed specifically at monastics. Monks are told, for example, to recycle their old robes and refrain from polluting water or grass with urine or excrement (Harvey, 2000, p.180). The monastic system is ecologically appropriate because it aims at 'sufficiency and sustainability by limiting resource consumption to satisfying basic needs and by self-restraint in wants and desires' (Sponsel and Natadecha-Sponsel, 1997, p.49). Monks and nuns are urged to live in this way in the interests of their own development rather than in order to save the earth's resources. However, such values may be increasingly appropriate as the increase in world population and the demands of developed nations threaten resources. Under these circumstances it is not only monks and nuns who need to limit their consumption. There are other examples in the Buddhist scriptures of teachings about simple living in which the resources of the earth are not squandered. Forests should not be burned without good reason, for example. Not killing living beings and not taking what is not given are two fundamental ethical precepts for lay Buddhists, both of which can be usefully applied to contemporary ecological problems.

Buddhists in other areas also become involved in positive action. For example, in Japan a ceremony to release birds and animals is regularly performed (Williams, 1997). But a question remains about whether such injunctions and actions are enough to construct a specifically Buddhist ethic. Monastic self-restraint and injunctions not to kill or to take what does not belong to one are not exclusively Buddhist. Because this is the case, they are useful aids to inter-faith and cross-cultural discussion on ecological issues and they therefore support Beyer's assertion that religious dialogue on environmental issues is essentially a liberal exercise. Based on evidence from Thailand, such injunctions, along with values such as empathy, cooperation and compassion, are sufficient to promote significant action to change the ways in which the earth is used. It is possible therefore to construct an argument that Buddhist teaching and practice is effective in promoting ecological awareness and changes in ways in which the land is used, regardless of whether there is a specifically Buddhist ethic which can be grounded in the canonical texts of Buddhism.

Harris and other likeminded scholars have not been content to leave the issue here, but have attempted to find support for an environmental ethic within a more rigorous reading of Buddhist doctrine. Although Buddhist texts have nothing to say about the late twentieth and early twenty-first century environmental crisis, they do promote a specifically Buddhist attitude to nature. It is to writings on this subject that scholars, such as Harris, turn in an attempt to construct an 'authentic' Buddhist environmental ethic. While acknowledging that Buddhists are encouraged to live lightly on the land, respecting the right to life of animals and other living beings, such scholars want to know whether Buddhist philosophy, as found in the early texts in particular, can support the kind of Buddhist environmental ethic which can be reconciled with scientific ecological thinking. Scholars who represent the two final categories of the Harris typology come to opposing views based on the same resources.

Lambert Schmithausen, a Buddhist scholar, especially of early Buddhist texts, represents Harris's fourth category. Harris describes the category as:

> Critical treatments which, while fully acknowledging the difficulties involved in reconciling traditional Asian modes of thought with those employed by scientific ecology, are optimistic about the possibility of establishing an authentic Buddhist response to environmental problems.

(Harris, 1995, p.3)

Schmithausen's arguments are grounded in the complexities of Buddhist doctrine. I shall therefore not present them in detail,[11] but rather, give an indication of the direction in which they move by selecting just one aspect for exploration.

One of the foundational Buddhist doctrines and one which is repeated often in the early texts is the teaching known as the Four Noble Truths. The first Noble Truth of Buddhism is that life actually or potentially is **dukkha**: unsatisfactory, painful and entailing the suffering of birth, old age, disease and dying. All things, including things which are usually regarded as good, wholesome or desirable are, in the long run, unsatisfactory because they are spoilt by the

---

[11] They do however deserve a careful reading; a rewarding activity for anyone familiar with Buddhist ideas.

disadvantages that accompany them. Bad things are obviously unsatisfactory, but good things are also unsatisfactory because they sometimes entail bad consequences or side-effects, and they are also spoilt by the knowledge that they will inevitably come to an end. This is because nothing lasts for ever; everything is subject to decay and is impermanent.

The second Noble Truth explains the cause of *dukkha*: the reason why life is unsatisfactory is that beings constantly grasp for, or crave things they cannot have. In particular, beings crave permanence but, according to the Buddhist account, nothing is permanent. Good things as well as bad things decay and end; there is no permanence in anything (except *nirvana*), including what we like to think of as ourselves. Indeed, according to Buddhism, no being or thing has a permanent unchanging Self. This craving for permanence keeps beings in the cycle of birth, death and rebirth, known as **samsara** and leads to yet more unsatisfactory life and to further rebirth and therefore to further *dukkha*.

The third Noble Truth is that it is possible for this craving to stop and that with its ceasing comes the end of *dukkha*; since craving causes *dukkha*, the cessation of craving stops the cause of more *dukkha*.

The fourth Noble Truth explains the Noble Eightfold Path, which, if followed, leads to the stopping of craving and therefore of dukkha: it leads to *nirvana* – a way of being that unenlightened beings cannot comprehend but which has none of the characteristics of life in *samsara*. The Noble Eightfold Path is the basis of Buddhist practices.

Given the Buddhist truth that everything is unsatisfactory, impermanent and without a fixed and unchanging Self, Schmithausen argues that there can be no ultimate value in nature, life, species or ecosystems.

> The ultimate value and goal of early Buddhism, absolute and definitive freedom from suffering, decay, death and impermanence, cannot be found in nature.
>
> (Schmithausen, 1997, p.5)

The ultimate goal of Buddhism – release from the constant round of life, death and rebirth which is caused by continued craving which in turn leads to *dukkha* – comes only when beings are no longer attached to life in *samsara*; that is, when they no longer crave for the things which *samsara* offers, including things which though good and wholesome cannot last for ever.

Thus far it looks as though Schmithausen is arguing that Buddhism devalues the natural world. If the natural world has no ultimate value it does not matter what happens to it. Attempts to save the world are therefore futile; there is no ultimate benefit to be gained from saving species or eco-systems. All ecological action is therefore a waste of time. Schmithausen does not stop here however. He goes on to show that if there is no ultimate value in nature – because it is impermanent and characterized by *dukkha* – then, equally, there is no value in the civilized or artificial world which is the result of taming or controlling nature. The benefits to be gained from cutting down forests (whether they are on balance benefits or liabilities in ecological and economic terms), which 'civilization' entails, have no more ultimate value than the natural world.

In promoting practices designed to end craving and the generation of further *dukkha*, Buddhism promotes detachment from the world and a form of indifference to it.[12] This is not the complete picture however. Advancement on the Buddhist path towards enlightenment and therefore increasing detachment from the world leads to a reduction in consumption which is itself conducive to ecological benefit, but only accidentally so; that is, it is a result of the advancement on the Buddhist path but not the reason for being conducive to ecological benefit. But further than this, according to Buddhist accounts, detachment from the world does not, as we might think, lead to a lack of love or compassion for the world and the beings in the world. On the contrary, Buddhist texts teach that enlightenment is not just the absence of suffering, which is a rather negative goal. Enlightenment is not annihilation but instead a positive state characterized by supreme happiness, freedom and liberation. Along with this liberation and happiness come qualities such as compassion, loving kindness and friendliness. If these qualities characterize beings as they achieve the goal, it follows that those who are well advanced on the Buddhist path to the goal are also increasingly characterized by these desirable qualities. If this is the case then it ought to be possible to develop an ecological ethic based on such qualities.

> This prevents a Buddhist from the short-circuit of misinterpreting the *ultimate* valuelessness of life as a permission to destroy life wilfully (by killing living beings, including, normally, oneself)... Should it not be equally justified to establish... nature too... as a value to be preserved, in spite of its *ultimate* valuelessness, in order to prevent the latter from being misinterpreted by deriving from it the permission to exploit and destroy nature relentlessly for our own short-term advantage or for any other reason?
>
> (Schmithausen, 1997, p.16)

---

[12] Note that Schmithausen's presentation of Buddhist *nirvana* is not the same as the understanding of *nirvana* offered by Joanna Macy on page 168.

Schmithausen is optimistic, if cautious, about the possibility of establishing a Buddhist environmental ethic based on the doctrines promoted by Buddhist canonical texts. By his own admission he is sympathetic to the view that humankind is responsible for maintaining intact ecosystems and biodiversity. He shares this concern with writers in the first three of Harris's categories. However, unlike those writers, he also holds the view that in order to establish a Buddhist environmental ethic it is necessary to ground that ethic within the Buddhist textual canon. He claims that the use of selective doctrinal formulae (for example, the interpenetration doctrine favoured by Macy) to support the idea that Buddhism teaches a way which is compatible with an ecological ethic is not sufficient to authenticate a specifically Buddhist approach. In this he comes close to Beyer's eco-traditionalist category (Harris, 1995, pp.5–6). He wants to discover whether the ideological tools needed to support a Buddhist environmental ethic are indeed to be found within traditional Buddhism.

Other writers, those who fall into Harris's fifth and final category, are much less optimistic about whether the Buddhism of the canonical texts can accommodate a modern environmental ethic. Like Schmithausen's, these writings engage with Buddhist texts and doctrine at a sophisticated level in ways that are not readily accessible to a non-specialist. However, the point is that the writers Harris cites, principally Japanese scholar Noriaki Hakamaya, are able to construct a vigorous denial that Buddhism supports an environmental ethic, based, just as Schmithausen's arguments are, on Buddhism's canonical texts (cited in Harris, 1995, p.3; Schmithausen, 1997, p.2; Samuel, 1998, p.133). Hakamaya claims that since what he calls 'true' Buddhism negates nature it is not possible to develop an environmental ethic based on nature's intrinsic value. His argument says that dealing with environmental issues represents a distraction from the proper activity of a Buddhist, which is to attain enlightenment. Harris himself tends, albeit reluctantly, to similar conclusions. He cannot agree with the general claims: that Buddhism attaches importance to wildlife and the protection of the environment; that based on Buddhist doctrines, habitats and species should be preserved; and that Buddhists of the past lived in harmony with nature (Harris, 1991, p.101). He admits that based on their philosophical coherence he wavers between categories four and five. According to his own account, his heart tells him that category four makes sense but his mind tends towards category five (Harris, 1994, p.1). Elsewhere Harris writes:

> Clearly there are difficulties involved in translating Western environmentalist discourse into an authentically Buddhist setting or,

indeed in calling on Buddhism to provide a rationale for ecological activity. This does not mean that the task is hopeless.

(Harris, 1997, p.396)

The disagreement between scholars such as Schmithausen and Hakamaya illustrates one of the problems of hermeneutics – the difficulty of using ancient texts to address modern problems. In all traditions, philologists and other scholars of the history of ideas whose studies are based on religious texts face problems when they try to address modern ethical problems using sources written at a time when these problems simply did not exist. While Buddhist texts certainly promote attitudes towards nature, it is anachronistic or, at the very least, fraught with difficulty, to relate these writings directly to modern-day problems – which are qualitatively and quantitatively different. Sociologist Beyer's view is that:

Religions, like all social forms, change: old forms decline; new ones arise. It is therefore theoretically inappropriate to research the latter using the historical standards of the former.

(Beyer, Part Two, p.277)

Damien Keown, a scholar of Buddhism, is more optimistic about this endeavour. He writes:

To interrogate the scriptures for guidance on new problems is to constantly rediscover and renew them, and in so doing to deepen one's insight into their meaning. It is remarkable how a text which at first glance has nothing to say about an issue can speak eloquently to the matter when read from a new perspective. The answers are certainly available, if not at the surface level then not too far below it. In this respect developing a Buddhist perspective on modern issues is a bit like assembling a jigsaw.

(Keown, 2000, p.1)

The problem with Keown's jigsaw, however, is that there is no picture on the puzzle box. If there were, commentators would agree on what it looks like and could make the pieces fit together with confidence. As we have seen, those who write in accordance with the first three of Harris's categories, are motivated to promote ecological activity and are content to rely on general Buddhist principles such as the precept not to kill or the benefits of using minimal resources. On the whole, such writers leave aside a detailed examination of Buddhist doctrines or use them in selective ways. Schmithausen on the other hand, while personally concerned about the 'ecological crisis', believes that as a scholar he must ask 'to what extent ecological ethics is, at least, in tune with, and susceptible of being integrated into' the Buddhist tradition (Schmithausen, 1997, p.1). He also argues that if Buddhism is:

> to remain a living tradition, it has to supply answers to new vital questions, and it may have to accommodate its heritage to the new situation by means of explication, re-interpretation, re-organization or even creative extension or change.
>
> (ibid., p.3)

Based on these two quotations it seems that while using the tools of the traditionalist – the texts – Schmithausen has the mindset of the liberal – he acknowledges that Buddhism may have to change. He therefore fits Beyer's eco-traditionalist category rather well.

At the beginning of this chapter I observed that the idea that there is a relationship between Buddhism and environmentalism derived initially from the west coast of North America. A recent collection entitled *Buddhism and Ecology: The Interconnection of Dharma and Deeds* includes essays by a number of representatives from Buddhist groups operating in North America, some of whom are developing communities based on ecological principles (Barnhill, Kaza & Yamauchi in Tucker and Williams, 1997). North American Buddhists have been the most prolific writers on this topic in the English language. We have seen that scholars and practitioners in Japan and in south-east Asia are also writing about this relationship and in the case of south-east Asia, in particular, that Buddhists are taking action to counter the destruction of forests and other natural features.

Harris's approach to environmental writings by Buddhists has been to challenge the idea that there can be an authentic Buddhist environmental ethic. He recognizes that some Buddhists – the Dalai Lama and monastic practitioners in Thailand are examples – appear to rely on their own status either as 'guardians of the truth' or as high-profile Buddhists to authenticate the positions they take. These positions, he argues, are not specifically Buddhist in character. Others attempt to find a Buddhist environmental ethic in the texts in more or less rigorous ways. One of the problems with this exercise is that most traditional interpretations of Buddhist texts have more to say to the specialist intent on *nirvana*, about escaping the world than about saving it.

An alternative approach to this issue is to look at the nature of traditional practice in Asian Buddhist countries, rather than at the texts which underpin that practice, and to understand environmental activity and Buddhist practice as aimed at contrasting, but complementary goals. This approach has something in common with accounts within Harris's third type but differs from them in that it looks to traditional patterns of practice, which are often ignored in western Buddhism, in order to argue that environmental activity can be connected to distinctively Buddhist ways of living.

One of the reasons why Buddhism has been successful in transplanting into diverse cultures is that it has the capacity to assimilate religious ideology and practices into its own worldview. Alternatively it can exist successfully alongside religious practices with aims which complement its own. Buddhists traditionally recognize that Buddhism can deal with certain problems but that other more worldly problems require help from other sources, for example, gods or spirits. Tibetan, Thai and Japanese Buddhists, for example, have no difficulty in holding religious systems in tension within their daily lives. In Japan Buddhists visit Shinto shrines as well as Buddhist temples (Reader, 1991), and in Tibet what we might label 'pagan' practices already operate alongside Buddhism and are complementary to it (Samuel, 1998, p.124). In the West there has been a tendency for converts to Buddhism to concentrate on practices aimed at enlightenment and to downplay other aspects of traditional Buddhist practice. For example, meditation, a specialist practice largely (but not entirely) reserved for monastics in Asia, often represents a first introduction to Buddhism for westerners. Other activities in Asia, associated with popular Buddhist practice and aimed at this-worldly goals, are often disregarded and may some-times be treated with disdain by westerners.[13] Since environmental activities are worldly activities this is an instance where a this-worldly focus is required by Buddhists – in the East and the West. Based, in particular, on accounts of environmental activity from Thailand, it seems that there is scope for Buddhist practices and ecological activity to operate alongside each other in a way which is not untraditional within Buddhist areas if we view environmental activity as part of religious activity aimed at this-worldly goals (Colour Plates 9 and 10). This would fit well with the idea that environmentalism is a worldly religion in its own right.

Consider the following account, based on two newsletter contri-butions – one by Dr Nick Scott, a former professional conservation worker and the other a dialogue between Scott and Ajahn Pasanno, a western-born monk acting as the abbot of a monastery in Thailand. Both men are affiliated to the Thai Forest Theravada **Sangha**.[14] This Buddhist monastic order runs monasteries in several countries including Britain and other European states, the USA, Australia and in Thailand, the country of its foundation. This is a western example

[13] For example, spells to offer protection.

[14] An account of this *Sangha* can be found in Waterhouse, 2001.

not one drawn from the East. In the traditional Buddhist heartlands of the East the idea that this-worldly and ultimate goals need complementary but contrasting practices is taken for granted and not in question. It is therefore in the west that such accounts are significant.

Scott reports how he suffered as a result of his commitment to the idea that he had to 'Save the World' (Scott, 1997, p.13). Of particular concern to him were first, the encroachment on the Cheviot Hills of subsidized, cash-crop conifer plantations which, he believed, spoiled the moorland habitat, and second, the choking of the seventeenth-century pond at Chithurst Buddhist monastery by willows and rushes. He constantly felt that he had a duty to take action and consequently he could not sit beside the pond or walk in the hills without becoming angry and upset – emotions which he believes got in the way of both Buddhist practice and effective action. His perspective changed when he realized that the Buddhist teaching about impermanence – the idea that all phenomena are subject to change and decay – applies as much to the planet, including the moorland of the Cheviot Hills and the ancient pond, as it does to anything else. With this in mind he was able to experience the pond in a new way. He writes that with this insight, 'the pond's transience made it seem even more beautiful'. When he shared these insights at an interfaith meeting however, he found that the people there preferred hope to acceptance. His conclusion is that many religious people, including those associated with New Age religion, prefer false hope to the sadness of recognizing that 'we are slowly ruining the planet and there is little we can personally do about it'. He is now trying to develop 'a more skilful approach to ecological issues' based on Buddhist practice (ibid.).

Scott's observations combine acceptance of a foundational Buddhist teaching – that of impermanence – with the recognition that he none the less feels an impetus to contribute something useful to ecological effort, although he now recognizes that he cannot do that single-handedly. These observations resonate with the view of Alan Sponberg who, as we have seen, argues that while efforts to safeguard the environment are not pointless, they are none the less 'at best a stop-gap measure, and not an ultimate solution' (ibid.). Scott continues to work in support of conservation projects, in particular Nature Care, an organization based in Thailand and operated under the auspices of the same Thai Forest Theravada organization. The Nature Care project aims to educate the population local to Poo Jom Gom, a retreat centre in a Thai National Park. It focuses on providing the populace with a sustainable means of livelihood which means that they will no longer need to destroy the forest land. Ajahn Pasanno, who runs the project, has a clear motivation for his activities which, as he expresses it, is neither based on not killing nor on not taking what is not given, nor on using minimal resources. Neither is it based on selective Buddhist doctrines. Instead, his motivation for ecological activity is that without forests there can be no forest monks.[15] As he says:

> If monasteries are set up in areas which are being encroached upon by settlements, or in degraded areas where there is no longer water or shelter, these are not conducive places to practise in. So definitely I am looking out for myself.
>
> (Scott and Pasanno, 1996, p.12)

The perspectives taken by Nick Scott and Ajahn Pasanno, lead to practical ecological action which does not compromise Buddhist practice but are recognized as something rather separate from, but arguable complementary to, that. This approach does not sit quite comfortably within any of Harris's categories. The activities of Pasanno and Nature Care resonate with the third category in that they involve activity undertaken by members of the Buddhist establishment within Thailand; however, the initiative in this case has been taken with the very practical purpose of facilitating the continuance of Buddhist practice. We might convincingly argue that Buddhism does not need forests in order to survive, but from the perspective of the practitioner it is desirable that suitable land continues to be available for isolated meditative practice.

Scott, who has been educated in the western, scientific conservation tradition and is committed to ecological activity, recognizes that there is a tension between such activity and the Buddhist tenet of impermanence. He admits that since the planet itself, like all things in it, is transient, it cannot ultimately escape its inevitable passing away. Though they do not engage extensively with Buddhist texts in these accounts, both men accept the constraints implied by Harris's fifth category and do not attempt to justify their activity by constructing a specifically Buddhist philosophical response. Both men continue to work for relatively small-scale conservationist projects but recognize that they cannot 'Save the World', not simply because they feel powerless in the face of government policies but because, by implication, according to Buddhist cosmological thinking the world cannot be saved. The motivation for their action therefore seems to be that although, in the broadest terms, what Harris calls a

---

[15] While 'forests' conjures up for us a large area covered by trees and undergrowth the point of 'forest' practice is that forests are depopulated places of degradation and the antithesis of cultivated space.

'thorough-going Buddhist environmental ethic' (Harris, 1994, p.1) cannot be justified by foundational Buddhist teachings, it is none the less demonstrably worthwhile to become involved in environmental activity if this can be shown to directly facilitate Buddhist practice both in personal terms, as in the case of Scott, and in terms of a community of monks, as in the case of Pasanno and Nature Care.

This example indicates that Buddhist practitioners are motivated to act to restrict and repair ecological damage, regardless of whether such action is entirely in keeping with the Buddhist way of looking at the world – its traditional cosmology. Whether or not an authentic environmental ethic can be found within Buddhist canonical writings, the impetus to act ecologically, and to write about that is strong. Such actions and writings may be required, as here, to protect areas for Buddhist monasteries or, as in Scott's case, they may have to be tempered to allow for the development of Buddhist understanding. They may also be useful to support a Buddhist homeland, as in the case of the Dalai Lama's writings about Tibet.

We have seen that environmentalism may be understood as representing a religion, or at least a quasi-religious doctrine, in its own right. It may be that Buddhism and environmentalism can operate alongside each other with the recognition that they aim for different but complementary goals. In this way ecological concerns may be served as well as legitimate Buddhist aims.

Conclusion

Environmentalism emerged as a concern in the 1960s, attracted the attention of religious leaders in the late 1980s and became widely popular in the 1990s. The ideology of environmentalism now attracts broad assent in spite of the fact that practices associated with environmentalism lag behind that ideology at both personal levels and at the level of government initiatives. Because the ideology of environmentalism is so widely accepted there is pressure on religions to show how that ideology can be supported within their particular teachings. This is problematic within all traditions not least because religious doctrine was largely developed at a time when the concerns which environmentalism promotes were not necessary; world population was comparatively small and scientific techniques which create problems as well as solving them were unknown.

If religions are to be relevant in the modern world, however, they must address modern problems and concerns. We might argue that they can and do take a lead in such concerns in certain circumstances. Religions are not and never have been static entities. While the truths they teach may be timeless, such truths cannot be disseminated without some degree of religious structure to act as a vehicle for that truth. This means that religious structures have the possibility to change and to adapt according to local and temporal conditions, and also that they can initiate social transformation. The challenge for religions has been to find ways of developing their thinking to incorporate the questions which the condition of the planet poses. All the world religions have attempted this but in this chapter we have confined our analysis to Buddhism.

Just as religions attempt to show how environmental issues fit into their traditional teachings and practices, so ecological groups have invoked traditional religion in support of their cause. An example has been the attempt by the Worldwide Find for Nature to draw on Buddhist teachings to support conservation projects. We see here a jostling between the two ideologies as they each try to gain the support of the other in order to achieve practical, mutually beneficial results.

We have seen that finding a place for environmental ideology within Buddhism is not straightforward in spite of the fact that Buddhism's high profile, particularly in the West, means that there is a certain assumption within some sectors that Buddhism must support an environmental ethic. While there are possibilities for an environmental ideology to operate alongside traditional Buddhist doctrine, it is not easy to find a justification for ecological awareness within Buddhist texts. The conclusions of scholars so far have been varied. Selective readings of Buddhist doctrine yield specific justifications for a Buddhist environmental ethic but, equally, such selectivity has its own drawbacks. Some scholars have argued that the ideology of Buddhism cannot support an environmental ethic at all while others appear to remain doggedly optimistic although failing to satisfy their own criteria. So far as the Buddhist response to the environmental crisis is concerned it is still early days. Scholarly work is in its early stages and there is no consensus. Indeed, it is unlikely that consensus will be achieved within Buddhism given its broad geographical spread and widely contrasting institutional forms. Meanwhile, however, practical initiatives which have the assent of Buddhist communities are already in place. Those who endorse such initiatives are untroubled by any apparent mismatch between environmentalism and the Buddhist worldview to which they adhere.

This material raises issues which are central to religion today and not just to Buddhism. The chapter is focused on one of the foremost concerns of the modern world, a concern which has promoted one of the major social transformations of the late twentieth and early twenty-first centuries. In the course of examining the relationship between environmentalism and Buddhism, we have also been obliged to consider liberalism, traditionalism, the impact of modern ways of living on religious worldviews, the capacity of religions to adapt to change, and the impact of religious ideology on social action. Are the traditional practices of Buddhism and other religious traditions relevant in the modern world or are other practices, with more tangible consequences, more appropriate? Or are the tangible problems of the planet ultimately unresolveable, with the need for transformation beyond the obvious and the physical being the more pressing concern? Such issues, which are central to any consideration of religion in the modern world, are illustrated here by the relationship between two ideologies, one of which, environmentalism, is thoroughly modern and the other, Buddhism, thoroughly traditional.

Appendix: World Charter for Nature (1982)

The General Assembly

Reaffirming the fundamental purposes of the United Nations, in particular the maintenance of international peace and security, the development of friendly relations among nations and the achievement of international cooperation in solving international problems of an economic, social, cultural, technical, intellectual or humanitarian character.

Aware that:

(a) Mankind is a part of nature and life depends on the uninterrupted functioning of natural systems which ensure the supply of energy and nutrients.

(b) Civilization is rooted in nature, which has shaped human culture and influenced all artistic and scientific achievements, and living in harmony with nature gives man the best opportunities for the development of his creativity, and for rest and recreation.

Convinced that:

(a) Every form of life is unique, warranting respect regardless of its worth to man, and, to accord other organisms such recognition, man must be guided by a moral code of action.

(b) Man can alter nature and exhaust natural resources by his action or its consequences and, therefore, must fully recognize the urgency of maintaining the stability and quality of nature and of conserving natural resources.

Persuaded that:

(a) Lasting benefits from nature depend upon the maintenance of essential ecological processes and life support systems, and upon the diversity of life forms, which are jeopardized through excessive exploitation and habitat destruction by man.

(b) The degradation of natural systems owing to excessive consumption and misuse of natural resources, as well as to failure to establish an appropriate economic order among peoples and among States, leads to the breakdown of the economic, social and political framework of civilization.

(c) Competition for scarce resources creates conflicts, whereas the conservation of nature and natural resources contributes to justice and the maintenance of peace and cannot be achieved until mankind learns to live in peace and to forsake war and armaments.

Reaffirming that man must acquire the knowledge to maintain and enhance his ability to use natural resources in a manner which ensures the preservation of the species and ecosystems for the benefit of present and future generations.

Firmly convinced of the need for appropriate measures, at the national and international, individual and collective, and private and public levels, to protect nature and promote international co-operation in this field.

Adopts, to these ends, the present World Charter for Nature, which proclaims the following principles of conservation by which all human conduct affecting nature is to be guided and judged.

I General Principles

1 Nature shall be respected and its essential processes shall not be impaired.

2 The genetic viability on the earth shall not be compromised; the population levels of all life forms, wild and domesticated, must be at least sufficient for their survival, and to this end necessary habitat shall be safeguarded.

3 All areas of the earth, both land and sea, shall be subject to these principles of conservation; special protection shall be given to unique areas, to representative samples of all the different types of ecosystems and to the habitat of rare or endangered species.

4 Ecosystems and organisms, as well as the land, marine and atmospheric resources that are utilized by man, shall be managed to achieve and maintain optimum sustainable productivity, but not in such a way as to endanger the integrity of those other ecosystems or species with which they coexist.

5 Nature shall be secured against degradation caused by warfare or other hostile activities.

II Functions

6   In the decision-making process it shall be recognized that man's needs can be met only by ensuring the proper functioning of natural systems and by respecting the principles set forth in the present Charter.

7   In the planning and implementation of social and economic development activities, due account shall be taken of the fact that the conservation of nature is an integral part of those activities.

8   In formulating long-term plans for economic development, population growth and the improvement of standards of living, due account shall be taken of the long-term capacity of natural systems to ensure the subsistence and settlement of the populations concerned, recognizing that this capacity may be enhanced through science and technology.

9   The allocation of areas of the earth to various uses shall be planned and due account shall be taken of the physical constraints, the biological productivity and diversity and the natural beauty of the areas concerned.

10   Natural resources shall not be wasted, but used with a restraint appropriate to the principles set forth in the present Charter, in accordance with the following rules:

   (a) Living resources shall not be utilized in excess of their natural capacity for regeneration;

   (b) The productivity of soils shall be maintained or enhanced through measures which safeguard their long-term fertility and the process of organic decomposition, and prevent erosion and all other forms of degradation;

   (c) Resources, including water, which are not consumed as they are used shall be reused or recycled;

   (d) Non-renewable resources which are consumed as they are used shall be exploited with restraint, taking into account their abundance, their rational possibilities of converting them for consumption, and the compatibility of their exploitation with the functioning of natural systems;

11   Activities which might have an impact on nature shall be controlled, and the best available technologies that minimize significant risks to nature or other adverse effects shall be used; in particular:

(a) Activities which are likely to cause irreversible damage to nature shall be avoided;

(b) Activities which are likely to pose a significant risk to nature shall be preceded by an exhaustive examination; their proponents shall demonstrate that expected benefits out-weigh potential damage to nature, and where potential adverse effects are not fully understood, the activities should not proceed;

(c) Activities which may disturb nature shall be preceded by assessment of their consequences, and environmental impact studies of development projects shall be conducted sufficiently in advance, and if they are to be undertaken, such activities shall be planned and carried out so as to minimize potential adverse effects;

(d) Agriculture, grazing, forestry and fisheries practices shall be adapted to the natural characteristics and constraints of given areas;

(e) Areas degraded by human activities shall be rehabilitated for purposes in accord with their natural potential and compat-ible with the well-being of affected populations;

12 Discharge of pollutants into natural systems shall be avoided and:

(a) Where this is not feasible, such pollutants shall be treated at the source, using the best practicable means available;

(b) Special precautions shall be taken to prevent discharge of radioactive or toxic wastes;

13 Measures intended to prevent, control or limit natural disasters, infestations and diseases shall be specifically directed to the causes of these scourges and shall avoid averse side-effects on nature.

III Implementation

14 The principles set forth in the present Charter shall be reflected in the law and practice of each State, as well as at the international level.

15 Knowledge of nature shall be broadly disseminated by all possible means, particularly by ecological education as an integral part of general education.

16 All planning shall include, among its essential elements, the formulation of strategies for the conservation of nature, the establishment of inventories of ecosystems and assessments of the effects on nature of proposed policies and activities; all of these elements shall be disclosed to the public by appropriate means in time to permit effective consultation and participation.

17 Funds, programmes and administrative structures necessary to achieve the objective of the conservation of nature shall be provided.

18 Constant efforts shall be made to increase knowledge of nature by scientific research and to disseminate such knowledge unimpeded by restrictions of any kind.

19 The status of natural processes, ecosystems and species shall be closely monitored to enable early detection of degradation or threat, ensure timely intervention and facilitate the evaluation of conservation policies and methods.

20 Military activities damaging to nature shall be avoided.

21 States and, to the extent they are able, other public authorities, international organizations, individuals, groups and corporations shall:

(a) Co-operate in the task of conserving nature through common activities and other relevant actions, including information exchange and consultations;

(b) Establish standards for products and other manufacturing processes that may have adverse effects on nature, as well as agreed methodologies for assessing these effects;

(c) Implement the applicable international legal provisions for the conservation of nature and the protection of the environment;

(d) Ensure that activities within their jurisdictions or control do not cause damage to the natural systems located within other States or in the areas beyond the limits of national jurisdiction;

(e) Safeguard and conserve nature in areas beyond national jurisdiction.

22 Taking fully into account the sovereignty of States over their natural resources, each State shall give effect to the provisions of the present Charter through its competent organs and in co-operation with other States.

23 All persons, in accordance with their national legislation, shall have the opportunity to participate, individually or with others, in the formulation of decisions of direct concern to their environment, and shall have access to means of redress when their environment has suffered damage or degradation.

24 Each person has a duty to act in accordance with the provisions of the present Charter, acting individually, in association with others or through participation in the political process, each person shall strive to ensure that the objectives and requirements of the present Charter are met.

Glossary

dharma (dhamma) The teachings, practices and goals of Buddhism.

dukkha (duḥkha) Unsatisfactoriness or suffering. One of the characteristics (along with impermanence and not-self) which characterize life in *samsara. Dukkha* is caused by attachment to fleeting phenomena, illness, old age and death.

environmental ethics Ethics based on the conviction that humankind is responsible for the preservation of nature.

interpenetration A Buddhist doctrine prominent within East-Asian traditions which argues that all things are interconnected and that nothing is independent of this.

karma The automatic and impersonal law by which actions and the intentions which motivate them lead to related consequences. Present circumstances are partly the result of past *karma* and future circumstances will be based partly on present karmic activity.

liberal A liberal approach to religion tends towards tolerance and open-mindedness. Literal or technical explanations of, for example, doctrine are usually regarded as less important than the presentation of what is viewed as the general spirit of a tradition.

nirvana (nirvāṇa, nibbana) The final goal of Buddhist practice. Liberation from the endless cycle of birth, death and rebirth; inexpressible since it is outside of the experience of beings within that cycle, but characterized by supreme happiness.

samsara The inexorable round of birth, death and rebirth in which all unenlightened beings are circling.

sangha The primary Buddhist social structure.

soteriological Concerning salvation, however that is envisaged.

tathagatagarbha the doctrine that all beings possess, in embryonic form, the potential to mature into Buddhas.

References

Barnhill, D.L. (1997) 'Great Earth *Sangha*: Gary Snyder's view of nature as community', in Tucker and Williams, 1997.

Batchelor, M. and Brown, K. (1992) *Buddhism and Ecology*, London: Cassell.

Beckerlegge, G. (ed.) (2001) *From Sacred Text to Internet*, Aldershot: Ashgate/Milton Keynes: The Open University.

Beyer, P. (1992) 'The global environment as a religious issue: a sociological analysis', *Religion*, 22, pp.1–19.

Beyer, P. (1994) *Religion and Globalization*, London: Sage.

Bocking, B. (1994) 'Japanese religions', J. Holm and J. Bowker (eds) *Attitudes to Nature*, London: Pinter.

Brown, B. (1993) 'Toward a Buddhist ecological cosmology', *Bucknell Review*, 37:2, pp.124–37.

Campbell, C. (1999) 'The Easternization of the West', in B. Wilson and J. Cresswell (eds) *New Religious Movements, Challenge and Response*, London: Routledge.

Dalai Lama. (1992) 'A zone of peace', in M. Batchelor and K. Brown (eds) *Buddhism and Ecology*, London: Cassell; also at www.tibet.com/DL/nobellecture.html (accessed June 2001).

Eckel, M.D. (1997) 'Is there a Buddhist philosophy of nature?', in Tucker and Williams, 1997.

Giddens, A. (1990) *The Consequences of Modernity*, Cambridge: Polity.

Harris, I. (1991) 'How environmentalist is Buddhism?', *Religion*, 21, pp.101–14.

Harris, I. (1994) 'Causation and *telos*: the problem of Buddhist environmental ethics', *Journal of Buddhist Ethics*, http://jbe.gold.ac.uk/1/harris1.html (accessed June 2001).

Harris, I. (1995) 'Getting to grips with Buddhist environmentalism: a provisional typology', *Journal of Buddhist Ethics*, http://jbe.gold.ac.uk/2/harris2.html (accessed June 2001).

Harris, I. (1997) 'Buddhism and the Discourse of Environmental Concern: Some Methodological Problems Considered', in Tucker and Williams, 1997.

Harris, I. (2000) 'Buddhism and ecology', in D. Keown (ed.) *Contemporary Buddhist Ethics*, Richmond: Curzon.

Harvey, P. (2000) *An Introduction to Buddhist Ethics*, Cambridge: Cambridge University Press.

Haught, J. (1996) 'Christianity and Ecology', in R. Gottlieb (ed.) *This Sacred Earth*, London: Routledge.

Kaza, S. (1997) 'American Buddhist response to the land: ecological practice at two West Coast retreat centres', in Tucker and Williams, 1997.

Keown, D. (ed.) (2000) *Contemporary Buddhist Ethics*, Richmond: Curzon.

Letcher, A. (2000) 'The scouring of the shires: fairies, trolls and pixies in eco-protest culture'. Paper delivered to the Contemporary and New Age Religion Conference, Bath Spa University College, 20 May.

Macy, J. (1990) 'The greening of the self', in A. Hunt Badiner (ed.) *Dharma Gaia*, California: Parallax Press.

Pearson, J. (ed.) (2001) *Belief Beyond Boundaries*, Aldershot: Ashgate/ Milton Keynes: The Open University.

Reader, I. (1991) *Religion in Contemporary Japan*, London: Macmillan.

Samuel, G. (1998) 'Paganism and Tibetan Buddhism: contemporary western religions and the question of nature', in J. Pearson, R. Roberts and G. Samuel (eds) *Nature Religion Today*, Edinburgh: Edinburgh University Press.

Schmithausen, L. (1997) 'The early Buddhist tradition and ecological ethics', *Journal of Buddhist Ethics*, http://jbe.gold.ac.uk/4/schm1.html (accessed June 2001).

Scott, N. (1997) 'How not to save the world', *Forest Sangha Newsletter*, no.39, p.13. Also at http://www.abn.ndirect.co.uk/fsn/35/forests.html (accessed June 2001).

Scott, N. and Ajahn Pasanno. (1996) 'Saving forests so there can be forest monks', *Forest Sangha Newsletter*, no.35, pp.10–12.

Sponberg, A. (accessed June 2001) 'The Buddhist conception of an ecological self', *Western Buddhist Review*, vol.2, www.westernbuddhistreview.com/ vol2/ecological_self.html.

Sponsel, L. and Natadecha-Sponsel, P. (1997) 'A theoretical analysis of the potential contribution of the monastic community in promoting a green society in Thailand', in Tucker and Williams, 1997.

Swearer, D. (1995) *The Buddhist Worlds of Southeast Asia*, New York: State University of New York Press.

Thomas, K. (1984) *Man and the Natural World*, Harmondsworth: Penguin Books.

Tucker, M.E. and Williams, D.R. (eds) (1997) *Buddhism and Ecology*, Cambridge, Mass: Harvard University Press.

Waterhouse, H. (2001) 'Representing western Buddhism: a United Kingdom focus', in Beckerlegge, 2001, pp.117–60.

White Jnr, L. (1967) 'The historical roots of our ecological crisis', *Science* 155, pp.1203–7.

Williams, D. (1997) 'Animal liberation, death , and the state: rites to release animals in medieval Japan', in M.E. Tucker and D. Williams (eds) *Buddhism and Ecology*, Cambridge, Mass: Harvard University Press.

Yamauchi, J. (1997) 'The greening of Zen Mountain Centre: a case study', in Tucker and Williams, 1997.

PART TWO

Theologians and the Renewal of Democratic Political Institutions*

JOHN P. BURGESS

On March 18, 1990, East Germans participated in their first and last free elections as East Germans. The party that emerged with the majority in the new Parliament, the Christian Democratic Union (CDU), campaigned on the platform of rapid unification. On October 3, 1990, union became official, and the GDR was a relic of the past.

The subsequent, difficult process of social and economic transition in eastern Germany has obscured the deeply formative political experience that originally accompanied the emergence of a public opposition to and the demise of the Marxist–Leninist state. While few of the new political groups were able to translate their original enthusiasm and idealism into a viable political program, all participated in a lively and significant exchange of views concerning the purpose of government and the nature of popular participation in politics.

Pastors and leaders of the Evangelische Kirche played a significant role in this debate. Some, like Heino Falcke, deliberately refrained from entering electoral politics. They called for a democratization of the church that would draw on the insights of the alternative groups. Others quickly gained prominence in the major German political parties. Even before unification, Manfred Stolpe, formerly the chief administrative officer of the East German Federation of Evangelische Kirchen, had important contacts in the West German Social Democratic Party (SPD). With unification, he won election as a Social Democrat, becoming minister-president of Brandenburg, one of the East's new federal states. Heinrich Fink, formerly the dean of the theological faculty at the Humboldt University – and briefly rector of

*This text first appeared in John P. Burgess, *The East German Church and the End of Communism*, New York and Oxford: Oxford University Press, 1997, pp.91–104.

the university itself – eventually ran for elected office as a member of the Party for Democratic Socialism (PDS), which succeeded the East German Communist Party.

Two Protestant theologians, Wolfgang Ullmann and Richard Schröder, played a particularly significant role in the debate by giving creative and systematic articulation to the issues at stake. Ullmann, born in 1929 in Saxony, part of the Soviet Zone after World War II, served as a parish pastor for nearly a decade, then became professor of church history at the Protestant seminary in Naumburg. In 1978 he was called to teach at the Protestant seminary in East Berlin. Ullmann's interest in the early church fathers, the Radical Reformation, the history of law, and the philosophy of Eugen Rosenstock-Huessy shaped his commitment to an alternative politics.

Schröder, also from Saxony, belonged to a younger generation. Born in 1943, his early memories were not of World War II, but the Cold War, when the East German state was consolidating its power and defining itself over against West Germany. Schröder's Christian upbringing put him at social disadvantage. Whereas Ullmann had been able to study in the West, Schröder did not even receive permission to attend high school. Completing his education in church institutions, he served as a parish pastor for four years, before being called, in 1977, to teach philosophy at the seminaries in Naumburg and East Berlin. Largely self-educated in philosophy, Schröder offered a classical approach that was unavailable at the state universities, where Marxist–Leninist ideology dominated. The Greeks, especially as interpreted through Hannah Arendt, shaped his commitment to politics as a matter of rational debate. He believed that the possibility of such debate depended especially on stable political institutions and on popular participation in politics.

This chapter describes and assesses the role that Ullmann and Schröder played in debating the terms in which democratization should proceed in East Germany. While unification brought about a practical political resolution to the debate, the debate itself remains significant. It illuminates the political attitudes of an entire generation of young East Germans who actively participated in the Wende, and it illustrates the degree to which different understandings of human nature and its capacities for community underlie different under-standings of popular participation in government.

As the hard work of shaping and running democratic institutions began in early 1990, the right to self-government unleashed a lively debate, especially among those in the Evangelische Kirche who had led the Wende. Ullmann and Schröder had been colleagues at the seminary in East Berlin. Both had been close to the alternative groups. Both had played a key role in the church's Conciliar Process for Peace, Justice, and the Integrity of the Creation, which had openly criticized the government's human rights record.[1] Yet Ullmann and Schröder developed two very different approaches to politics and came to find themselves in competing camps.

In the late 1980s, Ullmann emerged as a spokesman for the church-related alternative groups and eventually helped found one of the first public opposition groups, Demokratie Jetzt (Democracy Now).[2] During the tumultuous days of 1989, he regularly addressed mass gatherings in the East German churches, as well as the Western media.[3]

With the opening of the Berlin Wall on November 9, 1989, East Germany's future came into question. Economic and political collapse was imminent. The country needed a new government that could win broad political participation and legitimation. Replacing their leaders and initiating reform, the communists desperately fought to retain their power. They were able to win little popular support, however. As a result, the church, as well as prominent leaders of the new political parties, feared the possibility of civil war, and of a political coup, especially if reactionary forces in the military or secret police organized themselves.

In this context, Ullmann played a crucial role in working with church leaders, who alone enjoyed widespread popular support, to organize a national Round Table to bring government and opposition leaders together to negotiate political transition, including revision of the Constitution and preparation for free elections.[4] Leaders of the Evangelische Kirche, together with leaders of the Roman Catholic Church and the Protestant free churches, convened the first Round Table on December 7, 1989, and moderated its meetings until it

---

[1] See Ökumenische Versammlung von Kirchen und Christen in der DDR zu Gerechtigkeit, Frieden und Bewahrung der Schöpfung, *Ökumenische Versammlung für Gerechtigkeit, Frieden und Bewahrung der Schöpfung: Dresden-Magdeburg-Dresden, Eine Dokumentation* (Berlin: Aktion Sühnezeichen, 1990), 21–51., New York and Oxford: Oxford University Press, 1997, pp.91–104.

[2] For an overview of the development of Demokratie Jetzt, see the documents in Gerhard Rein, ed., *Die Opposition in der DDR: Entwürfe für einen anderen Sozialismus* (Berlin: Wichern Verlag, 1989), 59–83.

[3] Ullmann describes some of these events in interviews in Bernhard Maleck, *Wolfgang Ullmann: 'Ich werde nicht schweigen': Gespräche mit Wolfgang Ullmann* (Berlin: Dietz Verlag, 1991), 67–70.

[4] The Round Table model originated in Poland, then played an important role in several other Eastern European countries.

disbanded on March 12, 1990, shortly before parliamentary elections.[5]

Initially, the government refused to attend. But when Hans Modrow, the new communist premier, attempted to reorganize the hated secret police into a ministry of national security, the Round Table finally gave him an ultimatum. From the middle of January on, he participated in the Round Table, and it essentially assumed legislative powers, both vetoing government proposals and setting forth its own agenda, including measures relating to economic reform, environmental protection, property rights, and immigration.

Ullmann himself served as a minister without portfolio in Modrow's last cabinet. With the nation's first free elections, Ullmann was elected to the East German Parliament, and, within the Parliament, vice-president. With unification, he won a seat in the German Bundestag as a member of a small coalition, Bündnis '90, which was representative of the original opposition groups. While East Germany as a whole quickly distanced itself from these groups (and largely supported the two parties – the Social Democrats and the CDU – that had united with their Western counterparts), Ullmann continued to enjoy considerable respect, and his ideas represented an important, while clearly minority, political position.

Ullmann was deeply impressed by his experience with the Round Table, which included representatives of every major social organization and political party, both old and new. While these groups had varying degrees of public support, the Round Table invited each of them to send the same number of representatives (two), thereby establishing parity among them. Moreover, the Round Table operated on the principle of consensus. While not always attaining complete agreement, the Round Table took pains to allow all voices to speak, and to seek common ground.[6]

Ullmann argued that the Round Table represented a new way of doing politics. First, he saw it as providing for much broader social and political representation than most elected bodies, in which large coalitions rule and smaller groups are either marginalized or unable to attain enough votes to be represented at all. Second, it involved all

---

[5] During these months, church leaders also helped organize and moderate numerous round tables and citizen committees at the local level.

[6] The best book to date on the East German Round Table is Uwe Thaysen, *Der Runde Tisch: Oder: Wo blieb das Volk* (Opladen: Westdeutscher Verlag, 1990). For a brief but helpful overview of the Round Table and its work, see David A. Steele, 'At the Front Lines of the Revolution: East Germany's Churches Give Sanctuary and Succor to the Purveyors of Change,' in *Religion, the Missing Dimension of Statecraft*, ed. Douglas Johnston and Cynthia Sampson (New York: Oxford University Press, 1994).

participants in a search for the common good. It was not an exercise in mere power politics, with different interests competing for superiority, but a common striving for what was just *(Recht)*. It asked participants to speak the truth as best they knew it, confident that consensus would emerge as open, honest dialogue took place. Third, the Round Table was an effort to build and sustain intimate community. It was small enough to allow its members to get to know each other. Despite their differences, they had a sense of common purpose and mutual need.[7]

Prior to unification, members of the Round Table, including Ullmann, prepared and proposed a new East German constitution that incorporated elements of their experience with the Round Table.[8] Because the new East German Parliament was deeply divided on the question of a new constitution and increasingly focused on issues of unification with West Germany, the proposal soon died. Nonetheless, the treaty of unification included a provision for a parliamentary commission to study the possibility of writing a constitution to replace the West German *Grundgesetz* (the so-called foundational law that West Germany had adopted after the war in lieu of a constitution, in order to avoid appearing to legitimize the division of the country). In this way, the Round Table proposal stimulated the commission's work, even though the proposal itself found little acceptance.

As a member of the Bundestag, Ullmann continued to argue for the Round Table's proposal, and for alternative political structures that would embody the possibilities of the Round Table model. While recognizing the limitations of the Round Table, especially at the national level, he argued that no state could address and solve major social issues without widespread citizen involvement and support. At the local level, he saw the Round Table model as even more viable.[9]

In part, Ullmann wished to address what he saw as the current political malaise of the Western world. Democratic theory affirms the people's capacity for self-government; in practice, however, many

---

[7] Ullmann's most important essay on the Round Table is 'Vorschule der Demokratie: Kirche und Runder Tisch – der gemeinsame Boden einer geschichtlichen Erfahrung' in Wolfgang Ullmann, *Demokratie – jetzt oder nie! Perspektiven der Gerechtigkeit*, ed. Wolfram Bürger and Michael Weichenhan (Munich: Kyrill & Method Verlag, 1990), 157–167.

[8] Arbeitsgruppe 'Neue Verfassung der DDR' des Runden Tisches, *Verfassungsentwurf für die DDR* (Berlin: BasisDruck Verlagsgesellschaft/Staatsverlag der DDR, 1990).

[9] Wolfgang Ullmann, interview by author, July 10, 1991.

people, even in a democracy, feel alienated or apathetic.[10] They
sense that they have little real choice when they go to the polls, and
that they elect officials who have little direct accountability to them, at
least not until the next election. Ullmann saw the Round Table as a
model that could help ameliorate these frustrations and contribute
important impulses to democratic renewal.[11]

Ullmann's position rested on a particular theological and philosophical orientation and critique. He argued that Marxism-Leninism
had a mechanistic model of power and justice. The state sought to
organize society in such a way as to produce equality. The result was
the opposite: massive violation of human rights.[12] For Ullmann, the
West too was threatened by forms of power politics in which the
strongest party imposes its will and calls it justice. Drawing on the
example and teaching of Jesus, he argued for conceiving power and
justice in terms of equality rather than hierarchy.[13] This vision of a
new kind of community was not narrowly political, in the sense of
belonging only to the state. On the contrary, it found its ultimate
realization in the church. The church, however, could challenge the
state to embody this kind of community in its sphere, and to exercise
its power in ways that helped individuals claim their fundamental
right to self-government.[14]

Ullmann argued against an overly individualistic understanding of
rights. People would need to exercise their rights not against each
other but for each other. Only by working together would they be
able to address and solve the questions that threatened their survival.
Ullmann argued that such cooperation could best be achieved in
smaller political units. The renewal of democracy would therefore
depend on the decentralization of power and population. Only as
people live in communities in which they actually know each other
can they seek a common good.[15] When people exercise their rights
together, they give voice to justice (Recht) together.[16] Law ultimately

---

[10] Ullmann, *Demokratie – jetzt oder nie!*, 18.

[11] Ullmann, interviews by Maleck, *Wolfgang Ullmann*, 77.

[12] Ibid., 54, 64–65.

[13] Ullmann, *Demokratie – jetzt oder nie!*, 31.

[14] Ibid., 38–39; and Ullmann, interviews by Maleck, *Wolfgang Ullmann*, 60–63.

[15] Ullmann, *Demokratie – jetzt oder nie!*, 20, 52; and Ullmann, interviews by
Maleck, *Wolfgang Ullmann*, 79.

[16] Ullmann, *Demokratie – jetzt oder nie!*, 143, 150, 168–171; and Wolfgang
Ullmann, 'Für einen demokratischen verfassten Bund deutscher Länder,' in
Thaysen, *Der Runde Tisch*, 270–272.

depends on consensus in community. Ullmann argued that the Sermon on the Mount, while it remains an ideal that criticizes and corrects every earthly reality, finds realization in this kind of political community.[17]

Richard Schröder

To those who had prepared for, and participated in, the Wende, Schröder represented a major alternative to Ullmann. In the mid-1980s, Schröder had organized a reading and discussion group for students from the seminary in East Berlin. Meeting quietly in his home over several years, this group addressed major philosophical questions about the nature of the state, justice, and politics. Eventually, core members of the group began to chart an alternative political course for East Germany, and in the summer of 1989 they founded the East German Social Democratic Party, another of the first public opposition groups.

Schröder joined the Social Democratic Party and, like Ullmann, was elected to the new East German Parliament. He served as head of the Social Democratic faction and helped forge the 'great coalition' with the Christian Democrats that prepared the way for unification. With unification itself, he returned to teaching but remained active in politics. A gifted speaker and writer, he became one of the best-known East Germans in the united German SPD.[18]

Schröder agreed with Ullmann that the Round Table had been a necessary institution during a time of national emergency and transition. But he was also critical of its work, arguing that its drive to achieve consensus hindered its ability to confront and challenge the Marxist–Leninist government. Moreover, its control of legislation had been profoundly antidemocratic; none of its representatives had been popularly elected.[19]

---

[17] Compare Ullmann's remarks in Ullmann, *Demokratie – jetzt oder nie!*, 34–39, 167; and in Ullmann, interviews by Maleck, *Wolfgang Ullmann*, 60–63. It is not surprising that Ullmann has been especially interested in Thomas Müntzer, though Ullmann would reject his appeal to violence.

[18] With the merger of the East Berlin seminary with the Humboldt University, Schröder also served a term as dean of the theological faculty and actively participated in university politics.

[19] Richard Schröder, interview by author, June 13, 1991.

Schröder drew a sharp distinction between the private and the public.[20] In the private realm, characterized by such institutions as family and church, people meet each other in varying degrees of intimacy. They reveal themselves to each other. They form their deepest convictions and practices. In the public realm, by contrast, people have a persona; they wear a mask. Their private lives and beliefs are not necessarily relevant to the performance of their public duties.[21]

Schröder saw Ullmann's concerns – dialogue, consensus, intimate community – as belonging to the private realm. They were matters of individual choice and commitment. The state could neither produce nor guarantee them; at most, it could help foster the external circumstances that provided for them. Politics belongs to the public realm. It entails compromise rather than consensus, the possible rather than the ideal, justice rather than love.[22]

Nonetheless, these two realms are not entirely separable: The private conditions the public. If politics is to be more than power politics, it requires people to have a sense of justice. They must come to politics with convictions about what is morally right and wrong. Moreover, their convictions must give them a sense of political responsibility – that is, responsibility to a common good – rather than mere self-interest.[23]

Convictions, however, cannot always find political realization, for politics requires negotiation and compromise, and convictions, though they can be modified, cannot be negotiated or compromised.[24] In this sense, Schröder, like Ullmann, saw the Marxist–Leninist model of power and justice as deeply flawed.[25]

---

[20] Hannah Arendt's appeal to, and interpretation of, Aristotle on these matters has been especially influential in Schröder's thinking. See, in particular, part 2, 'The Public and the Private Realm,' in Hannah Arendt, *The Human Condition* (Chicago: University of Chicago Press, 1958.)

[21] Richard Schröder, *Denken im Zwielicht: Vorträge und Aufsätze aus der alten DDR* (Tubingen: Mohr, 1990), 92–94, 138, 143; and Richard Schröder, 'Abkehr von der Utopie: Gesprächmit dem DDR-Politiker Richard Schröder (SPD),' interview by Peter Hölzle and Hans Norbert Janowski, Evangelische Kommentare 23 (June 1990): 345.

[22] Schröder, Denken im Zwielicht, 88–94, 120; and Richard Schröder, 'Zu Hause in aller Welt, doch fremd im eigenen Land,' *Frankfurter Allgemeine Zeitung* (December 7, 1990).

[23] Schröder, *Denken im Zwielicht*, 88.

[24] Ibid., 90.

[25] Ibid., 78, 158–159.

Politics is a matter of *poesis,* not of the mechanical application of ideals or an ideology.

In contrast to Ullmann, however, Schröder argued that democracy rested on twin foundations. Ullmann called for the renewal of public life by the introduction of elements of intimate community into it. Schröder called for the renewal of both the public, governmental realm (e.g., through constitutional standards and safeguards, such as the separation of powers) and the private, nongovernmental realm – but apart from each other.[26]

Schröder argued that, in an age in which the social anonymity and instability of mass society seem to undermine intimacy and community, people are tempted to seek intimate community in the public rather than the private realm.[27] He feared that such a politics easily becomes moralistic, imposing a particular set of opinions or feelings as public policy.[28] He called instead for society to recover forms of 'binding community' *(verbindliche Gemeinschaft)* in the private realm.[29] As people acquire a sense of right and wrong, as well as skills of arguing, testing, and modifying their convictions, they begin to develop a 'political culture,' and to overcome the alienation, apathy, and conformity so characteristic of modern life. They slowly become capable of critical thinking, self-government, and political responsibility.[30] This political culture, though private (in Schröder's terms), is the precondition for the renewal of public life.

Rights, too, had a different significance for Schröder than for Ullmann. Ullmann saw rights as reflecting and establishing a fundamental equality among persons. This equality becomes the basis for shared experience, mutual concern, and intimate community. In this way, Ullmann again tended to blur the boundary between the private and the public. For Schröder, by contrast, rights functioned differently in the private and public realms, though they were in both cases grounded in an equality of human beings before

[26] Ibid., 89, 145; and Richard Schröder, "Wir hatten hier in geistiges Elend': Richard Schröder über die Folgen des Marxismus–Leninismus,' *Forum Ethik und Berufsethik,* Sonderheft (July 1990): 6. Schröder, interview by author, June 13, 1991.

[27] Schröder, interview by author, June 13, 1991.

[28] For his criticism of the *Bürgerbewegung* (citizens' movement) that Ullmann claimed to represent, see Richard Schröder, 'Politik von Anfang an: Gespräch mit Richard Schröder am 4. Mai 1990,' interview by Gerhard Rein, in *Die protestantische Revolution 1987–1990: Ein deutsches Lesebuch,* ed. Gerhard Rein (Berlin: Wichern Verlag, 1990), 389–390; and Richard Schröder, 'Warum Parteien nötig sind,' *Zeitschrift für Parlamentsfragen* (1990): 611.

[29] Schröder, *Denken im Zwielicht,* 147.

[30] Schröder, interview by Hölzle and Janowski, 'Abkehr von der Utopie,' 344–345.

God, as established by Christian doctrines of creation and redemption.[31]

This fundamental equality first finds expression in the private realm, especially the church. Christians have the rights of brothers and sisters. They share deep convictions about right and wrong; they seek open, honest discussion of what is true and good; they practice love and forgiveness.

This fundamental equality of human beings before God also has implications for the public realm. If every person has a relationship with God, whether acknowledged or not, others must respect and protect that person's private realm. The experience of the religious wars of the sixteenth and seventeenth centuries convinced people that this equality of conscience would be best protected through the law. Equality before God necessitates equality before the law, expressed in rights that find state protection.[32]

Like Ullmann, Schröder argued that rights always imply duties. One's rights do not simply protect one from others; they require one to respect others. In this sense, rights are the very foundation of community.[33] Unlike Ullmann, Schröder again saw private and public levels of community. The kind of community that one may experience in the church does not provide a model for political life. Nonetheless, the church can make an essential contribution to building the political culture that makes public, political life and democratic government possible.[34]

How, then, can individuals best participate in government? What is required of them, and how can they best represent their interests? In assessing the relationship of intimate community to political community, Ullmann and Schröder engaged in an implicit debate about the parameters of democratization. Their debate suggested that negotiating the rules of participation in the new political system would not simply be a matter of power politics. Nothing less than differing views of human nature and its capacities for community were at stake.

---

[31] Schröder, *Denken im Zwielicht*, 139–141.

[32] Ibid., 92–93, 143.

[33] Ibid., 147.

[34] On the special contribution that the church can make to recreating a political culture, see Schröder, *Denken im Zwielicht*, 346; and Richard Schröder, 'Naturschutzpark für "DDR-Identität"? Antwort auf die Thesen eines ökumenischen Initiativkreises,' *Neue Zürcher Zeitung* (April 22–23, 1990).

Issues of popular political participation

The members of the church-related alternative groups that helped lead the East German Wende agreed that democracy alone could guarantee people the fundamental political rights that find classic formulation in the American Bill of Rights: freedom of speech, assembly, and press; respect for the integrity of the individual; protection from government interference. Moreover, they shared a common concern that individuals exercise their rights for the sake of social, economic, and political renewal. The Marxist–Leninist state had devastated the nation's political, economic, and cultural life. It had proven itself incapable of addressing issues of both national and global survival, especially in relation to peace, justice, and environmental protection.

People who had once adapted, and even accommodated themselves, to political powerlessness now had the responsibility to reclaim a sense of civic duty. Demokratie Jetzt and Bündnis '90 drew people who argued for a kind of democracy that would provide for a much greater degree of popular participation than they saw in West Germany. Others, such as those who joined the Social Democratic Party or the reformed CDU, argued that the West German political system was basically sound – and, in any case, more desirable than any new experiment in 'democratic socialism.'

As the new East German political leadership negotiated the terms of democracy and of popular participation in government, three questions came to the fore; Ullmann and Schröder answered each differently:

(1) How does the question of truth relate to the question of power?

The alternative groups believed that Marxist–Leninist ideology had destroyed political life. People had lost the capacity for critical thinking. They had forgotten or ignored their ability to ask questions of fundamental truth. They had, to borrow Vaclav Havel's phrase, 'lived in a lie.' In gathering to discuss and examine pressing social issues, the groups saw themselves making the first moves toward 'living in truth.'

Ullmann further developed this position. The key skill for people who seek to govern themselves is dialogue. Through dialogue, they seek the truth, realizing that each has a contribution to make. Through dialogue, they ultimately come to consensus about the way things are and should be.[35]

---

[35] Ullmann, 'Für einen demokratischen verfassten Bund,' 270.

Schröder criticized this position. He argued that dialogue about truth, because it involves people's deepest convictions, is essentially a private affair.[36] Politics, as a public affair, begins with, but cannot stop at, dialogue. A government that waits until dialogue becomes consensus will never be able to act quickly or resolutely, for dialogue and consensus require more time than political reality ever allows. Politics is always conditioned by the necessities and limitations of the moment.[37]

To Schröder, Ullmann appeared to imply that those who have the truth have the right to exercise power. Schröder saw this position as problematic in two respects, both of which had parallels in Marxism-Leninism. First, despite Ullmann's rejection of Marxism-Leninism, his position still seemed to assume a mechanistic model of truth, as though truth were something that one simply grasps and applies, with a specific political result in mind.[38] Second, Schröder saw a position like Ullmann's as easily leading to the danger of political elitism. A particular group, in the name of the people, claims to discover and realize a shared truth on their behalf.[39]

(2)   What kind of competency gives one a right to participate in political decisionmaking?

The alternative groups argued for a 'competence of the affected' (Kompetenz der Betroffenheit). Insofar as their members felt threatened by global and domestic issues of peace, justice, and the environment, they argued that they had the right and responsibility to act politically. They not only organized seminars and protests, but also called for specific changes in laws and policies.

Ullmann's position drew on these insights. He argued that the state, in addressing major social issues, needed the advice and counsel of as many people as possible. It would want to draw on the insights of those with professional credentials, but also on the insights of those most affected by different courses of action.[40] Indeed, at the local level, affected laypeople bring great motivation to addressing

---

[36] Schröder, *Denken im Zwielicht*, 92.

[37] Ibid., 63, 92; and Schröder, 'Warum Parteien nötig sind,' 613.

[38] See Schröder, 'Warum Parteien nötig sind,' 613.

[39] Schröder, *Denken im Zwielicht*, 63; and Schröder, interview by Rein, 'Politik von Anfang an,' 389–390.

[40] Ullmann, interview by author, July 10, 1991.

and solving even the most pressing and complex issues, and can quickly develop any necessary expertise.[41]

Schröder argued strongly against the idea of a competence of the affected, maintaining that a politics that measures competency in terms of suffering is potentially 'terroristic,' imposing one group's opinions and feelings on all society.[42] Because the problems that threaten human survival are highly complex, wise political decisionmaking ultimately depends on consulting primarily those whose competence is based on knowledge and expertise.

Schröder acknowledged that popular discussion of these issues is essential. They affect every person to some degree. But he argued that this kind of discussion should take place in the private realm. True dialogue would depend, moreover, on more than a sharing of mere opinions and feelings. Those who are uninformed have a right to join in the conversation but also a responsibility to educate themselves, at least generally, about the issues that face them locally and globally.[43]

This private conversation nonetheless has public import. By becoming competent participants in the discussion of public issues, laypeople are able to demand accountability from those who, because of their expertise, shape public policy.[44]

Schröder agreed with Ullmann that government at the local level would offer the best opportunities for laypeople who feel 'affected' to become involved in policymaking and to develop an expertise that can make a genuine political contribution. In contrast to Ullmann, however, Schröder argued that problems of global and national magnitude – peace, justice, and the environment – are not necessarily best solved at the local level. They are simply too complex.[45]

(3)   What form of representation best respects one's right to participate in political decisionmaking?

The alternative groups practiced direct democracy in shaping their own life; with the fall of the Wall, they envisioned bringing elements of direct democracy into postcommunist political structures. They dismissed established political parties as interest groups that did not

---

[41] Ullmann, *Demokratie – jetzt oder nie!*, 21

[42] Schröder, 'Naturschutzpark für "DDR-Identitä"?; and Schröder, 'Warum Parteien nötig sind,' 613.

[43] Schröder, *Denken im Zwielicht*, 91, 147.

[44] Schröder, interview by author, June 13, 1991.

[45] Schröder, *Denken im Zwielicht*, 92–93.

necessarily reflect the public will. They saw representative democracy as disempowering ongoing public participation in political decisionmaking. Key to the experience of the alternative groups had been the political awakening of an entire nation, of crowds peacefully gathering in churches and streets, shouting 'We are the people' (Wir sind das Volk). As the communist government crumbled, self-organized 'citizen committees' had helped to organize and maintain public services, as well as to occupy and secure the buildings of the secret police. The people had demonstrated and proven their right to govern themselves.

Ullmann, too, was deeply impressed by these events. For him, the high point of the revolution was the mass demonstration that took place in East Berlin on November 4, 1989.[46] On that day, only a week before the Wall fell, a million East Germans peacefully gathered at Alexanderplatz, in the heart of the city. Organized by the nation's artists and writers, this demonstration called specifically for the state to respect people's political rights, especially freedom of speech, assembly, and the press.

Inspired by 'the people,' Ullmann called for a politics that could continue to empower them and to learn from their experience and wisdom.[47] For him, the renewal of democracy meant the reconstruction of politics from the ground up. Local groups, able to organize and govern themselves, would make many of the decisions currently made at the national level.[48] Ullmann also argued for incorporating elements of direct democracy into national decisionmaking. Citizen groups should have the authority to bring bills directly to the Parliament for consideration, and major laws should come to the people for decision by referendum.[49]

Schröder again offered a sharp critique of this position. More clearly than Ullmann and the alternative groups, he saw that the cry for German unification, Wir sind ein Volk (We are one people), would prove more enduring and significant than the earlier Wir sind das Volk (We are the people). He was concerned to draw on the political traditions and experience of the West.

---

[46] Ullmann, interviews by Maleck, Wolfgang Ullmann, 73.

[47] Ullmann, Demokratie – jetzt oder nie!, 151.

[48] Ibid., 51–52; and Ullmann, interviews by Maleck, Wolfgang Ullmann, 78–79, 120.

[49] For Ullmann's critique of representative democracy, see Ullmann, Demokratie – jetzt oder nie!, 31, 35.

While open to some elements of direct democracy, Schröder argued that its usefulness was limited.[50] In a highly complex world, there can be no return to a romanticized past of radical political decentralization. Moreover, a direct democracy poses the danger that policy will be made by assertion and acclamation, as under Marxism-Leninism, rather than by discussion and negotiation. When the focus is on swaying the masses, politics easily becomes an exercise in demagoguery rather than democracy. Schröder argued that representative democracy actually ensures rather than undercuts accountability. People can know who supports a particular position; a popular referendum leaves no such possibility. For this reason, parties also play an important role in a democracy. They help provide stability and continuity, and they enable the development of clear political positions that can come to public discussion and debate.[51]

Conclusion

Though Ullmann and Schröder never explicitly directed their polemics against each other, they were among the most articulate spokesmen in a debate that shaped East German politics in the brief time between the emergence of a public opposition to the Marxist–Leninist state in 1989 and unification with West Germany in 1990. With unification, the debate lost much of its urgency, for East Germans no longer needed to construct a new state.

Despite this practical resolution to the debate, East Germans have brought elements of it into their new political context. The positions that Ullmann and Schröder represent have found institutional homes nationally – Ullmann's in the recent alliance of Bündnis '90 with the Greens, Schröder's in the SPD. Though Ullmann and Schröder continue largely to represent the concerns of East Germans, they have achieved a degree of national prominence. In the summer of 1994, Ullmann was elected to a seat in the European Parliament. That same year, Schröder ran for the Bundestag, though unsuccessfully. As politicians, they have drawn on the East German experience to articulate a vision of a new Germany in a new Europe.

While it is difficult to gauge the actual political influence of either Ullmann or Schröder, their positions have become part of a larger debate about German politics. With the emergence of parties to the

---

[50] For those elements that he accepts, see Richard Schröder, 'Die Verfassungsfrage in der DDR seit dem Herbst 1990,' in *Markierungen auf den Weg zu einer gesamtdeutschen Verfassung: Ein Symposium*, ed. Martin Pfeiffer and Manfred Fischer (Bad Boll: Evangelische Akademie, 1990), 71.

[51] See Schröder, 'Warum Parteien nötig sind.'

extreme right, the resurgence of the former Communist Party in the eastern part of the country, the growing fragmentation of the political landscape in recent elections, and the relative decline of the Social Democratic and Christian Democratic parties, Germans are asking basic questions about the nature and viability of their democratic institutions. Political discontent with the established parties reflects a growing frustration that politics has become too much the business of professional politicians, rather than providing for popular partici-pation and self-government.[52]

In this context, the areas of agreement between Ullmann and Schröder are more significant than the areas of disagreement. While differing on what the nature of a new constitution should be, both have argued that the renewal of democratic institutions in Germany depends in part on popular ratification of one. While differing on the degree to which a constitution should provide for plebiscites and popular referenda, both have argued for more elements of popular participation in government. Each in his own way has argued that the future of German democracy depends on citizens' taking the political task seriously, and not abandoning it to others.

The Ullmann–Schröder debate also has significance for a deeper understanding of religion and democratization. It is noteworthy in itself that *theologians* played such a significant role in shaping a democratizing nation's political discourse, even if only for a short time, reflecting the unique role of the church in the East German context.

The role of theologians is also remarkable in light of the vulnerability of new democratic regimes to reactionary expressions of primal identities, that is, to new fundamentalisms of nation, ethnicity, and religion.[53] Analysis of the East German situation affirms that religious institutions and ideals can support, as well as impede,

---

[52] Schröder has recently noted and commented on some of these concerns in a book directed primarily to a West German audience: *Deutschland schwierig Vaterland: Für eine neue politische Kultur* (Freiburg im Breisgau: Herder, 1993).

[53] See Edward Friedman, 'Alternatives to Leninist Democratization: The Legitima-tion of Culture, Region, Nationalisms and Fundamentalism,' in *National Identity and Democratic Prospects* (Armonk, N.Y.: Sharpe, 1995). For other recent literature, see Boris Kagarlitsky, *The Thinking Reed: Intellectuals and the Soviet State from 1917 to the Present*, trans. Brian Pearce (London: Verso, 1988), 221–222; and Sergei Kapitza, 'Anti-Science Trends in the USSR,' *Scientific American* 265 (August 1991): 32–38.

democratization. Theologians like Ullmann and Schröder drew on theological categories to connect concerns about individual rights to a vision of a higher responsibility for building and preserving democratic political community.[54]

Yet it is striking that neither Ullmann nor Schröder developed extensive political theologies. Neither was concerned to establish a 'Christian' nation. Their appeals to Scripture and theology were limited to rather broad principles of freedom, justice, equality, and responsibility. They addressed issues of religion and politics, and of church and state, primarily to the end of calling for the renewal of a political culture in which people could acquire deep convictions about their political rights and responsibilities. Ullmann and Schröder sought to give political form to the church's free space, so that East Germans might practice the basic skills of critical analysis and debate so necessary for democratic life. Where they differed was in their understanding of the relationship between intimate community and public politics.

In the East German context, the Ullmann–Schröder debate was perhaps most significant in shifting the discussion of popular participation in government away from the enumeration and elucidation of personal rights, which East Germans were so quick to claim for themselves as the Wall fell. Ullmann and Schröder helped focus the debate on the broader issue of what self-government entails and requires. If political rights imply political responsibility, questions of consensus, competency, and representation become crucial. Rights and responsibility might not only support each other but also come into tension, depending on how one defines the nature of popular participation in government.

The Ullmann–Schröder debate seemed to confirm what several political scientists have recently suggested, namely, that democratization is not simply a matter of building new political institutions, such as an independent judiciary or free elections, but is above all the process by which the groups that have opposed the old political system negotiate the rules of participation in the new political system and define the exercise of political rights. The

---

[54] Vaclav Havel refers to and develops the notion of a higher responsibility in 'Help the Soviet Union on Its Road to Democracy,' *Vital Speeches of the Day* (March 15, 1990): 330. For various appeals to Christian values to undergird democratization, see Adam Michnik, 'Notes on the Revolution,' trans. Klara Glowczowski, *New York Times Magazine* (March 11, 1989): 44; Czeslaw Milosz:, 'From the East: A Sense of Responsibility,' *New Progressive Quarterly* (Spring 1990): 46; and Vaclav Havel, 'The Power of the Powerless,' trans. Paul Wilson, in *The Power of the Powerless: Citizens against the State in Central-Eastern Europe*, ed. Vaclav Havel (London: Hutchinson, 1988), 81.

viability of a new democracy depends on the successful completion of such negotiations, and any attempt to short-circuit them risks eventual disillusionment with the idea of democracy.[55] The Ullmann–Schröder debate demonstrated the terms in which such negotiations implicitly proceeded in one country. The renewal of the democratic promise elsewhere in the world will require attention to similar questions.

---

[55] For the recent literature, see Giuseppe Di Palma, *To Craft Democracies: An Essay on Democratic Transitions* (Berkeley: University of California Press, 1990). See also Giuseppe Di Palma, 'Democratic Transitions: Puzzles and Surprises from West to East' (paper presented at the Conference of Europeanists, Washington, D.C., March 23–25, 1990); and Edward Friedman, 'Consolidating Democratic Breakthroughs in Leninist States,' in *From Leninism to Freedom*, ed. Margaret Lotus Nugent (Boulder: Westview, 1992), 67–84.

A Feminist Interpretation of Women's Rights in Islam*

FATIMA MERNISSI

Fatima Mernissi (Morocco, born 1940), 'one of the best known Arab-Muslim feminists,' was part of the first generation of Moroccan women to be granted access to higher education. She studied at the Mohammed V University in Rabat and went on to receive her doctorate in sociology in the United States in 1973. She returned to Morocco to teach at her alma mater and currently works at a research institute in Rabat. 'She is a recognized public figure in her own country,' and her work has been translated into several European languages.[1] According to a fellow academic, Mernissi is the first Muslim woman in the Middle East to succeed 'in extricating herself from the issue of cultural loyalty and betrayal' that plagues so many Muslim feminists torn between their double identities.[2] According to a fellow African Muslim, Mernissi represents 'the aspirations of women

---

*This text first appeared in Mernissi, F. (1998) 'A Feminist Interpretation of Women's Rights in Islam', in C. Kurzman (ed.) *Liberal Islam: A Sourcebook*, New York and Oxford: Oxford University Press, pp.112–26. Previously published in Fatima Mernissi, *The Veil and the Male Elite: A Feminist Interpretation of Women's Rights in Islam*, translated by Mary Jo Lakeland. Reading, Mass.: Addison-Wesley, 1991, pp.1–4, 49–61, 62, 64, 70, 81. First published in French in 1987 © 1991 by Fatima Mernissi. Published with permission of Addison-Wesley and Edite Kroll Literary Agency.

[1] Amal Rassam, 'Mernissi, Fatima' in John L. Esposito, editor, *The Oxford Encyclopedia of the Modern Islamic World* (New York: Oxford University Press, 1995), volume 3 pp. 93–94.

[2] Leila Ahmas, 'Feminism and Feminist Movements in the Middle East,' *Women's Studies International Forum*, volume 5, number 2, 1982, pp. 153–168.

who, while remaining Muslims, wish to live in modernity.'[3] One of the recurring themes of Mernissi's work is the mistreatment of women in Islamic societies. In this excerpt, Mernissi argues that the Qur'an and other Islamic sources have been systematically misinterpreted on the subject of the position of women.

'Can a women be a leader of Muslims?' I asked my grocer, who, like most grocers in Morocco, is a true 'barometer' of public opinion.

'I take refuge in God!' he exclaimed, shocked, despite the friendly relations between us. Aghast at the idea, he almost dropped the half-dozen eggs I had come to buy.

'May God protect us from the catastrophes of the times!' mumbled a customer who was buying olives, as he made as if to spit. My grocer is a fanatic about cleanliness, and not even denouncing a heresy justifies dirtying the floor in his view.

A second customer, a schoolteacher whom I vaguely knew from the newsstand, stood slowly caressing his wet mint leaves, and then hit me with a *hadith* [tradition of the Prophet] that he knew would be fatal: 'Those who entrust their affairs to a women will never know prosperity!' Silence fell on the scene. There was nothing I could say. In a Muslim theocracy, a *hadith* is no small matter. The *hadith* collections are works that record in minute detail what the Prophet said and did. They constitute, along with the Qur'an (the book revealed by God), both the source of law and the standard for distinguishing the true from the false, the permitted from the forbidden – they have shaped Muslim ethics and values.

I discreetly left the grocery store without another word. What could I have said to counterbalance the force of that political aphorism, which is as implacable as it is popular?

Silenced, defeated, and furious, I suddenly felt the urgent need to inform myself about this *hadith* and to search out the texts where it is mentioned, to understand better its extraordinary power over the ordinary citizens of a modern state.

A glance at the latest Moroccan election statistics supports the 'prediction' uttered in the grocery store. Although the constitution gives women the right to vote and be elected, political reality grants them only the former. In the legislative elections of 1977, the eight women who stood for election found no favour with the six and a half million voters, of whom three million were women. At the opening of Parliament, there was not one woman present, and the

[3] Fatoumata Sow, '*Le Harem Politique*' (The Political Harem), in *Fippu, Journal de Yewwu Yewwi pour la libération des femmes* (*Fight Back, Journal of 'Liberation through Consciousness' for the Liberation of Women*) (Dakar, Senegal), number 2, April 1989, p.33.

men were settled among their male peers as usual, just as in the cafes. Six years later, in the municipal elections of 1983, 307 women were bold enough to stand as candidates, and almost three and a half million women voters went to the polls. Only 36 women won elections, as against 65,502 men![4]

To interpret the relationship between the massive participation of women voters and the small number of women elected as a sign of stagnation and backwardness would be in accordance with the usual stereotypes applied to the Arab world. However, it would be more insightful to see it as a reflection of changing times and the intensity of the conflicts between the aspirations of women, who take the constitution of their country seriously, and the resistance of men, who imagine, despite the laws in force, that power is necessarily male. This makes me want to shed light on those obscure zones of resistance, those entrenched attitudes, in order to understand the symbolic – even explosive – significance of that act which elsewhere in the world is an ordinary event: a woman's vote. For this reason, my misadventure in a neighborhood grocery store had more than symbolic importance for me. Revealing the misogynistic attitude of my neighbors, it indicated to me the path I should follow to better understand it – a study of the religious texts that everybody knows but no one really probes, with the exception of the authorities on the subject: the *mullas* [religious scholars] and *imams* [prayer leaders].

Going through the religious literature is no small task. First of all, one is overwhelmed by the number of volumes, and one immediately understands why the average Muslim can never know as much as an *imam*. [Muhammad ibn Isma'il] Al-Bukhari's [810–870] prestigious collection of traditions, *Al-Sahih* (*The Authentic*), is in four volumes with an abstruse commentary by one [Muhammad ibn 'Abd al-Hadi] al-Sindi [died 1726] , who is extremely sparing with his comments.[5] Now, without a very good commentary a non-expert will have difficulty reading a religious text of the ninth century. ... This is because, for each *hadith*, it is necessary to check the identity of the Companion of the Prophet who uttered it, and in what circumstances and with what objective in mind, as well as the chain of people who passed it along – and there are more fraudulent traditions than authentic ones. For each *hadith*, al-Bukhari gives the results of his

---

[4] Morocco, Ministère de l'Artisanat et des Affaires Sociales, *Les Femmes marocaines dans le développement économique et social, décennie 1975–1985* [*Moroccan Women in Social and Economic Development, the Decade 1975–1985*].

[5] Al-Bukhari, *Al-Sahih* (*Collection of Authentic Hadiths*) with commentary by al-Sindi (Beruit, Lebanon: Dar al-Ma'rifa, 1978). The *hadith* quoted by the school-teacher in volume 4. p.226.

investigation. If he speaks of X or Y, you have to check which Companion is being referred to, what battle is being discussed, in order to make sense of the dialogue or scene that it being transcribed. In addition, al-Bukhari doesn't use just one informant; there are dozens of them in the dozens of volumes. You must be careful not to go astray. The smallest mistake about the informant can cost you months of work.

What is the best way of making this check? First of all, you should make contact with the experts in religious science (*faqihs*) in your city. According to moral teaching and the traditional conventions, if you contact a *faqih* for information about the sources of a *hadith* or a Qur'anic verse, he must assist you. Knowledge is to be shared, according to the promise of the Prophet himself. *Fath al-bari* by [Ibn Hajar] al-'Asqalani (he died in year 852 of the *hejira* [1372–1449 AD] was recommended to me by several people I consulted. It consists of 17 volumes that one can consult in libraries during their opening hours. But the vastness of the task and the rather limited reading time is enough to discourage most researchers.

The schoolteacher in the grocery store was right: the *hadith* 'those who entrust their affairs to a woman will never know prosperity' was there in al-'Asqalani's 13th volume, where he quotes al-Burkhari's *Sahih*, that is, those traditions that al-Bukhari classified as authentic after a rigorous process of selection, verifications, and counter-verifications.[6] Al-Bukhari's work has been one of the most highly respected references for 12 centuries. This *hadith* is the sledgehammer argument used by those who want to exclude women from politics. One also finds it in the work of other authorities known for their scholarly rigor, such as Ahmad ibn Hanbal [780–855], the author of the *Musnad* and founder of the Hanbali school, one of the four great schools of jurisprudence of the Sunni Muslim world.[7]

---

[6] Ibn Hajar al-'Asqalani, *Huda al-sari, muqaddimat Fath al-bari* [*The Traveller's Guide, Introduction to 'The Creator's Conquest'*], commonly known as *Fath al-bari* [*The Creators Conquest*]. It comprises al-Bukhari's text with a commentary by al-'Asqalani. The *hadith* that concerns us here, on the necessity of excluding women from power, is found on p. 46 of volume 13 of the edition of Al-Matba'a al-Bahiya al-Misriya (1928) and on p. 166 of volume 16 of the edition of Maktaba Mustafa al-Babi al-Halabi fi Misr (1963). (Future page references are to the 1928 edition).

[7] The Muslim world is divided into two parts: the Sunnis (orthodox) and the Shi'ites (literally, schismatics). Each group has its own specific texts of *fiqh* (religious knowledge), especially as regards sources of the *shari'a* (legislation and laws). The Sunnis are split between four *madhahib* (schools). ... The differences between them most frequently relate to details of juridical procedures.

This *hadith* is so important that it is practically impossible to discuss the question of women's political rights without referring to it, debating it, and taking a position on it. ...

According to al-Bukhari, it is supposed to have been Abu Bukra [died circa 671] who heard the Prophet say: 'Those who entrust their affairs to a woman will never know prosperity.' Since this *hadith* is included in the *Sahih* – those thousands of authentic *hadith* accepted by the meticulous al-Bukhari – it is a priori considered true and therefore unassailable without proof to the contrary, since we are here in scientific terrain. So nothing bars me, as a Muslim woman, from making a double investigation – historical and methodological – of this *hadith* and its author, and especially of the conditions in which it was first put to use. Who uttered this *hadith*, where, when, why, and to whom?

Abu Bakra was a Companion who had known the Prophet during his lifetime and who spent enough time in his company to be able to report the *hadith* that he is supposed to have spoken. According to him, the Prophet pronounced this *hadith* when he learned that the Persians had named a woman to rule them. 'When Kisra died, the Prophet, intrigued by the news, asked: 'And who has replaced him in command?' The answer was: 'They have entrusted power to his daughter.'[8] It was at that moment, according to Abu Bakra, that the Prophet is supposed to have made the observation about women.

In 628 AD, at the time of those interminable wars between Romans and the Persians, Heraclius, the Roman emperor, had invaded the Persian realm, occupied Ctesiphon, which was situated very near the Sassanid capital, and Khusraw Pavis, the Persian king, had been assassinated. Perhaps it was this even that Abu Bakra alluded to. Actually, after the death of the son of Khusraw, there was a period of instability between 629 and 632 AD, and various claimants to the throne of the Sassanid empire emerged, including two women.[9] Could this be the incident that led the Prophet to pronounce the *hadith* against women? Al-Bukhari does not go that far; he just reports the words of Abu Bakra – that is, the content of the *hadith* itself – and the reference to a woman having taken power among the Persians. To find out more about Abu Bakra, we must turn to the huge work of Ibn Hajar al-'Asqalani.

In the 17 volumes of the *Fath al-bari*, al-'Asqalani does a line-by-line commentary on al-Bukhari. For each *hadith* of the *Sahih*, al-'Asqalani gives us the historical clarification: the political events that

---

[8] 'Asqalani, *Fath al-bari*, volume 13, p.46.

[9] See Hodgson, *Venture of Islam*, volume 1, p.199.

served as background, a description of the battles, the identity of the
conflicting parties, the identity of the transmitters and their opinions,
and finally the debates concerning their reliability – everything
needed to satisfy the curiosity of the researcher.

On what occasion did Abu Bakra recall these words of the
Prophet, and why did he feel the need to recount them? Abu Bakra
must have had a fabulous memory, because he recalled them a
quarter of a century after the death of the Prophet, at the time that the
caliph 'Ali [reigned 656–661] retook Basra after having defeated
'A'isha [wife of the Prophet, circa 614–678] at the Battle of the
Camel.[10]

Before occupying Basra, 'A'isha went on pilgrimage to Mecca,
where she learned the news of the assassination of 'Uthman [caliph,
644–656] at Medina and the naming of 'Ali as the fourth caliph. It was
while she was in Mecca that she decided to take command of the
army that was challenging the choice of 'Ali. Days and days of
indecision then followed. Should she go to Kufa or Basra? She needed
to have an important city with enough malcontents to aid her cause
and let her set up her headquarters. After numerous contacts,
negotiations, and discussions, she chose Basra. Abu Bakra was one of
the notables of that city and, like all of them, in a difficult position.
Should he take up arms against 'Ali, the cousin of the Prophet and the
caliph, challenged maybe but legitimate, or should he take up arms
against A'isha, the 'lover of the Beloved of God' and the 'wife of the
Prophet on earth and in paradise'?[11] If one realizes, moreover, that he
had become a notable in that Iraqi city, which was not his native city,
one can better understand the extent of his unease.

It can be said that Islam brought him good fortune. Before being
converted, Abu Bakra had the hard, humiliating life of a slave in the
city of Ta'if, where only the aristocracy had the right to high office. In
year 8 AH (630 AD) the Prophet decided that it was time for him to
undertake the conquest of Ta'if. He had just conquered Mecca,
making a triumphal entry into that city, and now felt himself strong
enough to subdue the inhabitants of Ta'if who were still resisting
Islam. But they put up a strong defense. The Prophet camped outside
the city and besieged the citadel for 18 days. In vain. The chief tribe
that controlled the city, the Banu Tamim, and their allies were

---

[10] 'Asqalani, *Fath al-bari*, volume 13, p.46.

[11] On this dilemma and the division that it occasioned, see 'Asqalani, *Fath al-bari*,
volume 13, p.49. On the political implications and the philosophical debates that
the Battle of the Camel aroused, see the extraordinary description by [Abu Ja'far
Muhammad] Tabari [died 922] in his *Tarikh al-umam wa al-muluk* [*History of
Imams and Kings*] (Beirut, Lebanon: Dar Al-Fikr, 1979), volume 5, pp. 156–225.

entrenched in the fort and used bows and arrows against the attackers, causing casualties among Muhammad's army. Twelve of his men were killed, causing him distress, as he had hoped to win without losses. Each soldier was a Companion: he knew their families; this was not an anonymous army. He decided to lift the siege and depart. But before doing so, he sent messengers to proclaim around the fort and the besieged city that all slaves who left the citadel and joined his ranks would be freed.[12] A dozen slaves answered his call, and Abu Bakra was one of them. The Prophet declared them free men, despite the protests of their masters, and after their conversion to Islam they became the brothers and equals of all.[13] In this way, Abu Bakra found both Islam and freedom.

And then we see him a few years later, a notable in an Iraqi city, the incarnation of Muhammad's dream – that all the poor, the humiliated of the world, could accede to power and wealth. The rapid rise of this one Companion summarizes very well what Islam meant for a man like Abu Bakra, who would never have been able to imagine leaving his native city as a free man and especially changing his social status so quickly: 'You, the Arabs, were in an unspeakable state of degradation, powerlessness, and profligacy. The Islam of God and Muhammad saved you and led you to where you are now.'[14] In fact, since his conversion Abu Bakra had scaled the social ladder at a dizzying pace: 'Abu Bakra was very pious and remained so throughout his life. His children were among the notables of Basra as a result of their fortune and their erudition.'[15]...

So why was he led to dig into his memory and make the prodigious effort of recalling the words that the Prophet was supposed to have uttered 25 years before? The first detail to be noted – and it is far from being negligible – is that Abu Bakra recalled his *hadith* after the Battle of the Camel. At that time 'A'isha's situation was scarcely enviable. She was politically wiped out: 13,000 of her supporters had fallen on the field of battle.[16] Ali had retaken the city of Basra, and all those who had not chosen to join 'Ali's clan had to justify their action. This

[12] [Muhammad] Ibn Sa'd [784–845], [*Kitab*] *al-tabaqat al-kubra* [*The Great Book of Classes*] (Beirut, Lebanon: Dar Sadir, no date), volume 3, p. 159.

[13] Ibn Sa'd, *Al-Tabaqat*, p.159.

[14] 'Asqalani, *Fath al-bari*, volume 13, p.622.

[15] ['Izz al-Din] Inb al-Athir [1160–1233]. *Usd al-ghaba fi* [*ma'rifat*] *al-sahaba* [*The Lions of the Forest, on Knowing the Companions of the Prophet*] (Beirut, Lebanon: Dar al-Fikr li al-Tiba'a wa al Tawzi', no date) volume 5, p.38.

[16] Mas'udi [died 956], *Muruj* [*al-zahab*] [*Meadows of Gold*] volume 2, p.380; and the French translation of this work *Les Prairies d'or* [*Prairies of Gold*], volume 3, p. 646.

can explain why a man like Abu Bakra needed to recall opportune traditions, his record being far from satisfactory, as he had refused to take part in the civil war. Not only did he refrain from taking part, but, like many of the Companions who had opted for nonparticipation, he had made his position known officially. 'A'isha, who often used to accompany the Prophet on military expeditions, knew the procedure for the negotiations that took place before the military occupation of a city and had conducted matters correctly. Before besieging the city, she had sent messengers with letters to all the notables of the city, explaining to them the reasons that had impelled her to rebel against 'Ali, her intentions, and the objectives that she wanted to attain, and finally inviting them to support her.[17] It was a true campaign of information and persuasion, a preliminary military tactic in which the Prophet excelled. And 'A'isha was going to use the mosque as the meeting place for a public discussion to inform the population before occupying the city. Abu Bakra was thus contacted from the beginning in his capacity as a notable of the city.[18]

'A'isha did not take this course of action only because of faithfulness to Mohammad's methods. There was a more important reason. This was the first time since the death of the Prophet that the Muslims found themselves on opposite sides in a conflict. This was the situation that Muhammad had described as the worst possible for Islam: *fitna*, civil war, which turned the weapons of the Muslims inward instead of directing them, as God wished, outward, in order to conquer and dominate the world. So 'A'isha had to explain her uprising against 'Ali. She reproached him for not having brought the murderers of 'Uthman, the assassinated third caliph, to justice. Some of those who had besieged 'Uthman and whose identity was known were in 'Ali's army as military leaders. Many Muslims must have thought as 'A'isha did, because a large part of the city of Basra welcomed her, giving her men and weapons. After driving out the governor who represented 'Ali, 'A'isha set up her headquarters in Basra, and with her two allies, Talha [ibn 'Ubayd Allah al-Taymi, died 656] and al-Zubair [ibn al-'Awwam, seventh century], members of the Quraysh tribe like herself, she continued her campaign of information, negotiation, and persuasion through individual interviews and speeches in the mosques, pressing the crowds to support her against the 'unjust' caliph. It was year 36 A.H. (656 AD), and public opinion was divided: should one obey an 'unjust' caliph (who did not

---

[17] Tabari, *Tarikh*, volume 5, p. 182.

[18] 'Asqalani, *Fath al-bari*, volume 13, p. 46.

punish the killers of 'Uthman), or should one rebel against him and support 'A'isha, even if that rebellion led to civil disorder?

For those who held the first opinion, the gravest danger that the Muslim nation could face was not that of being ruled by an unjust leader, but rather of falling into civil war. Let us not forget that the word '*islam*' means 'submission.' If the leader was challenged, the fundamental principle of Islam as order was in danger. The others thought that the lack of justice in the Muslim chief of state was more serious than civil war. A Muslim must not turn his back when he sees his leader commit injustices and reprehensible acts (*munkar*): 'The Prophet said: 'If people see *munkar* and they do not try to remedy it, they incur divine punishment." Another version of this *hadith* is: 'Let him who sees a situation in which *munkar* is being perpetrated endeavor to change it.'[19] This was the argument of the group that assassinated Anwar Sadat [1918–1981] of Egypt, and is representative of the very prolific literature of the Muslim extremists of today.[20]

At Basra in year 36 the dilemma that confronted a Muslim – whether to obey an unjust caliph or to take up arms against him – was not just being posed in the circles of the ruling elite. The mosques were veritable plenary assemblies where the leaders came to discuss with the people they governed the decisions to be taken in the conflict between 'A'isha and 'Ali, and it must be pointed out (after reading the minutes of those meetings) that the people spoke up and demanded to be informed about what was going on. The ordinary people did not even know what the quarrel was about: for those citizens the important problem was the absence of democracy. It seemed mad to them to get involved without knowing the motives that were driving the leaders and the conflicts that divided them. They gave as the reason for their refusal to get involved on either side the lack of democracy in the selection of the caliph. In one of the debates that took place at the Basra mosque when 'A'isha's partners were invited by the people to explain their motives, a young man who did not belong to the elite made a speech that illuminated a whole area that was not very clear in the dynamics of Islam at the beginning and is often 'forgotten' today – the nondemocratic dimension of Islam, which was noted and felt as such by the ordinary people. This young man took the floor in the Basra mosque, an act that would cost him his life, and addressing the allies and

[19] 'Asqalani, *Fath al-bari*, volume 13, pp. 50 and 51 for the first version, and p. 44 for the second.

[20] See the analysis of Hamied N. Ansari, 'The Islamic Militants in Egyptian Politics,' *International Journal of Middle East Studies*, volume 16, number 1, 1984, pp. 123–144.

representatives of 'A'isha who were pushing him towards subversion, said to them:

> It is true that you *Muhajirun* [the original migrants from Mecca][21] were the first to respond to the Prophet's call. You had the privilege of becoming Muslims before all the others. But everyone had that privilege later and everyone converted to Islam. Then, after the death of the Prophet, you selected a man from among you without consulting us [the common people, who were not part of the elite]. After his death, you got together and you named another [caliph], still without asking our advice. ... You chose 'Uthman, you swore your allegiance to him, still without consulting us. You became displeased with his behavior, and you decided to declare war without consulting us. You decided, still without consulting us, to select 'Ali and swear allegiance to him. So what are you blaming him for now? Why have you decided to fight him? Has he committed an illegal act? Has he done something reprehensible? Explain to us what is going on. Why are you fighting?[22]

Thus the decision not to participate in this civil war was not an exceptional one, limited to a few members of the elite. The mosques were full of people who found it absurd to follow leaders who wanted to lead the community into tearing each other to pieces. Abu Bakra was not in any way an exception.

When he was contacted by 'A'isha, Abu Bakra made known his response to her: he was against *fitna*. He is supposed to have said to her (according to the way he told it after battle):

> It is true that you are our *umm* [mother, alluding to her title of 'Mother of Believers,' which the Prophet bestowed on his wives during his last years]; it is true that as such you have rights over us. But I heard the Prophet say: 'Those who entrust power [*mulk*] to a woman will never know prosperity.'[23]

Although, as we have just seen, many of the Companions and inhabitants of Basra chose neutrality in the conflict, only Abu Bakra justified it by the fact that one of the parties was a woman.

According to al-Tabari's account, Basra, after 'A'isha's defeat, lived through many days of understandable anxiety. Was 'Ali going to take revenge on those who had not supported him, one of whom was Abu Bakra? 'In the end 'Ali proclaimed a general amnesty. ...All those who threw down their arms, he announced on the day of the battle, and

---

[21] [Bracketed comments in indented quotations in this chapter are the author's, not the editor's. – Editor].

[22] Tabari, *Tarikh*, volume 5, p. 179.

[23] 'Asqalani, *Fath al-bari*, volume 13, p. 46.

those who returned to their homes would be spared.'[24] ' 'Ali spent some days on the battlefield; he buried the dead of both sides and said a common funeral prayer for them before returning to the city.'[25]

Nevertheless, everything was not quite so simple, if we take the example of Abu Musa al-Ash'ari [614–662], another Muslim pacifist who had refused to get involved in a civil war that he regarded as senseless. Abu Musa al-Ash'ari lost both position and fortune. However, it is true that the situations of Abu Musa and Abu Bakra are not comparable, except for their refusal to get involved. Abu Bakra's support was solicited by 'A'isha, the losing party, while that of Abu Musa was sought by 'Ali, the victor. Abu Musa was none other than a governor in 'Ali's service, his representative, and the symbol of the Muslim state as the head of the Iraqi town of Kufa. 'Ali, before proceeding to Basra, then occupied by 'A'isha, sent emissaries to Abu Musa demanding that he mobilize the people and urgently send him troops and weapons. Not only did Abu Musa personally choose not to obey his caliph, but he also thought himself obligated to 'consult with' the population he governed. He decided to involve the people, whom he called together in the mosque for information and discussion, and to enlighten them about the position of the Prophet on the subject of civil war. Abu Musa recited to them the *hadith* condemning *fitna*, and ordered them to disobey the caliph and not answer his call to enlist. For him, the duty of a Muslim in the case of *fitna* was absolute opposition to any participation. He recited many *hadith* at the Kufa mosque, all of them against *fitna* – against civil war plain and simple. It was not a question of the sex of the leader![26] Al-Bukhari assembled all *hadith* on the subject of civil war in a chapter entitled '*Al-Fitna*'; among them was Abu Bakra's *hadith* – the only one to give as a reason for neutrality the gender of one of the opponents.[27]

What is surprising to the modern reader who leafs through the chronicles of that famous Battle of the Camel is the respect that the people, whatever their position toward the war, showed to 'A'isha. Very rare were the occasions on which she was insulted – and even then it was never by one of the political leaders, but by some of the ordinary people.[28] The historians recall that only the Shi'i chroniclers (the pro-'Ali ones) find fault with 'A'isha. Why, then, did Abu Bakra

[24] Mas'udi, *Muruj*, volume 2, p. 378; and the French translation, volume 2, p. 644.

[25] Tabari, *Tarikh*, volume 5, p.221.

[26] Tabari, *Tarikh*, volume 5, p. 188.

[27] Bukhari, *Sahih*, volume 4, pp. 221ff.

[28] Mas'udi, *Les Prairies d'or*, volume 2, p. 645.

distinguish himself by a completely unprecedented misogynistic attitude?

Abu Musa al-Ash'ari was dismissed from his post and banished from Kufa by 'Ali. He was replaced by a governor who was less of a pacifist, and above all more tractable.[29] If this happened to Abu Musa, the situation of other 'pacifists' who were less highly placed was very delicate indeed. It would seem providential to also remember having heard a *hadith* that intimated an order not to participate in a war if a women was at the head of the army.

Abu Bakra also remembered other *hadith* just as providential at critical moments. After the assassination of 'Ali, Mu'awiya [ibn Abi Sufyan] the Umayyad [circa 605–680] could only legitimately claim the caliphate if Hasan [624–669], the son of 'Ali and thus his successor, declared in writing that he renounced his rights. And this he did under pressure and bargaining that were more of less acknowledged.[30] It was at this moment that Abu Bakra recalled a *hadith* that could not have been more pertinent, under political circumstances that had unforeseen repercussions. He is supposed to have heard the Prophet say that 'Hasan [the son of 'Ali] will be the man of reconciliation.'[31] Hasan would have been a very small baby when the Prophet, his grandfather (through his daughter Fatima), would have said that! Abu Bakra had a truly astonishing memory for politically opportune *hadith* which curiously – and most effectively – fitted into the stream of history.

Once the historical context of a *hadith* was clarified, it was time to go on to its critical evaluation by applying to it one of the methodological rules that the religious scholars had defined as principles of the process of verification.[32] The first of these rules was to consider 'this religion as a science,' in the tradition of Imam Malik ibn Anas (born in year 93 A.H. [710–796 AD], who was considered, with [Abu 'Abdallah Muhammad] Shafi'i [767–820] and Abu Hanifa

---

[29] Tabari, *Tarikh*, volume 5, p. 190.

[30] 'Asqalani, *Fath al-bari*, volume 13, pp. 51ff; Mas'udi, *Muruj*, volume 3, pp. 4ff; and al-Tabari, *Mohammed, Sceau des prophètes* [*Muhammad, Seal of the Prophets*] (Paris: Sindbad, 1980), volume 6, p.95.

[31] 'Asqalani, *Fath al-bari*, volume 13, p. 56.

[32] For assistance with the research for this chapter, I am indebted to Professor Ahmed al-Khamlichi, Chairman of the Department of Private Law, Faculté de Droit, Université Mohammed V, Rabat, Morocco.

[circa 699–767], one of 'the three most famous *imams* in Islam because of their contribution to the elaboration of the knowledge that enables the believer to distinguish the permitted from the forbidden.'[33] Malik ibn Anas never ceased saying:

> This religion is a science, so pay attention to those from whom you learn it. I had the good fortune to be born [in Medina] at a time when 70 persons [Companions] who could recite *hadith* were still alive. They used to go to the mosque and start speaking: The Prophet said so and so. I did not collect any of the *hadith* that they recounted, not because these people were not trustworthy, but because I saw that they were dealing in matters for which they were not qualified.[34]

According to him, it was not enough just to have lived at the time of the Prophet in order to become a source of *hadith*. It was also necessary to have a certain background that qualified you to speak: 'Ignorant persons must be disregarded.' How could they be considered sources of knowledge when they did not have the necessary intellectual capacity? But ignorance and intellectual capacity were not the only criteria for evaluating the narrators of *hadith*. The most important criteria were moral.

According to Malik, some persons could not under any circumstances transmit a *hadith*:

> Knowledge [*al-'ilm*] cannot be received from a mentally deficient person, nor from someone who is in the grip of passion and who might incite *bid 'a* [innovation], nor from a liar who recounts anything at all to people.... And finally, one should not receive knowledge from a shaykh, even a respected and very pious one, if he has not mastered the learning that he is supposed to transmit.[35]

Malik directs suspicion at the transmitters, emphasizes the necessity for Muslims to be on their guard, and even advises us to take the daily behavior of sources into consideration as a criterion for their reliability:

> There are some people whom I rejected as narrators of *hadith*, not because they lied in their role as men of science by recounting false *hadith* that the Prophet did not say, but just simply because I saw them

---

[33] Ibn 'Abd al-Barr [978–1070], *Al-Intiqa' fi fadl al-thalath al-a'imma al-fuqaha* [*The Selection, on the Merits of the Three Founding Jurists*] (Beirut, Lebanon: Dar al-Kutub al-'Ilmiya, no date), pp. 10, 16.

[34] Ibn 'Abd al-Barr, *Al-Intiqa'* p.16.

[35] Ibn 'Abd al-Barr, *Al-Intiqa'* p.16.

lying in their relations with people, in their daily relationships that had nothing to do with religion.[36]

If we apply this rule to Abu Bakra, he would have to be immediately eliminated, since one of the biographies of him tells us that he was convicted of and flogged for false testimony by the caliph 'Umar ibn al-Khattab [reigned 634–644].[37] This happened during a very serious case that 'Umar punished by execution – a case involving *zina* [fornication], an illicit sex act. In order to end the sexual licentiousness and promiscuity that existed in pre-Islamic Arabia and in an effort to control paternity, Islam condemned all sexual relations outside marriage or ownership as *zina*, encouraging women and men to marry and labeling celibacy as the open door to temptations of all kinds. It gave men the right to have several wives and to divorce them easily and replace them by others, provided that it was all within the framework of Muslim marriage.

'Umar, the second caliph of a new community still under the influence of pre-Islamic customs, had to act rapidly and severely to see that a key idea of Islam, the patriarchal family, became rooted in the minds of believers. Capital punishment for *zina* would only be applied if four witnesses testified to having seen the adultery with their own eyes and at the same time. These were conditions so difficult to prove that it made this punishment more of a deterrent than a realistic threat. It was necessary, moreover, to avoid having enmities and slanders lead to the condemnation of innocent persons. If there were only three witnesses who saw the accused *in flagrante delicto*, their testimony was not valid. In addition, any witness who slandered someone by accusing him of the crime of *zina* would incur the punishment for slander – he would be flogged for false testimony.[38]

Now this was what happened in the case of Abu Bakra. He was one of the four witnesses who came before 'Umar to officially make the accusation of *zina* against a well-known person, a Companion and a prominent political man, al-Mughira ibn Shu'ba [died 670]. The four witnesses testified before 'Umar that they had seen al-Mughira ibn Shu'ba in the act of fornication. 'Umar began his investigation, and one of the four witnesses then admitted that he was not really

[36] Ibn 'Abd al-Barr, *Al-Intiqa'* p.15.

[37] Ibn al-Athir, *Usd al-ghaba*, volume 5, p. 38.

[38] 'Umar ibn al-Khattab institutionalized the recourse to capital punishment for fornication. his contemporaries were not at all in agreement with his position. See Bukhari, *Sahih*, volume 4 pp. 146ff. ... 'Umar ibn al-Khattab ... was [also] the instigator of the wearing of the veil and was in complete disagreement with the Prophet about the way to treat women.

sure of having seen everything. The doubt on the part of one of the witnesses made the others subject to punishment by flogging for slander, and Abu Bakra was flogged.

If one follows the principles of Malik for *fiqh* [Islamic jurisprudence], Abu Bakra must be rejected as a source of *hadith* by every good, well-informed Malikite Muslim.

To close this investigation, let us take a brief look at the attitude of the religious scholars of the first centuries toward that misogynistic *hadith* that is presented to us today as sacred, unassailable truth. Even though it was collected as *sahih* (authentic) by al-Bukhari and others, that *hadith* was hotly contested and debated by many. The scholars did not agree on the weight to give that *hadith* on women and politics. Assuredly there were some who used it as an argument for excluding women from decision making. But there were others who found that argument unfounded and unconvincing. Al-Tabri was one of those religious authorities who took a position against it, not finding it a sufficient basis for depriving women of their power of decision making and for justifying their exclusion from politics.[39]

After having tried to set straight the historical record – the line of transmitters and witnesses who gave their account of a troubled historical epoch – I can only advise redoubled vigilance when, taking the sacred as an argument, someone hurls at the believer as basic truth a political axiom so terrible and with such grave historical consequences as the one we have been investigating. Nevertheless, we will see that this 'misogynistic' *hadith*, although it is exemplary, is not a unique case.

Throughout my childhood, I had a very ambivalent relationship with the Qur'an. It was taught to us in a Qur'anic school in a particularly ferocious manner. But to my childish mind only the highly fanciful Islam of my illiterate grandmother, Lalla Yasmina, opened the door for me to a poetic religion. ...This dual attitude that I had toward the sacred text was going to remain with me. Depending on how it is used, the sacred text can be a threshold for escape or an insurmountable barrier. It can be that rare music that leads to dreaming or simply a dispiriting routine. It all depends on the person who invokes it. However, for me, the older I grew, the fainter the music became. In secondary school the history of religion course was studded with traditions. Many of them from appropriate pages of al-Bukhari, which the teacher recited to us, made me feel extremely ill at ease: 'The Prophet said that the dog, the ass, and woman interrupt

---

[39] 'Asqalani, *Fath al-bari*, volume 13, p.47.

prayer if they pass in front of the believer, interposing themselves between him and the *qibla* [the direction of Mecca].'[40]...

By lumping [woman] in with two familiar animals, the author of the *hadith* inevitably makes her a being who belongs to the animal kingdom. It is enough for a woman to appear in the field of vision for contact with the *qibla* – that is, the divine – to be disturbed. Like the dog and the ass, she destroys the symbolic relation with the divine by her presence. One has to interrupt one's prayer and begin again.

Arab civilization being a civilization of the written word, the only point of view we have on this question is that of Abu Hurayra [died 678]. According to [Shams al-Din] Ibn Marzuq [1311–1379], when someone invoked in front of 'A'isha the *hadith* that said that the three causes of interruption of prayer were dogs, asses, and women, she answered them: 'You compare us now to asses and dogs. In the name of God, I have seen the Prophet saying his prayers while I was there, lying on the bed between him and the *qibla*. And in order not to disturb him, I didn't move.'[41] The believers used to come to 'A'isha for verification of what they had heard, confident of her judgment, not only because of her closeness to the Prophet, but because of her own abilities:

> I have seen groups of the most eminent companions of the Prophet ask her questions concerning the *fara'id* [the daily duties of the Muslim, the rituals, etc.], and Ibn 'Ata' said: "A'isha was, among all the people, the one who had the most knowledge of *fiqh*, the one who was the most educated and, compared to those who surrounded her, the one whose judgment was the best.'[42]

Despite her words of caution, the influence of Abu Hurayra has nevertheless infiltrated the most prestigious religious texts, among them the *Sahih* of al-Bukhari, who apparently did not always feel obliged to insert the corrections provided by 'A'isha. The subject of many of these *hadith* is the 'polluting' essence of femaleness.

To understand the importance for Islam of that aspect of femaleness, evoking disturbance and sullying, we would do well to look at the personality of Abu Hurayra, who, as it were, gave it legal force. Without wanting to play the role of psychoanalytical detective, I can say that the fate of Abu Hurayra and his ambivalence toward women are wrapped up in the story of his name. Abu Hurayra,

[40] Bukhari, *Sahih*, volume 1, p.99.

[41] Bukhari, *Sahih*, volume 1, p.199.

[42] Ibn Hajar al-'Asqalani, *Al-Isaba fi tamyiz al-sahaba* [*A Biographical Dictionary of the Companions of the Prophet*] (Cairo: Maktaba al-Dirasa al-Islamiya Dar al-Nahda, no date), volume 8, p.18.

meaning literally 'Father of the Little Female Cat,' had previously been called 'Servant of the Sun' ('Abd al-Shams).[43] The Prophet decided to change that name, which had a very strong sense of idolatry about it. 'Servant of the Sun' was originally from Yemen, that part of Arabia where not only the sun, a female star in Arabic, was worshipped, but where women also ruled in public and private life. Yemen was the land of the Queen of Sheba, Bilqis [tenth century BC], that queen who fascinated King Solomon [reigned 962–922 BC], who ruled over a happy kingdom, and who put her mark on Arab memory, since she appears in the Qur'an:

> [Hud-hud] said: 'I have found (a thing) that thou apprehendest not, and I come unto thee from Sheba with sure tidings'

> Lo! I found a woman ruling over them, and she hath been given (abundance) of all things, and hers is a mighty throne.

> I found her and her people worshipping the sun instead of God. ... (Sura 27: Verses 22–24)

Abu Hurayra came from the Yemeni tribe of the Daws.[44] At the age of 30 the man named 'Servant of the Sun' was converted to Islam. The Prophet gave him the name 'Abdallah (Servant of God) and nicknamed him Abu Hurayra (Father of the Little Female Cat) because he used to walk around with a little female cat that he adored.[45] But Abu Hurayra was not happy with this nickname, for he did not like the trace of femininity in it: 'Abu Hurayra said: 'Don't call me Abu Hurayra. The Prophet nicknamed me Abu Hirr [Father of the Male Cat], and the male is better than the female".[46] He had another reason to feel sensitive about this subject of femininity – he did not have a very masculine job. In a Medina that was in state of full-blown economic development, where the Medinese, especially the Jews, made an art of agriculture, and the immigrant Meccans continued their commercial activities and managed to combine them with military expeditions, Abu Hurayra preferred, according to his own comments, to be in the company of the Prophet. He served him and sometimes 'helped out in the women's apartments.'[47] This fact might

---

[43] 'Asqalani, *Al-Isaba*, volume 7, p. 427.

[44] 'Abd al- Mun'im Salih al-'Ali al 'Uzzi, *Difa an Abi Hurayra* [*In Defense of Abu Hurayra*], second edition (Beirut, Lebanon: Dar al-Qalam; Baghdad: Maktaba al-Nahda, 1981), p. 13.

[45] 'Asqalani, *Al-Isaba*, volume 7, p.426.

[46] 'Asqalani, *Al-Isaba*, volume 7, p.434.

[47] 'Asqalani, *Al-Isaba*, volume 7, p.441.

clear up the mystery about his hatred of women, and also of female cats, the two seeming to be strangely linked in his mind.

He had such a fixation about female cats and women that he recalled that the Prophet had pronounced a *hadith* concerning the two creatures – and in which the female cat comes off much better than the woman. But 'A'isha contradicted him, a Companion recounted:

> We were with 'A'isha, and Abu Hurayra was with us. 'A'isha said to him: 'Father of the Little Cat, is it you who said that you heard the Prophet declare that a woman went to hell because she starved a little female cat and didn't give it anything to drink?'
>
> 'I did hear the Prophet say that,' responded Father of the Little Cat.
>
> 'A believer is too valuable in the eyes of God,' retorted 'A'isha, 'for Him to torture that person because of a cat. ...Father of the Little Cat, the next time you undertake to repeat the words of the Prophet, watch out what you recount.'[48]

It is not surprising that Abu Hurayra attacked 'A'isha in return for that. She might be 'The Mother of the Believers' and 'The Lover of the Lover of God,' but she contradicted him too often. One day he lost patience and defended himself against an attack by 'A'isha. When she said to him, 'Abu Hurayra, you relate *hadith* that you never heard,' he replied sharply, 'O Mother, all I did was collect *hadith*, while you were too busy with make-up and your mirror.'[49]

One of the constant themes of conflict in Islam from the very beginning is what to do about menstrual periods and the sex act. Are periods the source of sullying? 'A'isha and the other wives of the Prophet never lost any opportunity to insist that the Prophet did not have the phobic attitude of pre-Islamic Arabia on that subject. Did the Prophet purify himself after making love during the holy month of Ramadan? 'I heard Abu Hurayra recount that he whom the dawn finds sullied (*janaban*, referring to sullying by the sex act) may not fast.'[50] Upon hearing this new law decreed by Abu Hurayra, the Companions hastened to the wives of the Prophet to reassure themselves about it: 'They posed the question to Umm Salama [wife of the Prophet, circa 596–682] and 'A'isha. ... They responded: 'The Prophet

[48] Imam [Muhammad ibn Bahadur al-] Zarkashi [circa 1344–1392], *Al-Ijaba li-iad ma istadrakathu 'A'isha ala al-sahaba* [*Collection of 'A'isha's Corrections to the Statements of the Companions*], second edition (Beirut, Lebanon: Al Maktab al-Islami, 1980), p.118.

[49] 'Asqalani, *Al-Isaba*, volume 7, p.440.

[50] Imam Zarkashi, *Al-Ijaba*, p.112.

used to spend the night sullied without making any ritual of purification, and in the morning he fasted."[51] The Companions, greatly perplexed, returned to Abu Hurayra:

> 'Ah, so. They said that?' he responded.
>
> 'Yes, they said that,' repeated the Companions, feeling more and more troubled, because Ramadan is one of the five pillars of Islam. Abu Hurayra then confessed, under pressure, that he had not heard it directly from the Prophet, but from someone else. He reconsidered what he had said, and later it was learned that just before his death he completely retracted his words.[52]

Abu Hurayra was not the only one to report a *hadith* about the purification ritual, and this was a real bone of contention between 'A'isha and the Companions. '['Abdallah] ibn 'Umar [died 693] ordered women who were doing the purification ritual to undo their braids [before touching their hair with wet hands].' 'A'isha' is supposed to have responded when someone reported to her the teaching that he was propounding: 'That's strange. ...Why, when he was about it, didn't he order them to shave their heads? When I used to wash myself with the Prophet, we purified ourselves with the same bucket of water. I passed my wet hand over my braids three times, and I never undid them!'[53] 'A'isha insisted on these corrections because she was conscious of the implications of what was being said. Pre-Islamic Arabia regarded sexuality, and the menstruating woman in particular, as a source of pollution, as a pole of negative forces. This theory about pollution expressed a vision of femaleness that was conveyed through a whole system of superstitions and beliefs that Muhammad wanted to condemn. He saw it as, on the one hand, the essence of the *jahiliya* [pre-Islamic era], and, on the other hand, the essence of the beliefs of the Jewish community of Medina.

The religious scholars who took part in the debate on the subject of pollution, recorded at length in the religious literature, came down on the side of 'A'isha. Their argument was that her version of the *hadith* seemed to agree more with the attitude of the Prophet, who tried by all means to 'struggle against superstition in all its forms.'[54]

This was not a matter that interested only the *imams*. The caliphs were also greatly concerned about it: 'Mu'awiya ibn Abi Sufyan [reigned 661–680] asked Umm Habiba, the wife of the Prophet [circa

---

[51] Imam Zarkashi, *Al-Ijaba*, p.112.

[52] Imam Zarkashi, *Al-Ijaba*, pp.112, 113.

[53] Imam Zarkashi, *Al-Ijaba*, p.111.

[54] Imam Zarkashi, *Al-Ijaba*, p.115.

588–680], if the Prophet – may God pray for him – had ever prayed in the garments in which he had made love. She said yes, he had, because he saw nothing bad in it.'[55] Imam al-Nasa'i explains to us why he laid such stress on the subject of menstruation in his chapter on the purification ritual. The Prophet, he said, wanted to react against the phobic behaviour of the Jewish population of Medina, who declared a woman who was having her period unclean: 'He ordered them [the male believers who had asked him questions on this subject] to eat with their wives, drink with them, share their bed, and do everything with them that they wanted except copulate.'[56]

The books of *fiqh* devote whole chapters to the purification rituals that every Muslim must carry out five times a day before praying. It is undeniable that Islam has an attitude bordering on anxiety about bodily cleanliness, which induces in many people an almost neurotic strictness. Our religious education begins with attention focused on the body, its secretions, its fluids, its orifices, which the child must learn to constantly observe and control. The sex act imposes a more elaborate ritual for the grown man and woman, and after menstruating the woman must wash her entire body according to a precise ritual. Islam stresses the fact that sex and menstruation are really extraordinary (in the literal meaning of the word) events, but they do not make the woman a negative pole that 'annihilates' in some way the presence of the divine and upsets its order. But apparently the Prophet's message, 14 centuries later, has still not been absorbed into customs throughout the Muslim world, if I judge by the occasions when I was refused admittance at the doors of mosques in Penang, Malaysia, in Baghdad, Iraq, and in Kairouan, Tunisia.

According to the meticulous al-Nasa'i Maymuna [circa 593–672], one of the wives of the Prophet (he had nine at the time, that concerns us here, the last years of his life in Medina), said: 'It happened that the Prophet recited the Qur'an with his head on the knee of one of us while she was having her period. It also happened that one of us brought his prayer rug to the mosque and laid it down while she was having her period.'[57] Already at the time that Imam al-Nasa'i was writing (he was born in year 214 or 215 A.H., 830 AD), the scholars suspected that there was a message there that was disturbing the misogyny ingrained in the peoples of the Arab Mediterranean area, before and after the Prophet, and they made great efforts not to

---

[55] Imam [Abu 'Abd al Rahman al-Nasa'i [830–915], *Sunan* [*Hadith Collection*] (Cairo: Al-Matba'a al-Misriya, no date), volume 1, p. 155.

[56] Nasa'i, *Sunan*, volume 1, p.155.

[57] Nasa'i, *Sunan*, volume 1, p. 147.

betray that very disturbing aspect of the Prophet's message. These religious scholars, who saw in misogyny the danger of betrayal of the Prophet, doubled their precautions and did a thorough investigation of the sex life of the Prophet by listening to the reports of his wives, the only credible sources on this subject. They accumulated details about his life at home as well as in the mosque. Ibn Sa'd devoted a chapter of his book to the layout of the Prophet's house. This chapter, as we shall soon see, is extremely important for the clarification of a key dimension of Islam: the total revolution it represented vis-à-vis the Judeo-Christian tradition and the pre-Islamic period with regard to women. However, very quickly the misogynistic trend reasserted itself among the religious scholars and gained the upper hand. We will see the resurgence in many *hadith* of that superstitious fear of femaleness that the Prophet wanted to eradicate.

One can read among al-Bukhari's 'authentic' *hadith* the following one: 'Three things bring bad luck: house, woman, and horse.'[58] Al-Bukhari did not include other versions of this *hadith*, although the rule was to give one or more contradictory versions in order to show readers conflicting points of view, and thus to permit them to be sufficiently well informed to decide for themselves about practices that were the subject of dispute. However, there is no trace in al-Bukhari of 'A'isha's refutation of this *hadith*:

> They told 'A'isha that Abu Hurayra was asserting that the Messenger of God said: 'Three things bring bad luck: house, woman, and horse.' 'A'isha responded: 'Abu Hurayra learned his lessons very badly. He came into our house when the Prophet was in the middle of a sentence. He only heard the end of it. What the Prophet said was: 'May God refute the Jews; they say three things bring bad luck: house, woman, and horse.'[59]

Not only did al-Bukhari not include this correction, but he treated the *hadith* as if there was no question about it. He cited it three times, each time with a different transmission chain. This procedure generally strengthens a *hadith* and gives the impression of consensus concerning it. No mention was made of the dispute between 'A'isha and Abu Hurayra on this subject. Worse yet, al-Bukhari followed this misogynistic *hadith* with another along the same lines which reflected the same vision of femaleness as a pole of destruction and ill luck: 'The Prophet said: 'I do not leave after me any cause of trouble more fatal to man than women.''[60] The source of this *hadith* is

[58] Bukhari, *Sahih*, volume 3, p. 243.

[59] Imam Zarkashi, *Al-Ijaba*, p. 113.

[60] Bukhari, *Sahih*, volume 3, p. 243.

'Abdallah ibn 'Umar (the son of 'Umar ibn al-Khattab, the second caliph), who was known for his rare asceticism and for nights interrupted by prayers and purifications.[61] 'Abdallah was a source very highly valued by Bukhari. He was the author of another famous *hadith*, in which he throws women into hell: "Abdallah ibn 'Umar said: 'The Prophet said: 'I took a look at paradise, and I noted that the majority of the people there were poor people. I took a look at hell, and I noted that there women were the majority.' " '[62]

What conclusion must one draw from this? That even the authentic *hadith* must be vigilantly examined with a magnifying glass? That is our right, Malik ibn Anas tells us. Al-Bukhari, like all religious scholars, began his work of collecting by asking for God's help and acknowledging that only He is infallible. It is our tradition to question everything and everybody, especially the religious scholars and *imams*. And it is more than ever necessary for us to disinter our true tradition from the centuries of oblivion that have managed to obscure it. But we must also guard against falling into generalizations and saying that all the imams were and are misogynistic. That is not true today and was not true yesterday. The example of this is Imam Zarkashi, who, luckily for us, recorded in writing all of 'A'isha's objections.

Imam Zarkashi was of Turkish origin, but born in Egypt in the middle of the 14th century AD (year 745 AH). Like all the scholars of his time, he traveled throughout the Muslim world in search of knowledge. He specialized in religious knowledge and left behind no less than 30 compendiums. Many of these are lost to modern researchers, and we know only their titles. Among those that have come down to us is a book devoted to 'A'isha's contribution to Islam, her contribution as a source of religious knowledge. The book begins as follows:

> 'A'isha is the Mother of the Believers.... She is the lover of the Messenger of God.... She lived with him for eight years and five months; she was 18 years old at the time of the death of the Prophet.... She lived to be 65 years old. We are indebted to her for 1,210 *hadiths*.[63]

---

[61] The biography of 'Abdallah ibn 'Umar can be found in 'Asqalani, *Al-Isaba*, volume 4, pp. 182ff

[62] Bukhari, *Sahih*, volume 4, p. 137.

[63] Imam Zarkashi, *Al-Ijaba*, pp. 37, 38.

And he explains:

> This book is devoted to her particular contribution in this field, especially the points on which she disagreed with others, the points to which she supplied added information, the points on which she was in complete disagreement with the religious scholars of her time.... I have entitled this book *Collection of 'A'isha's Corrections to the Statements of the Companions*.[64]

This book remained in manuscript form until 1939. [Jamal al-Din] Al-Afghani [1838–1897] discovered it while doing research for his biography of 'A'isha in the al-Dahiriya Library of Damascus, Syria. Why did Imam Zarkashi, one of the greatest scholars of the Shafi'i school of his time, undertake his work on 'A'isha? A work that, by all accounts, he must have considered extremely important, since he dedicated his book to the Judge of Judges *(qadi al-qudat)* – the equivalent of the Minister of Justice today, the supreme authority in religious matters in a Muslim city. Because, he says, 'the Prophet recognized 'A'isha's importance to such an extent that he said: 'Draw a part of your religion from little *al-humayra* [red woman].''[65] One of the Prophet's favorite pet names for 'A'isha was *al-humayra*, referring to her very white skin made radiant by a light sunburn, something rather rare in the Hijaz, the northern part of Arabia.[66]

'A'isha disputed many of Abu Hurayra's *hadith* and declared to whoever wanted to hear it: 'He is not a good listener, and when he is asked a question, he gives wrong answers.'[67] 'A'isha could take the liberty of criticizing him because she had all excellent memory: 'I never saw anyone who had so much knowledge about religion, poetry, and medicine as 'A'isha.'[68] Abu Hurayra knew how to rile her. 'But who has heard about that from Abu al-Qasim [the Prophet's surname]?' she exclaimed when someone recounted to her another of Abu Hurayra's traditions, this time describing what the Prophet did after making love.[69]

It is not wasted effort for us to tarry over the personality of Abu Hurayra, the author of *hadith* that saturate the daily life of every modern Muslim woman. He has been the source of an enormous

---

[64] Imam Zarkashi, *Al-Ijaba*, p. 32.

[65] Imam Zarkashi, *Al-Ijaba*, p. 31.

[66] Zahiya Qaddura, *'A'isha, Umm al-mu'minin ['A'isha, Mother of the Faithful]* (Beirut, Lebanon: Dar al-Kitab al-Lubnani, 1976).

[67] Imam Zarkashi, *Al-Ijaba*, p. 116.

[68] 'Asqalani, *Al-Isaba*, volume 8, p.17.

[69] Imam Zarkashi, *Al-Ijaba*, p. 120.

amount of commentary in the religious literature. But he was and still is the object of controversy, and there is far from being unanimity on him as a reliable source. The most recent book about him, jointly published by a Lebanese and an Iraqi firm, is a tribute written by one of his admirers who devotes not less than 500 pages to defending him. 'Abd al-Mun'im Salih al-'Ali gave his book a rather eloquent title: *In Defense of Abu Hurayra.*[70] It was obviously a success, since a new edition was published in 1983. The author begins by asserting that 'the Zionists and their allies and supporters have found another weapon against Islam; it is to introduce doubt about the narrators of traditions ... and especially about those who were the source of many *hadith*.'[71] This gives an idea of the intensity of the controversy surrounding Abu Hurayra. What is certain is that Abu Hurayra, long before Zionism, was attacked by Companions of his own generation. He had a very dubious reputation from the beginning, and al-Bukhari was aware of it, since he reports that 'people said that Abu Hurayra recounts too many *hadith*.'[72] 'Abd al-Mun'im, to his credit, cites all the incidents in which he was strongly challenged, including by those other than 'A'isha. He assures us that 'Umar ibn al-Khattab, the second orthodox caliph, did not say that 'the worst liar among the narrators of *hadith* is Abu Hurayra.'[73] He disputes the claim that 'Umar threatened to exile him, to send him back to his native Yemen, if he continued to recount *hadith*.[74]

'Umar, who enjoyed an unparalleled influence on the Prophet and the Muslim community of yesterday (and still does today) because of his prestige as a man of politics, his boldness in military matters, his strong personality, and his horror of lying, avoided recounting *hadith*. He was terrified at the idea of not being accurate. For that reason, 'Umar was one of those Companions who preferred to rely on their own judgment rather than trust their memory, which they considered dangerously fallible.[75] He was very irritated by the facile manner in which Abu Hurayra reeled off *hadith*: 'Umar al-Khattab,' we can read in al-'Asqalani's biography of him, 'is supposed to have remarked as follows about Abu Hurayra: 'We have many things to

---

[70] [Al-'Ali] al- 'Uzzi, *Difa'*.

[71] [Al-'Ali] al- 'Uzzi, *Difa'*, p.7.

[72] Bukhari, *Sahih*, volume 1, p. 34.

[73] [Al-'Ali] al- 'Uzzi, *Difa'*, p. 122.

[74] [Al-'Ali] al- 'Uzzi, *Difa'*, p.122.

[75] Muhammad Abu Zahra, *Malik* [Malik ibn Anas, 710–796] (Cairo: Dar al-Fikr al-'Arabi, no date), p. 146.

say, but we are afraid to say them, and that man there has no restraint."[76]

For the pious Companion the fallibility of memory was an occasion for meditating on the fragility of existence in the face of the flowing river of time, which steals not only youth, but especially memory. 'Umar ibn Hasin [seventh century], another Companion who was conscious of the treacherousness of memory, said:

> If I wanted to, I could recite traditions about the Prophet for two days without stopping. What keeps me from doing it is that I have seen some of the Companions of the Messenger of God who heard exactly what I myself heard, who saw what I saw, and those men recounted *hadith*. Those traditions are not exactly what we heard. And I am afraid of hallucinating, as they hallucinate.[77]

The Arabic word is *yushba*, literally 'to hallucinate,' that is, to see a reality that does not exist but that has the appearance of reality.

Abu Hurayra, on the contrary, for the three years that he spent in the company of the Prophet, would accomplish the *tour de force* of recalling 5,300 *hadith*.[78] Al-Bukhari listed 800 experts who cited him as their source.[79] Here is how Abu Hurayra explains his excellent memory: 'I said to the Prophet: 'I listen attentively, I take in many of your ideas, but I forget many.'"[80] Then the Prophet is supposed to have told him to spread out his cloak while he was speaking to him, and afterwards to pick it up at the end of the session. 'And this is the reason that I no longer forgot anything.'[81] Telling the story of the cloak was not the best way to be convincing in a religion like Islam, which has a horror of mysteries of all sorts, where Muhammad resisted the pressure of his contemporaries to perform miracles and magical acts, and where the religious scholars became well-versed from very early on in an exaggerated pragmatism.

Abu Hurayra also gave another explanation that was a bit more realistic than the first. The other Companions, he said, put their energy into business matters and spent their time in the bazaars drawing up contracts and increasing their fortunes, while he had

---

[76] 'Asqalani, *Al-Isaba*, volume 7, p. 440.

[77] Abu Zahra, *Malik*, p. 145.

[78] 'Asqalani, *Al-Isaba*, volume 7, p. 432.

[79] Bukhari, *Sahih*, volume 1, p. 34.

[80] Bukhari, *Sahih*, volume 1, p. 34.

[81] Bukhari, *Sahih*, volume 1, p. 34.

nothing else to do but follow the Prophet everywhere.[82] 'Umar ibn al-Khattab, who was well known for his physical vigor and who awoke the city every day to say the dawn prayer, disliked lazy people who loafed around without any definite occupation. He summoned Abu Hurayra on one occasion to offer him a job. To his great surprise, Abu Hurayra declined the offer. 'Umar who did not consider such things it joking matter, said to him:

> 'You refuse to work? Better people than you have begged for work.'

> 'Who are those people who are better than me?' inquired Abu Hurayra.

> 'Joseph, the son of Jacob, for example, said 'Umar to put an end to a conversation that was its getting out of hand.

> 'He,' said Abu Hurayra flippantly, 'was a prophet, the son of a prophet, and I am Abu Hurayra, son of Umayma [his mother].'[83]

With this anecdote we come back to our point of departure, the relationship of 'Father of the Little Female Cat' to femaleness and to the very mysterious and dangerous link between the sacred and women. All the monotheistic religions are shot through by the conflict between the divine and the feminine, but none more so than Islam, which has opted for the occultation of the feminine, at least symbolically, by trying to veil it, to hide it, to mask it. Islam as sexual practice unfolds with a very special theatricality since it is acted out in a scene where the *hijab* [veil] occupies a central position. This almost phobic attitude toward women is all the more surprising since we have seen that the Prophet has encouraged his adherents to renounce it as representative of the *jahiliya* and its superstitions. This leads me to ask: Is it possible that Islam's message had only a limited and superficial effect on deeply superstitious seventh-century Arabs who failed to integrate its novel approaches to the world and to women? Is it possible that the *hijab*, the attempt to veil women, that is claimed today to be basic to Muslim identity, is nothing but the expression of the persistence of the pre-Islamic mentality, the *jahiliya* mentality that Islam was supposed to annihilate?

---

[82] 'Asqalani, *Al-Isaba*, volume 7, p. 517.

[83] 'Asqalani, *Al-Isaba*, volume 7, p. 517.

Kali, the Savior*

LINA GUPTA

Atop the golden peak of a mighty mountain, the goddess (Devi) Durga appeared mounted on her lion. Seeing the smiling Durga, the demons Canda and Munda approached with their army to seize her. Realizing she was about to be attacked, Durga became enraged, her face became as black as ink, and suddenly the goddess Kali appeared from her forehead with protruding fangs, a gaping mouth, and a lolling tongue. With a fierce roar she tore the demons into pieces with her hands, crushing and devouring them and their horses. In this magnificent myth depicted in the *Devi Mahatmya* (otherwise known as *Durga Saptasati*) Durga is an unconquerable, invincible warrior-maid, incarnated out of the collective wrath of all the gods joined in a council to save the world from the demons (*Devi Mahatmya* 7.3–22).[1] In Durga we have a manifestation of the dark goddess known to Hinduism as Kali. Who is this goddess? Is she merely another projection of the hostility and masculine fear of the feminine that characterizes patriarchal traditions within Hinduism and many of the other world faiths? Or does the goddess embody traits that can be a source of social and spiritual liberation for all women and men? Is she the mythic Great Mother whose symbolism depends on male fascination with female biology, or is she the goddess who represents the ultimate principle of Hinduism that transcends any form of duality? I argue that we can understand her in either of these ways, and that we can and must emphasize the latter understanding if we are to move into a healthier, more just world after patriarchy.

The evidence that the systematic subjugation of women has often been sanctioned by mythological stories, symbols, and images in world religions is too overwhelming to overlook. However, we have reached a point in history when it is simply not enough merely to

---

*This text first appeared in Paula M. Cooey, William R. Eakin and Jay B. McDaniel (eds) *After Patriarchy: Feminist Transformations of the World Religions*, New York: Orbis Books, 1991, pp.15–38.

[1] Many of the Puranas are available in English translation. For a selected bibliography relating to Indian goddesses, see Hawley and Wulff, 383–403.

recognize and analyze the patriarchal mindset and its effects on our religious and social lives. It is essential for us to seek new forms of religious experience and expression, either through the reinterpretation and reconstruction of our traditions or through alternative models of Ultimate Reality that will emphasize as well as include female experience. In search of an alternative, feminists have realized the overwhelming need for women to identify personally with positive images and role models, models that can reassert the importance of the 'feminine' in all religious experience. With this realization has come the recognition of the general lack of such images and stories in most traditions.

I believe that Hinduism does indeed contain a model and image that could be used to fit the needs of today's women, and that this model lies at the very heart of Hinduism itself. This image centres on the goddess Kali and her many manifestations. I also believe this image must be extricated from patriarchal interpretations and understandings that have clouded its essential meaning even while tapping into – and using – the many layers of meaning that surround it. In part, such extrication must occur using a method similar to that of Rosemary Ruether, in which feminists select as resources those aspects of tradition that support the well-being of women (and men). In part, such extrication involves reappropriating the essential messages of the scriptures as those messages are made clear in the Tantric writings.

Even though portrayals of female characters in the Hindu epics and the Hindu scriptures called the Puranas[2] appear to depict traditional roles of mothers and wives, deeper egalitarian connotations and religious interpretations of these images and stories have been accepted by many traditional Hindus. That is, Hinduism is not inherently patriarchal; the equal importance of the gods and goddesses in the pantheon would seem to support this. But despite the equality and importance of the goddesses found in various scriptures, traditional Hindu life by and large has remained patriarchal. The significance of the goddesses in Hinduism is undeniable; even so, the lives of women as subservient daughters and wives is also very real. It seems to me that patriarchal understanding has appropriated the goddesses and the feminine aspects of the Ultimate Reality at the heart of Hinduism in ways that sanction the unequal treatment of women. Still, in the absence of a clearly or totally patriarchal tradition, the question of a post-patriarchal version of Hinduism must be dealt with carefully.

---

[2] The Puranas are Hindu scriptures that were written down after the (earlier) Vedic scriptures.

What new religious paradigm for understanding and appropriating the feminine in Hindu traditions is available to post-patriarchal Hindu women? Hinduism itself offers clues for such a paradigm in the image of Kali, not in Kali as she has been understood through patriarchy – although this understanding does indeed involve some truth – but Kali in her deepest and most essential meaning. The goddess, the archetype of Devi, is considered to be one of the most enduring and endearing of all archetypes in Hinduism. In getting to the deepest meaning of the goddess, we approach more completely the central meanings of scriptural Hinduism itself.

After a thousand years of denial and devaluation, the archetype of the goddess is re-entering the West; Western feminists have relearned the power of the goddess. It is not so much recent interest in the goddess, however, as my own experience as a woman growing up in the Hindu tradition that leads me to this particular essay on Kali. Looking back, I realise how important Kali was to me. As far as I can remember, both daily worship of Kali at home and weekly visits to the Daksineshwar temple with my parents were part of my life. As a child I saw Kali as something to fear, but also something inspiring and empowering. At the temple I watched as people – male and female, old and young, sick and healthy – joined together in worship, waiting patiently to see their beloved goddess at least once. It was incredible to see the joy and reverence expressed at the slightest hint that the temple door would open.

Soon my daily experiences made me aware of discrepancies between a religious view of the goddess and the everyday lives of women. The scriptures and religious tradition proclaim that the beloved Devi resides in women. But these same women are not simply revered and protected; they are also dominated and excluded from the decision-making process that gives male members of Hindu society significant power and authority. This discrepancy was difficult for me to comprehend; although I personally can recall no direct experience of oppression, a subtle pressure to conform to an ideal form of womanhood was constant, and as a female, I felt at once hindered and exalted by ambiguities implicit in that pressure.

This essay will attempt to review the myth of the Great Goddess, whose power, beauty, independence, and religious importance presents an alternative vision to the limitations of patriarchal consciousness. I shall focus on the goddess as a dramatic embodiment of conflicts found in the struggle of women to assert their social rights through spiritual freedom from within the limiting structure of a patriarchal society. I will show how male domination violates the basic principle of equality integral to Hinduism, and how patriarchal ideology found in certain areas of Hinduism is based on a mistaken assumption about the nature of 'femaleness.' By taking a critical and reflective approach to the stories of the Puranas and their interpretations in Tantric literature, I will emphasize what I take to be the egalitarian core of Hinduism. According to Tantric interpretations, Kali represents, not only to women but to all people, a way of facing and transcending any limitation, whether the limitation is self-created or imposed by others, thus offering a way of liberating tradition itself from its patriarchal bias.

Women and the laws of Manu

In order to understand Kali from a post-patriarchal point of view as a resource for liberation and empowerment, one must see the goddess's femininity and femininity in general both in light of patriarchal interpretations found in the Hindu lawbooks collectively known as the *Dharmasastras (The Rules of Right Conduct)* and in the religious and more liberating interpretations found in various Tantric and Vedanta texts.

Hindu law was first codified by Manu in the seventh century BCE. Under this reform women lost much of their freedom. Restrictions were put upon their autonomy, their movements, and their associations with men. Child marriage became the norm, and women were required to be virgins and chaste. Women were placed under the supervision of their fathers first, later their husbands, and then their sons. In short, the role of women was relegated to wife and mother. Anything other was considered unacceptable. It seems to me that the sources on which the later patriarchal Hindu tradition is based have been interpreted only by Hindu men who had vested interests in, and who were responsible for, defining the sociological and religious status of Hindu women.

The following passages from *Manu Samhita (Laws of Manu)* clarify the basic rules of conduct for women. Here we find examples of restrictions put upon the nature and potentiality of women. Once stated as laws, these passages and countless more established the monolithic structure of the *Dharmasastras* that promoted and perpetuated the patriarchal mentality:

> Let the [husband] employ his [wife] in the collection and expenditure of his wealth, in keeping [everything] clean, in [the fulfillment of] religious duties, in the preparation of his food, and in looking after the household utensils (Manu, 329).

> Drinking [liquor], associating with wicked people, separation from the husband, rambling abroad, sleeping [at unreasonable hours], and

dwelling in other men's houses are the six causes of the ruin of women (Manu, 329).

She who drinks spirituous liquor or is of bad conduct, rebellious, diseased, mischievous, or wasteful, may at any time be superseded by another wife (Manu, 341).

Her father protects [her] in childhood; her husband protects [her] in youth; and her sons protect [her] in old age; a woman is never fit for independence (Manu, 328).

Day and night women must be kept in dependence by the males [of] their families and, if they attach themselves to sensual enjoyments, they must be kept under control (Manu, 328).

[When creating them] Manu allotted to women [a love of their] bed, [of their] seat, and [of] ornament, impure desires, wrath, dishonesty, malice, and bad conduct (Manu, 330).

For women no [sacramental] rite [is performed] with texts; thus the law is settled; women who are destitute of [the knowledge of] Vedic texts are [as impure as] falsehood [itself]; that is a fixed rule (Manu, 330).

It is obvious that societal and psychological constraints inherent in these restrictions leave a woman with very few life options to explore. These restraints create a sense of dependency, a disability that further narrows her chance to fulfill her own creativity in any areas other than allocated household chores. By interfering with their potentiality, Manu seems to be encouraging women to resort to passivity by making them appendages to men. A women loses not only her freedom to make her own life choices but her self-worth as well.

In order to follow the reasoning behind such restrictions, one needs to consider how the nature of femaleness is defined within the context of these writings. How is the feminine viewed and valued in the *Manu Samhita?* The following passages are revealing:

through their passion for men, through their mutable temper, through their natural heartlessness, they become disloyal towards their husbands, however carefully they may be guarded (Manu, 330).

Where women are honored, there the gods are pleased; but where they are not honored, no sacred rites yield rewards (Manu, 330).

The houses in which female relations are not being duly honored, pronounce a curse, perish completely, as if destroyed by magic (Manu, 85).

Knowing their disposition ... [every] man should most strenuously exert himself to guard them (Manu, 330).

And to this effect many sacred texts are sung also in the Vedas in order to [make] fully known the true disposition of [women] (Manu, 330).

Why is it that 'every man should most strenuously exert himself to guard women'? What is the nature or disposition of women that necessitates such precaution on the part of men? Manu speaks of an ambiguous nature of woman. She has a mutable temper and heartlessness, but despite this she is to be revered and honored. Her sacredness is to be preserved and appreciated, otherwise god will be displeased. Most important, there is nothing worse than a dishonored woman whose curse spells danger for the household. Her femininity reflects her paradoxical nature. She is to be guarded because of her profane nature; she is to be revered for her sacredness.

Why is there such an elaborate system of rules to control and protect her unless men are afraid of her inherent power? It is her inherent power that creates man's fear as well as his reverence toward her and finally prompts him either to control her through social restrictions or to honor her through gestures of respect and protectiveness.

Kali

It is in the goddess Kali that I find the inherent power of women made explicit. This is true when we understand Kali in the stories of the Puranas on a superficial level, and it is true even when we examine her in the terms patriarchy has used in dealing with her. It is most powerfully true when we examine more deeply the essential religious, cosmological, and epistemological implications of the goddess.

In order to understand Kali, it is also essential that we clarify the notion of Devi. The word *Devi* in its truest sense refers to Para Brahman, the Ultimate Reality, which is beyond all names and forms. In this sense Devi is neither male nor female, it is a state of being. In the *Yamala*, Siva says:

> Devi may, My beloved, be thought of as female or male, or the *Saccidanandarupini* may be thought of as *Niskala Brahman*. But in truth She is neither a female, male, neuter being, nor an inanimate thing. But like the term *Kalpavalli* [a word in feminine gender denoting 'tree'] feminine terms are attributed to Her (Avalon, 1965, 31).

Since mind cannot grasp the genderless reality of the Devi, she appears in physical forms; she is usually contemplated in her female form. Out of the countless manifestations of Devi, Kali is considered to be one of the most important. Characterization of Kali is not a simple matter because stories and personifications of Kali are extraordinarily diverse. She appears with different names as well as with different forms, manifesting in countless goddesses such as Durga, Dat, Parvati, and so on. Nevertheless, through all these diversities two obvious characterizations of Kali are most pertinent to my topic: Kali the mother and the destroyer, and Kali the independent woman (Kali the Great Mother and Kali the Great Goddess). Each of these characterizations could be understood in a variety of ways. In what follows I will look at Kali's superficial and/or physical iconography. I will examine Kali's behavior and baffling companions and her relationship with Siva, her husband. This [...] should also help us understand Kali in her deeper significance and how she can serve as a liberating force for women – and men. The patriarchal perspective often depicts the goddess as nothing more than a great but biologically dependent mother and wife; such interpretations, I suspect, have been used to legitimate the kind of patriarchal hierarchy espoused by Manu. But I will argue that in terms of scripture and the Tantric interpretations, Kali can be taken to symbolize the Ultimate Principle that transcends any form of duality and that, in doing so, the Great Goddess can be taken as a fruitful post-patriarchal model of the feminine, in whom the beauty, power, and independence of the female can be understood and appreciated.

The iconography of Kali

Kali is almost always pictured in ways that terrify the onlooker; red eyes, dishevelled hair, blood trickling at the corners of her mouth, lips saturated with fresh blood, a dangling tongue, long sharp fangs, a gaunt, dark-skinned body, a sunken stomach, and protruding breasts. Her adornment and *lack* of adornment intensify her frightening appearance: she is mostly naked; her necklace contains fifty human heads; her waistband is a girdle made of severed human arms; she is wearing two dead infants for earrings (Avalon 1965, 45). Each of her four arms holds a different object or projects a particular gesture. She holds a blood-smeared cleaver in her upper left hand and a blood-dripping severed head in the lower left. With her upper right hand she says 'Fear not,' and with her lower right she beckons 'Come unto me' (Avalon 1965, 46). A first impression of this terrifying appearance reaffirms the conviction that Kali is a goddess of death and destruction, disorder and chaos.

Seen *simply* in her destructive image, goddess Kali seems neither to portray a specifically patriarchal model of a woman nor to offer any appropriate model for contemporary women. Hindu responses to and understandings of Kali are ambiguous. Even as the numen of the untamed feminine who threatens stability and order, she is approached as the beloved all-protective mother by the Hindus. Gruesome as she may appear, Hindus worship her as the source of power, strength, equality, and justice.

While some Puranic myths as well as Tantric texts paint such a horrifying picture of Kali, other texts and later writings describe Kali in gentler images. The Tantric text *Karpuradi-Stotra* at times depicts her as a young, beautiful woman. According to the text she is *atiyuvatin:* always the same, fresh, unchanging, and unwasting (Avalon 1965, 71). Her fierce laughter often gives way to a bewitching smile. *Karpuradi-Stotra* describes her as *smeravadanam,* as having a gently smiling face (Avalon 1965, 92). Being Bliss herself, she is ever blissful.

Which of these images of Kali can be taken as reflecting the fundamental principle of Hinduism? Is Kali the terrible destroyer who laughs at her enemies and devours them with pleasure? Or is she the beautiful mother who nourishes and preserves her created beings? There is truth in both these images.

Patriarchal understandings of these images have been used to limit the power of women. Kali in her nakedness and unusually gross adornments seems to be affirming the patriarchal description of women as lustful and out of control found in the *Laws of Manu.* In speaking of the relationships of women with men, Manu says: 'Women do not care for beauty, nor is their attention fixed on age, [thinking it is enough that] he is a man; they give themselves to the handsome and to the ugly' (Manu, 330). Patriarchal claims regarding the unrefined and emotional nature of women are evident in this passage; this and similar claims would seem to be supported by Kali's image and behavior.

Not only her nakedness and unusual adornments, but also her dark complexion have been the focus of patriarchal mentality, a mentality that typifies black and white as symbols of evil and good. Dislike toward black complexion is quite evident in a story of the *Vamana Purana.* According to the Puranic story, the goddess Parvati at times is called Kali, the Black One, by her husband Siva. Hearing Siva call her by this name, she becomes insulted and enraged. In order to get rid of her dark complexion she undergoes severe austerities, finally receiving a golden complexion as her reward (*Vamana Purana* 25–29).

Kali's dark complexion possibly indicates her ancient origin as a tribal fertility goddess worshipped by the dark-skinned indigenous people who populated India prior to the Aryan invasion. Her dark color apparently suggests her connection to the earth and its fertility and therefore establishes her as the Great Mother. The universal devaluation of women could be explained in terms of the assumption that women are closer to the earth than men; it is natural, in this thinking, for men to dominate and subjugate women just as one tries to dominate the earth. In this view the dark Kali reflects a reality to be dominated (specifically by Siva), as women (and wives) must be dominated by men (their husbands).

Kali's image in Tantra

Tantric interpretation provides us with a means to understand the deeper significance of Kali's iconography and reveals how her presence can be empowering and liberating in a post-patriarchal context. In seeking to understand the essence of Kali in Hinduism we need to go beyond the mythic layer that presents the Great Goddess merely in terms of a Great Mother who represents the biologically dependent female, and therefore dependent wife. The *Karpuradi-Stotra*, a Tantric text, explains and interprets the image of Kali in the following way:

> Kali's 'body is imagined to be blue of color because, like the blue sky, she pervades the world.'

> Kali 'is imagined black because she is colorless and above the color gunas.'

> Kali's 'hair is disheveled because though herself changeless she binds infinite numbers of jivas [individual selves] by bonds of Maya [illusion]' and 'because she liberates Brahma, Vishnu, and Mahesvara, who are her kesa [hair]' (Avalon, 1965, 45).

The Sanskrit word *kesa* in the above quotation refers to 'K' as Brahma (god of creation), 'A' as Vishnu (god of preservation), and 'Isha' as Rudra (god of destruction) (Avalon, 1965, 45). That is, Kali's destructive image can be best understood in light of forms she assumes for the purpose of creation and preservation, as well as destruction. She embraces all these processes; indeed, she embraces all. Embracing creation, preservation, and destruction, Kali is a symbol of all that is; she is, at the deepest level, Brahman, or the unmanifested One. As such, she is capable both of placing consciousness and the devotee into bondage – the bondage of illusion and ignorance – and of releasing the devotee into absolute liberation (Avalon, 1965, 59).

In the Tantric interpretation parts of Kali's physical appearance represent qualities of consciousness and of all that is: Kali's white teeth represent *sattva guna,* potential consciousness; her lolling tongue refers to *raja guna,* the source of activity; and her wine drinking stands for *tamas gunas,* the source that resists activity

(Avalon 1965, 45). By destroying the *tamas gunas,* inertia, and by increasing one's *sattva guna,* potential consciousness, Kali finally grants her devotees liberation.

The human skull in her hand is the seat of the ultimate knowledge that finally leads one from bondage to liberation. With her upper left hand depicted as holding a sword of wisdom, she severs the bonds of illusion and mistaken identity that are holding her devotees in bondage. She is naked because she is beyond the shackles of *Maya* [deceptive creative power that deceives us into seeing the world as real] or illusion.

The fifty human heads of her necklace refer to the fifty letters of the Sanskrit language. These fifty letters are used for hymns and mantras; they are Brahman itself in the form of sound energy. Her girdle of human arms with folded palms suggests how to perform action without any attachment in order to avoid further entrenchment in the bondage of the cycle of cause and effect (the law of karma). Her heavy hips and *yoni* (sexual organ) stand for the creative process. Her three eyes represent energy radiated in three directions: as moon, sun, and fire. The well-developed breasts of the goddess Kali are filled with over-flowing milk. With the over-flowing milk of one breast she sustains the created world, and with the other she feeds and shows the path of liberation to her devotees. Like a child sleeping safely and peacefully in the lap of its mother, every human being at the end of worldly life rests in eternal peace in the crematorium ground, the dwelling place of mother Kali and the god Siva (Avalon, 1965, 84).

Kali as a contemporary role model

In Western tradition the depiction of goddesses' nakedness (Eve, Diana, Aphrodite, or – on the opposite pole – Medusa, whose head and snaky hair call to mind the exposed female sex organ) leads to the temptation and spiritual destruction of men. Kali's nudity, however, does not seem primarily to reflect this projection of men's inner fear at the power of women's sexuality or the cause of man's downfall. Rather, her choice to be naked reveals a choice to be free from social constraints. Kali neither adorns herself for others nor conceals her natural being. She is what she is.

In my mind, Kali's use of jewelry and adornment, while it would never make the cover of *Vogue* magazine, also offers us interesting insights into the way her myths reveal a subtle critique of the limitations of patriarchal consciousness. Kali's iconography, as we have pointed out, depicts her with necklaces of skulls and severed heads. Here the mythic image takes the *form* of a traditional female subservience to male desires in which the female turns herself into an adorned, bejewelled object for the approval of the men that gaze on her; but Kali totally reverses that form's function. Instead of rubies and diamonds, similar to those of other goddesses, Kali wears frightening skulls and corpses whose violent overtones suggest a hidden hostility or rage at this need to adorn and 'objectify' oneself. The transformation of jewels into emblems of death also hints at the power of women, with their close connection to the natural cycle of giving birth and nurturing life. Kali's flaunting of her association with nature's destructive powers, symbolized by the skulls, reinforces the link that binds women with mysteries of both life and death.

In addition, Kali, through her peculiar adornments, seems to communicate to others the predicaments she herself faces. Kali asks us to confront the inevitability of death and the unavoidable loss of our identity in death. The Dark Mother teaches us that it is only in accepting our fear and the dark within us that we recognize our true identity as being within a totality of all that is, a recognition that liberates us from all impositions and restrictions. Darkness absorbs all colors. In this sense Kali represents a totality that transcends all forms of duality and separation.

[...]

A creative and interactive reading in the light of Tantric scriptural interpretation of the Great Goddess can allow Kali with her terrifying appearance to emerge as a powerful symbol of life and liberation to women in their passage to post-patriarchy. Beyond mother and wife, she encourages us to challenge our assumptions, ambiguities, negativities, uncertainties, and fears about 'others.' Under her assurance we confront who we are in reality as opposed to what we perceive ourselves to be through the subjugated roles we play. [...]

It is difficult to criticize Manu's way of thinking without appearing to question the entire fabric of Hinduism. However, the whole fabric of Hinduism is not to be understood in terms of Manu's presuppositions about the dangerous emotional disposition of women. Manu's idea is not a solution; rather, we find in Manu a clear statement of a problem, which has an irreplaceable value in making our task so explicit. I find it a clear statement of how a denigrating view and evaluation of femaleness is ingrained in the social structure. Language, which is the prime reflection of attitudes held, reveals how a society defines the nature of male and female and assigns power accordingly. The more the concept of Purusa [masculine, associated with mind and consciousness] or Siva is defined in terms of spirit or consciousness without acknowledging its deeper connotation and the oneness of Purusa or Siva with Prakrti [nature, seen as feminine] or Sakti [energy, female power], the more the concept of

Sakti or Prakrti assumes the role of an unconscious raw power to be restricted and subjugated. The rationality of Purusa automatically assigns irrationality to Prakrti, to Kali, and to the female. It is this kind of understanding that a post-patriarchal reading must de-emphasize, and that a post-patriarchal appropriation of Kali through scriptural analysis will help us overcome.

Kali's behavior and associations

Not only do the images and iconography of Kali reveal her essence, her behavior also offers a clue to her true nature. Most of the Puranic stories present her as a deity who delights in death and destruction. Her madness is evident in her diabolical howl and in the way she deals with her enemies in war. She appears to be out of control both on and off the battlefield. She is often found 'intoxicated on blood,' eating raw and rotten flesh with a smile on her face. She sits on corpses drinking their blood from a human skull. She doesn't appear to be in need of any 'proper' friend other than her constant companions: snakes, jackals, and ghosts. Her human associates come from what traditional Hinduism has seen as the lowest caste, the sudras. Moreover, she is the 'patron deity' of thugs and thieves. She is found in two preferred localities – battlefields and cremation grounds – and appears fully at ease in both places.

Kali's behavior

There are many legends that illustrate the bloodthirsty and malevolent aspects of this goddess in her fury. According to the story of the *Devi Mahatmya,* the baffled Durga, in her battle with the demon Raktabija, who has incredible power to recreate himself from every drop of his own blood, summons Kali for assistance. Kali as Camunda, who sprang from Durga's body in her previous battle with the demons Canda and Munda, appears suddenly in her usual fury. She sucks the last drop of blood out of Raktabija's body and makes him unable to regenerate himself any further. She then murders his countless progeny by swallowing them whole, and finally rescues Durga from the imminent danger she faces on the field of war.

In the *Malati-Madhaba* of Bhabhuti we find that near Padmavati there was a temple of the goddess Camunda, who was worshipped with human sacrifice. Aghoroghanta, a devotee of Kali, was reported to have kidnapped a heroine in order to sacrifice her at the goddess's altar (see Kate). This reveals that Kali's worshippers reflect the same tendencies to violence as their deity, who appears to be satisfied with nothing less than the spilling of blood as a reflection of her power. In the *Bhagavata-Purana* Kali is approached by a leader of a band of thieves who plans to sacrifice the young Brahmin boy whom he kidnapped in order to obtain a blessing. As they approach the altar, the purity of the Brahmin burns the goddess and in her anger she decapitates the band of thieves and consumes their blood completely (*Bhagavata-Purana* 5.9 12–20).

In light of these stories Kali's behavior seems baffling and unpredictable. Although her benevolent side cannot be ignored, as when she saves the young boy's life and constantly aids other gods and goddesses in their distress, her malevolence is undeniable. The paradoxical mixture of compassion and violence evident in these stories is only the beginning of mysteries and ambiguities that surround her character. Although she is known as the Mother Goddess, she herself is barren. Although she is the wife of Siva, she is rarely found with her mate. She is not a hermit, but she lacks a proper household; in fact, she lives mostly outdoors and haunts the crematoriums. She is a woman, yet she excels in the normally male domains. Why is it so difficult to comprehend Kali's nature? Is it because we are trying to understand her divine nature in terms of the 'femininity' she portrays and because she reflects a form of femininity that does not conform to the established role of women in Hinduism or in *any* other tradition informed by patriarchy?

The concept of liberation within a Hindu context is understood in terms of realizing one's true nature as Brahman. Liberation within the social context could then be understood as realizing one's potential as an individual, as well as a woman. Kali, in her actions, shows that the world of action is not compartmentalized into masculine and feminine spheres. These sexual roles are, rather, only modes of operation one assumes as he or she attempts to fulfil an inner potentiality with regard to what is being presented in a particular time and place. Neither her physical constitution nor her social status constrains or determines Kali's behavior. Her body is not in her way and definitely does not stop her from anything she plans on doing. Whether in her role at the battlefields or at the cremation ground, she neither highlights the sexual difference nor obliterates it but overcomes both possibilities in a meaningful way.

The myth of Kali offers a story of a woman in a plight. She is the personified wrath of all women in all cultures. As we read Kali's stories, we repeatedly encounter her wrathful image appearing from various goddesses who are portrayed to be either docile daughters or devoted wives. In the *Devi Mahatmya* Kali appears as the personified anger of Durga as she faces the demons. In the *Adbhuta Ramayana*, a late work highly favored by the Kashmiri Saktas, Sita, having killed

Ravana, assumes the form of Kali *(Adbhuta Ramayana* xxv.29–31). Kali plays a similar role in Parvati, who is otherwise known to be a benevolent goddess. Kausiki appears from the muscles of Parvati, turns black, and becomes known as Kalika, dwelling in the Himalayas (Bhattacharya, 149). In another such story Sati becomes angry when her husband Siva refuses to allow her to attend her father's sacrificial ceremony (Avalon, 1960, 208–13). In her anger she assumes the form of Kali and appears in ten directions in her terrifying forms.

Kali's anger is an expression of a deep, long-buried emotion, a character trait that symbolizes deep emotional response to her situations and surroundings. She is not simply malevolent. Her 'terrifying howls' are also a demand for equality where femininity is equated with meekness and subservience, since such anger is the only language that can be heard.

Power, especially the power of the warrior, has always been thought of in exclusively masculine terms. When a female deity is described as excelling in any male function – as Kali does on the battlefield – she is described either as a masculinized female or as out of control and destructive, as if strength and valor are constructive character traits only as long as they are part of a male deity. When these 'destructive' traits are part of a female deity in a patriarchal system, the goddess no longer portrays a positive role model. But despite her violence and bloodthirstiness, Kali does indeed portray a model of strength and of self-liberation from constraint for post-patriarchal women.

Kali's associations

Kali's association with animals that are not domesticated – such as jackals and so on – suggests her relationship goes beyond any type of hierarchical structure. Moreover, her relationship with animals such as snakes verifies her interconnectedness with every life form, regardless of how lowly it may be. From the psychological standpoint animals may very well suggest various parts of the human psyche, and familiarizing oneself with one's own thoughts and feelings regardless of their nature, confronting and associating with one's own inner being, however difficult that may be, is the first step to freedom.

Furthermore, she associates with the sudras. Sudras, according to the social stratification of the Hindu caste system, fall at the bottom of the social structure and lack any possibility of ever transcending that role and status in one lifetime. Consequently they are looked down upon by the rest of the community. Social stratification becomes counterproductive because it segregates and separates people and ultimately leads to oppression and bondage. Kali's companionship with the sudras throws an interesting insight on her rebellion against any structure that is oppressive in any form, and on her determination to reverse that destructive order. For example, the conception of the nation in the form of Divine Mother proved to be a strong basis for India's movement for freedom from the British. Narendra N. Bhattacharya articulates this view very clearly:

> a constant characteristic of the Sakta religion, which we must not overlook or underestimate, is that throughout the ages the Female Principle stood for oppressed peoples, symbolizing all the liberating potentialities in the class-divided, patriarchal, and authoritarian social set up of India, the rigidity of which was mainly responsible for the survival and development of the opposite principles represented mainly by Saktism (Bhattacharya, 165).

Kali's habitations

This interpretation gains further support in Kali's choice of dwelling place, namely cremation grounds. In the Hindu community cremation grounds usually are located at the fringe of human localities, almost at the borderline of the world and beyond. Most important, until recently women were not allowed to go to the cremation ground. One of the reasons for such a restriction is that a woman was assumed to be too emotional to witness the finality of death. Kali, by contrast, breaks away from the existing structure in search of an alternative. To her, the cremation ground is no more natural or unnatural than any other place in the world. Just as the cremation ground does not exist separately from society, death does not exist separately from life. To Kali, the dichotomy does not exist.

Breaking away from existent structures, stereotypes, and limitations necessitates facing an unknown and uncertain future. Similarly, the freedom and absolute liberation, which Kali in the cremation ground signifies, goes beyond the restrictions imposed on our understanding, on our perception and energy; it implies freedom from one's ego and from one's attachment to particularity and separateness.

Kali and Siva

Lastly, and most importantly, we must examine Kali from the point of view of her relationship with her husband Siva. As a wife, she can be taken – as she has been understood in patriarchy – solely as a loving mother and spouse. In some versions of her myth, indeed, this appears to be a valid reading. But when we look toward Kali's other,

most striking characteristics, and when we look toward her most
essential meaning, we are able to see her as moving beyond the
patriarchal view of womanhood and marriage.

The virtuous wife in the laws of Manu

For Manu there are some clear expectations for an ideal wife:

Though destitute of virtue, or seeking pleasure [elsewhere], or devoid
of good qualities, a husband must be constantly worshipped as a god
by a faithful wife (Manu, 196).

She who, controlling her thoughts, words, and deeds, never slights her
lord, resides [after death] with her husband [in heaven] and is called a
virtuous wife (Manu, 197).

Whatever be the qualities of the man with whom woman is united,
according to the law, such qualities even she assumes, like a river
[united] with the ocean (Manu, 331).

An ideal wife for Manu is a virtuous wife. Although a woman is
devoid of natural virtues, as a wife she must earn them through her
fidelity to her husband. She is to strive to control all facets of her
thoughts and behavior with regard to her husband. Most important of
all, a wife should worship her husband as her god. A woman, married
according to religious and social law, must relinquish her identity and
individuality and assume her husband's character traits, regardless of
their nature. An ideal wife, therefore, is one who neither questions
the validity of the rules nor disobeys them, but rather follows them
with her whole being. Although a husband also has to follow certain
restrictions, and the text contains a few injunctions with regard to his
husbandly conduct, it is the wife who must account for the success or
failure of a marriage and be the responsible partner for the happiness
or unhappiness therein. Moreover, it is also her virtue as a wife that
guarantees her own individual fulfillment as a woman here and
hereafter in heaven. Manu seems to be defining the institution of
marriage in terms of the total submission of a wife to her husband. In
his definition of a virtuous wife he is emphasizing adherence to a
person – the husband – more than adherence to any moral principle.
That is, a wife's virtue solely depends on her total surrender and
submission to her husband's will and power – and nothing else.

Kali as wife

When Kali is seen with a god, she is always with Siva as his consort,
Sakti. True to her nature, in her relationship she is paradoxical. There
are times when she is not only the domineering one in the

relationship, but even the active, initiating partner in the destructive, cosmic dance. In one south Indian story we find Kali celebrating her victory over Sumbha and Nishumbha with a destructive dance (Sivaramamurti, 378–79, 381; also summarized in Kinsley 1986, 119). A devotee of Siva appeals to Siva to remove Kali from the forest. But Kali refuses to move from the area or to stop her destruction. Instead, at the end of the story we find Siva in the forest with Kali, engaged in the same destructive dance. Kali has a disruptive influence on Siva; at the same time, it is in his presence that her own destructive behavior continues.

On the other hand, Siva sometimes brings out the hidden, gentler instinct in her. According to one Puranic story, after defeating her enemies on the battlefield and getting drunk with the blood of her slain enemies, Kali becomes absorbed in her destructive dance. Fearing imminent destruction of the world, Siva appears in the middle of the battlefield in the guise of an infant crying out in thirst. As Kali sees the crying infant, she stops her dancing and puts the infant in her arms. Here, as in other stories, she is presented as a loving mother moved by the sight of the slightest distress in her child. In another story Siva places himself on the battlefield like a corpse in order to stop Kali from her destructive dance and to protect the stability of the world itself. Though intoxicated and mad in her dance, she stops as she recognizes her husband lying under her feet. Like a proper Hindu woman she bites her tongue in shame (Kinsley 1975, 108; Nivedita).

In other stories she behaves like a devoted wife who is unconcerned about her own safety and concerned for the well-being of her husband. Kali is the helpmate who repeatedly risks her life as she is called by her husband to assist him on the battlefield. Still other stories present her as a gentle mother and wife.

But in most of her myths Kali appears to be independent and unattached without any consort or male deity at her side. Even when she appears as the spouse of Siva, Kali projects a form of womanhood through her relationship with Siva that is beyond any normative behavior prescribed by Manu. Kali is a wife, yet she is far too domineering and destructive to be a wife as Manu envisioned. She appears to be an affectionate and devoted mate, but her changeable and unpredictable behavior does not let her continue in the role as a 'proper wife.' In short, she does not fulfill any of her wifely duties and obligations. Most important, her defiant nature reminds one of her unrestricted raw energy, which if uncontrolled, according to Manu, leads to chaos and calamity, but which, taken from another perspective, can serve as an imagistic resource for moving beyond patriarchy.

Patriarchal vs scriptural readings

The biological differences between men and women are undeniable, but the hierarchical order established by Manu on the basis of such differences can neither be verified nor established in Vedic or Upanishadic terms. The Veda says that all things are Brahman. All distinctions – including the one that allows men of the priestly class but not women to say Vedic mantras – are 'wholly opposed to the Spirit of the Great Word (*MahaVakya*).' One Brahman becomes dual, appears as Siva and Sakti, man and woman, two complementary principles involved in the process of creation. They are one and the same. The duality of Siva and Sakti is grounded in the unity and oneness of the Brahman. As Avalon notes, 'In the Tantrasastra also Siva has said that there is no difference between them who are inseparably connected. He who is Siva is also Sakti, and she who is Sakti is also Siva' (Avalon 1965, 31).

That is, *scripturally*, both the husband and the wife are considered to be reflections of the divine nature. Therefore any hierarchical order such as that present in Manu's vision of marriage negates the very premise on which it appears to be based. Manu used the symbols of duality found in the principles of Siva and Sakti (or Purusan and Prakrti) to support a hierarchical and patriarchal system in which women's understanding and experience of their own power have been severely restrained. In doing so he violated the very spirit of those symbols.

The more the patriarchal mind recognized the force of the creative power present in the divine female, the more it created an environment for the feminine to be restricted and restrained. The more one understood Prakrti as mere potentiality, who needs the presence of Purusa for her evolution, the more the sovereignty and absolute authority of the husband became established. In the relationship of man and woman Manu legitimated a sexually imbalanced society where man is to be regarded as a god. In this relationship it is the female who has been imagined to be acting out the unintegrated negative aspect (Prakrti, Avidya [ignorance, wrong knowledge, that which binds], Maya) of this union. Prakrti or woman as *object,* in this reading, requires a subject or the Purusa for fulfillment and existence itself. Marriage, according to Manu, is a form of union between a man and a woman where the feminine is required to be the subservient, dependent companion to the masculine. Rather than speaking of a union in terms of the transcendence of sexual differences and individual ego in a meaningful unity, Manu advocates gender difference that allows for a negative vision of the female.

But the patriarchal reading neglects the source of both subject and object, the One, unmanifested Brahman who is neither a subject nor an object, male nor female. Both subject and object in reality are the same. Union transcends sexual differences and the individual ego. Kali illustrates this. Not conscious of the kind of union Manu advocates, Kali symbolizes a form of marriage that necessitates equality and individuality. Her femininity belongs to her and not to her husband. Kali as a woman, as a wife, knows what her status should be. As she dances the dance of destruction she communicates her responses to the way things are and the way they should be. That is, in her destructive dance she creates her own reality. Only by moving beyond Manu to a less gender-centered reinterpretation of Kali's supposed destructiveness can we appreciate her as the fountain of creative energy she is.

Conclusion: the presence of Kali

Behind the diverse characters of Sati, Sita, Durga, and Parvati, lies the single, unchanging face of the true hero, the wrathful goddess Kali, the savior. As these goddesses face oppressing realities of life, Kali the true hero appears in all of them and saves them in their battle of life. How can contemporary women identify themselves with a mythical character? I think there is an interaction between a contemporary woman's psyche and the mythic behavior patterns of the goddess, patterns that inform and are played out in a woman's life. For example, when a woman is outraged by her husband's lack of understanding or refusal to follow through on a request, her acting out is comparable at some level to the story of outraged Sati, who appears as Kali to confront and terrify an uncooperative Siva. When a woman feels a tremendous need to subordinate her welfare to the welfare of the other, she is encountering self-sacrificing Sita. By identifying ourselves with the ways Kali acts on the mythic level, with the actual and potential embodiments of Kali, we begin to find a transpersonal source of liberation within her character and nature. As we listen to the various stories of the goddess Kali we see them take shape into a definite pattern of experience. In emphasizing or de-emphasizing certain elements – in particular, those dealing with the potential of women – we can see how some of the stories were told from a male point of view. By reviewing these stories over and over again, understanding them in their most liberating sense, as do the Tantric interpretations, and reappropriating from them those elements which are most powerful as resources for the liberation of both men and women – taking as authentic and genuinely spiritual those aspects that promote our over-all welfare – we can eliminate the inessential details and the patriarchal distortions and finally identify the sources and patterns of our oppressed past and present. It is this pattern that finally reveals the way we are now and what we could possibly become. It shows the ways in which the images and the stories of Kali can be liberating and empowering to all through exposing an essence that goes beyond male and female, beauty and ugliness, life and death, and all forms of alienation and separation.

In seeking to go beyond the patriarchal view of the goddess, and woman, as untamed and unsubjugated and therefore in need of control and restriction, we must understand Kali at various levels, at more essential levels than superficial, patriarchal readings reveal. On one level she is Brahman, the all-inclusive Reality that is beyond any form of alienation or separation. On another level Kali is the divine principle that provides us with a tradition of female language and images with which we can speak of the divine: Sakti, Prakrti, Maya, and Avidya. She is also called the Devi, the goddess, literally 'the self-manifested one' (Avalon 1965, 66). The term *devi* comes from the root *div* meaning 'the shining one.' That is, Devi is someone who shines through all that has been imposed upon her. She is also referred to as *Asita* (Avalon 1965, 95), which means that she is free from bondage (*sita* is 'bound'; *asita*, 'unbounded' or 'ultimately liberated'). She is called *Kalika,* 'a long-standing cloud threatening to rain.' She is *Tara,* 'the savior.' She saves the world from all forms of oppression (Avalon 1965, 101).

She is called *Matah,* 'mother of creation.' The Sanskrit term for mother is in the feminine when it refers to mother; it also refers to the knower or measurer, and appears when it does so in the masculine gender. Here, in Kali as Matah or Mother, we have the two aspects – Siva, the masculine knower, and the feminine Sakti, the mother, the creator. Neither masculine nor feminine image and language, then, contains the final truth; neither can be absolutized. They are both aspects of the same, single reality.

On still another level she reflects the behavioral reality of a subjugated woman in search of her identity. The dark goddess is perpetually present in the inner and outer struggles faced by women at all times. Her darkness represents those rejected and suppressed parts of female creativity, energy, and power that have not been given a chance to be actualized. As Sister Nivedita writes, 'Our daily life creates our symbol of God' (Nivedita, 461).

In and through the dark images we learn to accept the equality of all names, forms and genders, taken up as they are within the principles of Siva and Sakti and, finally, in the One. Indeed, Kali is the emblem of two opposites that constitute a composite whole, a power and a wonder that goes beyond all distinctions.

Works cited

Avalon, A., ed. *Principles of Tantra: The Tantratattva of Sriyukta Siva Candra Vidyamava Bhattacarya Mahodaya*. Madras: Ganesh and Company, 1960.

Avalon, A., ed. and trans. *Hymn to Kali (Karpuradi-Stotra)*. Madras: Ganesh and Company, 1965.

Avalon, A., trans. *Tantra of the Great Liberation (Mahanirvana Tantra)*. New York: Dover Publications, 1972.

Bhattacharya, Narendra Nath. *History of Sakta Religion*. New Delhi: Munishiram Manohaslar Pub. Pvt. Ltd, 1974.

Deutsch, Elliot. *Advaita Vedanta: A Philosophical Reconstruction*. Honolulu: The University Press of Hawaii, 1973.

Hawley, John Stratton, and Donna Marie Wulff, eds. *The Divine Consort: Radha and the Goddesses of India*. Boston, Beacon Press, 1982.

Kate, M.R., ed. and trans. *Bhavabhuti's Malaimadhava, with the Commentary of Jagadhara*. Delhi: Motilal Banarasidass, 1967.

Kinsley, David, *The Sword and the Flute: Kali and Krsna, Dark Visions of the Terrible and the Sublime in Hindu Mythology*. Berkley and Los Angeles: University of California Press, 1975.

Kinsley, David, 'Blood and Death Out of Place: Reflections on the Goddess Kali.' In *The Divine Consort*. See Hawley and Wulff, 1982.

Kinsley, David, *Hindu Goddesses*, Los Angeles: University of California Press, 1986.

Manu, *The Laws of Manu*. Sacred Books of the East, 25. Trans. G. Buhler. Delhi: Motilal Banaraidass, 1964.

Nivedita, *Kali the Mother*. I. Calenlta: Ramkrishna Sarada Mission, 1967.

Ruether, Rosemary, *Sexism and God-Talk*. Boston: Beacon Press, 1983.

Satprakashananda, *Methods of Knowledge*. Calcutta: Advaita Ashram, 1976.

Sivaramamurti, C. *Natarajain Art, Thought and Literature*. New Delhi: National Museum, 1976.

The Global Environment as a Religious Issue: a Sociological Analysis*

PETER BEYER

The article examines the possible sociological import of recent environmental concern by various religious actors and organizations. It argues that the rise to dominance of instrumental systems such as the world economy and global system of states has brought about globalization and the global spread of values like equality and progress. The holistic style of religion prevents it from developing as a parallel instrumental system but also suits it for addressing resultant problems like vast inequalities and environmental degradation. Both of these raise questions of theodicy and the meaning of the whole. We should therefore expect the conjunction of liberal religious concern with social justice and ecological issues. There is, however, also ambiguity as progress towards social justice may contradict preservation of the natural environment.

To some, writing on religion and the global environment at the present time may seem rather suspect: Is it not simply an attempt to ride the currently popular wave of environmental concern? Perhaps; but it is not the broad popularity of the trend that is at issue. Rather it is the fact that major, especially Western, religious organizations and leaders seem to have joined the trend in a way they had not previously. For example, in late 1989, Pope John Paul II issued 'Peace with God the creator, peace with all of creation',[1] the first papal

---

*This text first appeared in Peter Beyer, 'The global environment as a religious issue: a sociological analysis', *Religion* (1992) 22, 1–19.

[1] *Osservatore Romano* (English Edn), no. 51–52 (1120) (18–26 December 1989), pp. 1–3.

statement devoted exclusively to ecology. In October of that same year, the Harvard Divinity School held its first conference on theology and environment. And in the spring of 1990, the 307 member World Council of Churches met in Seoul under the rubric of 'Justice, peace, and integrity of creation'.[2]

To be sure, concern about environmental issues on the part of religious leaders and theologians is not new. There is a sizeable theological literature on the topic that dates back at least to the early 1970s.[3] It has also received mention in various Christian church documents and at various meetings.[4] Yet only in the last few years have environmental issues moved from the margins and mushroomed as a dominant concern within a large number of especially Christian[5] organizations. Indeed, as the theme of the recent WCC meeting and the pope's statement indicate, the topic has been elevated to join the two great contemporary liberal religious ideals of peace and justice.

It is my purpose here to take some preliminary steps in assessing the possible macrosociological significance of this development. Specifically, I pose the following question: What can it tell us about

---

[2] The Official Report for this Assembly has not yet been published. Numerous preliminary documents, however, exist. See e.g. from the WCC's *Church and Society Documents* series, J.N.K. Mugambi, 'God, humanity and nature in relation to justice and peace', no.2 (September 1987); World Council of Churches, 'Reintegrating God's creation: a paper for discussion', no. 3 (September, 1987); 'Caring for creation: call to the Latin American churches (Costa Rica Forestry and Environment Workshop)', no. 6 (August, 1988).

[3] See e.g. Ian G. Barbour (ed.), *Earth Might Be Fair: Reflections on Ethics, Religion, and Ecology,* Englewood Cliffs, NJ, Prentice-Hall 1972; Frederick Elder, *Crisis in Eden: A Religious Study of Man and Environment,* Nashville, TN, Abingdon 1970; and H. Paul Santmire, *Brother Earth: Nature, God, and Ecology in Time of Crisis,* New York, Thomas Nelson 1970.

[4] See e.g. 'Justice in the world', in Michael Walsh and Brian Davies (eds), *Proclaiming Peace and Justice: Documents from John XXIII to John Paul II,* London, Collins/CAFOD 1984, p. 191; and David M. Paton (ed.), *Breaking Barriers, Nairobi 1975,* The Official Report of the Fifth Assembly of the World Council of Churches, Nairobi, 23 November–10 December, 1975, London & Grand Rapids, SPCK/Eerdmans 1976.

[5] There is, however, a meaningful participation by representatives of other religions in the growing discussion. See e.g. O. P. Dwivedi and B. N. Tiwari, *Environmental Crisis and Hindu Religion,* New Delhi, Gitanjali 1987; Eugene C. Hargrove (ed.), *Religion and Environmental Crisis,* Athens, GA, University of Georgia 1984; Adel T. Khoury and Peter Hünermann (eds), *Wie sollen wir mit der Schöpfung umgehen?* Freiburg B., Herder, 1987. For a very recent assessment of Buddhist efforts, see Ian Harris, 'How environmentalist is buddhism?', *Religion* 21 (April 1991) pp. 101–14.

the role of religion as a form of social communication under the conditions of globalization? I am therefore looking at the phenomenon not just for itself, but also as a symptom of larger social processes.

There is, of course, a certain risk involved in attempting to analyse such a very recent development. We have not been able to observe this phenomenon over any length of time and therefore have little idea of what direction it may take or how institutionalized it will become. In fact, little scientific research exists on this topic. Of the very few studies that have been done, most concentrate on the microsociological connections between individual religious belief/involvement and environmental concern.[6] More macrosociological analyses of the inner-organizational dynamics that led to these institutional shifts, or the larger socio-structural and cultural forces that encourage them are almost entirely lacking.[7] It is in this last category that the present effort belongs. I attempt to assess the broad global context in which the religious organizations and mobilization operate; and to show how this analysis can help us better understand the possible changes that religion in our world is undergoing.

My presentation is divided into two parts. In the first section, I begin by outlining the basic social structures that are bringing about the increasing globalization of society; as well as the core values that resonate with those structures. This is followed by a functional analysis of the place of religion with relation to those structures and values. A second section then shows why we should expect ecological issues under conditions of globalization to become a central concern of certain religious outlooks, if not all of them; and that the linking of these issues with those that fall under the 'peace and justice' rubric is just as likely. The section includes a discussion of the inherent ambiguity of including environmental concerns among the central tasks of religion that reflects globalization and its core values. As such, the analysis concentrates on this type of religion,

---

[6] See Douglas Lee Eckberg and T. Jean Blocker, 'Varieties of religious involvement and environmental concerns: testing the Lynn White thesis', *Journal for the Scientific Study of Religion* 28 (1989), pp. 509–17; C. Hand and K. Van Liere, 'Religion, mastery-over-nature, and environmental concern', *Social Forces* 63 (1984), pp. 555–570; Ronald G. Shaiko, 'Religion, politics, and environmental concern', *Social Science Quarterly* 68 (1987), pp. 265–81.

[7] The above-cited studies all refer to Lynn White's thesis, see 'The historical roots of our ecological crisis', *Science* 155 (1967), pp. 1203–7, that posits a causal relation between features of Judaism and Christianity and environmental problems. All the studies either confirm or at least do not falsify White's thesis. Recent actions on the part of major Christian organizations would, on this basis, seem to be somewhat of an 'about-face' and therefore call for an explanation.

which I call, if only for the sake of having a label, liberal religion. I do not mean to imply that other, more conservative or radical forms of religion are not going to be concerned with environmental issues. The focus is rather a way of keeping this study within manageable bounds by restricting it to the sort of religion that has in fact made environmental issues one of its central preoccupations.

Global systems, global values, and religion

At the centre of the current globalization discussion within the social sciences is the notion that no analysis of larger social processes in the contemporary world is complete unless it situates them, if only residually, in a global context.

As Roland Robertson has succinctly put it, globalization means that, increasingly, the world is 'a single place',[8] a fact that contextualizes a great deal of social communication. While participants in the discussion agree on this singleness, there are significant differences in what are to be seen as its basic structures and what, if any, global culture and values resonate with it. My own position is heavily influenced by the work of Niklas Luhmann,[9] but incorporates important elements from other contributors, notably, but certainly not exclusively, Immanuel Wallerstein[10] and Roland Robertson.[11]

I begin my description with the observation that globalization is a direct consequence of modernization. The epochal transformation of social structures and ideas that began in Western Europe has had as

[8] 'Church–state relations and the world system', in Thomas Robbins and Roland Robertson (eds), *Church–State Relations: Tensions and Transitions,* New Brunswick, NJ, Transaction, p. 43.

[9] See 'The world society as a social system', in Niklas Luhmann, *Essays on Self-Reference,* New York, Columbia University 1990, pp. 175–90; 'Tautology and paradox in the self-descriptions of modern society', ibid., pp. 123–43; 'The self-description of society: crisis fashion and sociological theory', *International Journal of Comparative Sociology* 25 (1984), pp. 59–72; and *Ecological Communication,* John Bednarz, Jr, trans. and intro., Cambridge, Polity Press 1989.

[10] See *The Capitalist World-Economy,* Cambridge, Cambridge University 1979; and 'Culture as the ideological battleground of the modern world-system', *Theory, Culture & Society* 7:2–3 (1990), pp. 31–55.

[11] See 'The sacred and the world system', in Phillip Hammond (ed.), *The Sacred in a Secular Age: Toward Revision in the Scientific Study of Religion,* Berkeley, CA, University of California 1985, pp. 347–58; 'Mapping the global condition: globalization as the central concept', *Theory, Culture & Society* 7:2–3 (1990), pp 15–30; and Robertson and JoAnn Chirico, 'Humanity, globalization, and worldwide religious resurgence: a theoretical exploration', *Sociological Analysis* 46 (1985), pp. 219–42.

one of its most important consequences the spread of key aspects of modernity to encompass the entire globe, particularly a world capitalist economy[12] and the system of sovereign states.[13] These, however, are only the clearest and most powerful aspects of the globalizing social system. Other globalizing systems of social communication have developed in tandem with the world economy and world polity. There are, for instance, the world-wide scientific–technological systems, health systems, and education systems.[14] Like the first two, these are not uniform or without internal divisions and local variations. They represent differentiated means of specialized communication which have a strong tendency to co-opt, undermine, and otherwise challenge previously existing cultural and personal boundaries, including those of the initial, European carriers.

Historically, these functionally specialized social systems began their rise to prominence in the Western Europe of the early modern era. There they gradually replaced the established community-group and status-group structures as the dominant systems of the society. One of the important consequences has been a significant increase in the perceived autonomy of individual persons as no one of the newly dominant subsystems of society encompasses all aspects of their lives. As I discuss below, two of the prevailing values that correspond to this structural shift are those that emphasize individual freedom and equality among individuals. The reverse side of this individuation, however, is the 'impersonality' of the systems: each of these centres on a different means of communication and not directly on the persons involved. Thus, for instance, the world capitalist economy operates in terms of money, the global political system in terms of bureaucratically organized power, the scientific system in terms of verifiable truth, and so forth. Moreover, the

[12] See Immanuel Wallerstein, *The Modern World System: Capitalist Agriculture and the Origins of the European World-Economy in the Sixteenth Century,* New York, Academic Press 1974; *The Modern World-System II: Mercantilism and the Consolidation of the World Economy 1650–1750,* New York, Academic Press 1980; and *The Modern World-System III: The Second Era of Great Expansion of the Capitalist World-Economy, 1730–1840s,* New York, Cambridge University Press 1989.

[13] See John W. Meyer, 'The world polity and the authority of the nation-state', in Albert Bergesen (ed.), *Studies of the World System,* New York, Academic Press 1980, pp. 109–37.

[14] See Niklas Luhmann, *Ecological Communication;* and John W. Meyer and Michael T. Hannan, (eds), *National Development and the World System: Educational, Economic, and Political Change, 1950–1970,* Chicago, IL, University of Chicago 1979.

instrumental orientation of these systems gears them toward constant increase of their specific means, yielding such cultural values as progress, efficiency, and technical rationality.

If this view is accepted, then modernity results simultaneously in the increased individuation of persons and the increased impersonal power of the overarching social systems. Saying this does not complete the picture, however. Precisely because the differentiated functional systems concentrate on specialized means of communication and not on the total lives of the people that carry them, they leave a great deal of social communication undetermined, if not unaffected. From the casual conversation with the neighbour across the fence, to the voluntary organization, to the social movement, there is much that escapes the determination of these nevertheless dominant systems. These systems are totalizing in the sense that they are applicable to anything in their environment; but they are not thereby all-encompassing. Everything has its price, but not everything is commodified. Everything potentially affects our health, but not everything is medicalized. Different aspects of what remains have been variously called the private sphere, the life-world, or the domain of expressive action.

To be sure, the functional systems I am discussing are very powerful. Their development and spread has brought about globalization. There is virtually no part of the world in which the money economy does not operate; no land area that is not under the jurisdiction of a sovereign state; few areas where modern medicine, schools, and technology have not reached. They have profound influence on the overwhelming majority of our lives and on the non-human world around us. Among the results are vast inequalities among people in terms of wealth, power, and life-chances; exacerbated cultural conflicts as people of very different outlooks find themselves living in the same society; greatly accelerated population growth; and the significant alteration of the physical environment.

A look at the main cultural values that accompany and reflect globalization can carry the discussion further.'[15] In early modern

---

[15] Choosing to focus on values as cultural correlates of structural globalization may seem somewhat arbitrary. The justification lies in the important role that such values have in the self-conceptions (or identity) of a society, which, as I make evident below, is also a religious concern. In saying this, I am *not* also claiming that these values 'integrate' global society and are therefore somehow constitutive of the global system as society. For a more detailed argument, see Peter F. Beyer, 'Globalism and inclusion: theoretical remarks on the non-solidary society', in William H. Swatos, Jr, (ed.), *Religious Politics in Global and Comparative Perspective*, Westport, CN, Greenwood 1989, pp. 39–53.

Western society, as functional communication began to challenge status-group communication for dominance, the old social boundaries had to be challenged. In particular this meant that the social prerogatives of the nobility and the cognitive/normative ascendancy of the church had to be dismantled and replaced by the abstract rule of monied capital, positive law, and the scientific method. The personal freedom espoused by the bourgeoisie and the Enlightenment intelligentsia was at the same time the freedom of capital and rational enquiry. Equality meant the removal of status-group membership as a criterion of discrimination: henceforth only personal ability in manipulating the rising instrumentalities should serve in this role. The result was to be, not chaos, but rational progress. Indeed, the intimate link between personal freedom and equality on the one hand, and progress on the other shows that all three fundamental values were but different aspects of the same overall development.

In the third of its core values, fraternity, the French Revolution expressed a further key value attendant upon modernization and globalization. Personal freedom and equality also had a group or communal component. Much as the rise in dominance of the functional structures meant the increase of individuation, it also left room for the continued but recontextualized salience of group identities, especially through the political system in the form of the nation-state and nationalism. While no analysis of globalization can be complete without an understanding of this factor,'[16] it is not of central concern in the present discussion. Accordingly, in what follows, reference to global values implicitly includes both their individual and group manifestations.

The process of modernization in the West was, of course, not smooth or inevitable; nor did it go unchallenged. Various anti-systemic movements arose, for instance, among those who wished to restore the old aristocratic society or those who sought to prevent their own marginalization through the new techniques. Yet, historically, these and others like them were unable to prevent the eventual ascendancy of the functional systems, and of the values that were an essential part of their rise. More importantly, in the present context, the power of these systems enabled their eventual global spread.

The imperial and global extension of the Western-bred systems and their core values has a long and exceedingly complex history.

---

[16] This 'national' or ethnic factor is very central to Roland Robertson's contributions to the globalization debate. See Roland Robertson, 'A new perspective on religion and secularization in the global context', in Jeffrey K. Hadden & Anson Shupe (eds), *Secularization and Fundamentalism Reconsidered, Religion and the Political Order,* vol. III, New York, Paragon pp. 63–77; Robertson & Chirico, op. cit.

Here cannot be the place for even a cursory outline. Suffice it to say that the diffusion of the core values, especially equality and progress, has gradually become a key symptom of this globalization.[17] That is to say, it has not just been the dominant Westerners who have come to espouse these values, but also a sizeable portion of the indigenous elites in most areas of the world as these have become incorporated into the global system. One critical consequence has been that the great inequalities generated within the same system have come to be seen by many as a negation of those values and a failing of the global system, and this by people in both the advantaged core and the disadvantaged peripheral regions. Put slightly differently, the global system has built into it inherent contradictions between systemic effects and systemic values. While it would be unwarranted to conclude from this the inevitable demise of the system, the tension does augment the dynamism of a system that is already oriented towards constant increase and hence constant change. It favours action intended to redress inequalities rather than acceptance of their legitimacy. Such action, therefore, is anti-systemic and pro-systemic at the same time. We should distinguish it, at least analytically, from more purely anti-systemic action[18] which rejects both the structures and the cultural values of the global system, often in favour of particularistic and communicatively delimited groups (e.g. sects, 'fundamentalisms') that focus on problems of personal and collective identity.[19]

[17] John W. Meyer and his collaborators (see Meyer, op. cit., Meyer & Hannan, op. cit.) see the global extension of these values as a key element of global culture with which they explain, in part, the integration of the world system.

[18] Let me emphasize, in passing, that anti-systemic positions are by no means marginal or unimportant in the global system. They are not, however, the focus of this paper.

[19] Much of the theory and discussion about the significance of new social movements centres on this distinction, albeit with varying ways of drawing the line between the two. For an analysis of this discussion along with suggestions for how it affects the study of religion, see James A. Beckford, *Religion and Advanced Industrial Society,* London, Unwin Hyman 1989. See also, from among many, John A. Hannigan, 'Apples and oranges or varieties of the same fruit? New religious movements and new social movements compared', *Review of Religious Research* 31 (1990), pp. 246–58; and Dieter Rucht, 'Themes, logics, and arenas of social movements: a structural approach', in Bert Klandermans, Hanspieter Kriesi, and Sidney Tarrow (eds), *From Structure to Action: Comparing Social Movement Research Across Cultures, International Social Movement Research: A Research Annual,* vol. 1, Greenwich, CN, JAI 1988, pp. 305–28, for further constructive suggestions and applications.

The role of religion

An attempt to situate religion in the globalizing context can begin by asking whether or not religion is or can be a functionally oriented subsystem. Elements of this approach can be found in those versions of the still-powerful secularization thesis that stress the consequences of functional or institutional differentiation for religion.[20] Following Luhmann's variation on this thesis, religion under conditions of modernity faces the challenge of structuring religious communication in a way that more or less parallels similar structures in other systems. Without going into the matter in detail, this means focusing it around a bipolar code with one positive value-pole and its negative counterpart. Thus, for instance, the economic system operates with the polarity of owning/not owning, the health system with healthy/ sick, the scientific system with true/false. In religion, immanence/ transcendence takes this place.[21] Here, however, the situation is complicated by the holistic view of religion: just as religious commitment implies the whole person, so the religious dichotomy uses the whole world as its positive term, immanence. In other words, the world that, for instance, science approaches with the difference between true and false statements, religion identifies as the immanent. Since the whole cannot as such be the topic of communication – i.e. it does not distinguish itself from anything that is not itself – the transcendent functions to give it definition. But, as every major religious tradition shows only too clearly, the transcendent is not anything that can be talked about except in immanent terms. Hence, religion always deals with the simultaneity of immanence and transcendence, as in the Middle Eastern concept of divine creation or the Hindu concept of maya.

Like other functional spheres, therefore, religion is potentially applicable to everything. Just as anything can be commodified or politicized, so anything, as Durkheim stated, can be sacralized. What distinguishes religion from the others, however, is that it deals specifically with the overall conditions for the possibility of any communication. It thematizes those conditions, styling them as a special type of 'divine' communication accessible only in religiously

[20] See, for instance, Talcott Parsons, 'Religion in a modern pluralistic society', *Review of Religious Research* 7 (1966), pp. 125–46; Peter L. Berger, *The Sacred Canopy: Elements of a Sociological Theory of Religion,* Garden City, New York, Doubleday Anchor 1967; Niklas Luhmann, *Funktion der Religion,* Frankfurt, Suhrkamp 1977; and Bryan Wilson, *Religion in Sociological Perspective,* Oxford, Oxford University 1982.

[21] See Luhmann, *Ecological Communication,* p. 95.

controlled ways such as revelation, myth, mystical experience, ancestral wisdom, and so forth. Yet, because religion is about what is actually beyond all human communication, functional differentiation aimed at the creation of a specialized system of purely religious communication runs the serious risk of making religion generally relevant in all situations, but specifically relevant in comparatively few. More concretely, before the ascendancy of such functionally specialized social systems as for economic production, political decision-making, scientific explanation, or academic education, religious modalities provided essential support for a much larger portion of communication in these domains. Religious ritual was indispensable for the good harvest, the successful military campaign, the maintenance of health, and recovery from illness. Religious specialists played important roles in these matters and as teachers, scribes, and general sources of knowledge and wisdom. With the development of instrumentally specialized systems, however, religious approaches to these problems and functions have largely been displaced, marginalized, or privatized in most areas as these become enmeshed in the global system.[22] In addition, the global spread of these systems has often brought with it anti-religiousness and anti-clericalisms part of the delegitimation of the old and the promotion of the new.

The response of religion to these developments has, of course, been quite varied. Religious adherents, organizations, specialists and leaders around the world have adopted many strategies ranging from resistance and condemnation to acquiescence and approval. To understand the situation of religion under conditions of modernization and globalization, however, it is not enough simply to catalogue this diversity and leave it at that. It is also inadequate to judge the 'religious authenticity' of any given response in proportion to how resistant it is to modernity or the globalization of the

---

[22] Elsewhere, I have analysed this problem adapting the Luhmannian distinction between religious function and performance. See Peter F. Beyer, 'Privatization and the public influence of religion in global society', *Theory, Culture & Society* 7:2–3 (1990), pp. 347–69. A related analysis is, of course, embedded in the prevailing secularization thesis. See Bryan R. Wilson, 'Secularization: the inherited model', in Phillip E. Hammond (ed.), *The Sacred in a Secular Age: Toward Revision in the Scientific Study of Religion,* Berkeley, CA, University of California 1985, pp. 1–20. The problem also echoes in the discussion about whether the function of religion is primarily to provide meaning or whether we must also speak about religion necessarily furnishing power. See Meredith McGuire, 'Discovering religious power', *Sociological Analysis* 44 (1983), pp. 1–10; and James A. Beckford, 'The restoration of "power" to the sociology of religion', in Thomas Robbins and Roland Robertson (eds), *Church–State Relations: Tensions and Transitions,* New Brunswick, NJ, Transaction 1987, pp. 13–37.

functionally differentiated systems. Even the seemingly most resistant responses such as mid- and late- 19th century Roman Catholicism or segments of late 20th century Shi'a Islam include significant accommodation to modern structures.[23] And historically, various religious traditions from Buddhism to Judaism accommodated to changed social contexts as a condition for their growth or survival. Religions, like all social forms, change: old forms decline; new ones arise. It is therefore theoretically inappropriate to research the latter using the historical standards of the former.[24]

A sufficiently abstract analysis of what, sociologically speaking, religion is can help to address this limitation. I continue, therefore, with the idea that religion is a mode of communication centring around the dichotomy of immanent/transcendent. If we accept this description, then the core challenge for religion in modernity is that its way of relating to the world is too broadly based to allow the sort of instrumental specialization typical of functional subsystems like

[23] In the case of Roman Catholicism, I refer in particular to the development of social Catholicism out of the 19th century reaction, see Alec R. Vidler, *A Century of Social Catholicism,* London, SPCK 1964; Richard L. Camp, *The Papal Ideology of Social Reform. A Study of Historical Development 1878–1967,* Leiden, Brill 1969. In the case of Shi'a Islam, I refer to the Islamic Republic of Iran which has pursued global values such as egalitarian and redistributive 'social justice', and strengthened the modern state apparatus under the banner of a 'fundamentalist' theology which specifically condemns globalization of the Western-bred and Western-dominated systems/culture in symbolic phrases like 'Death to America', and 'global arrogance'. See Said Amir Arjomand, 'The rule of God in Iran', *Social Compass* 36 (1989), pp. 539–48; Shaul Bakhash, 'The politics of land, law, and social justice in Iran', in R. K. Ramazani (ed.), *Iran's Revolution: The Search for Consensus,* Bloomington, Indiana, Indiana University 1990, pp. 27–47; R. K. Ramazani, 'Iran's Foreign Policy: Contending Orientations', in ibid., pp. 48–68; and Daniel Pipes, *The Rushdie Affair: The Novel, the Ayatollah, and the West,* New York, Birch Lane 1990.

[24] Stark & Bainbridge in Rodney Stark and William Sims Bainbridge, *A Theory of Religion,* New York, Peter Lang 1987, are a good case in point. They quite correctly see that much of what is discussed under the heading of secularization is a result of periodic decline and growth, a feature of all ages, and not just the modern one. Yet in looking for the promising religious forms of the present, they limit themselves to, in their terms, cults and sects that resemble as closely as possible religion of the past. For another example of this rather common tendency, see, from among many, Reginald W. Bibby, *Fragmented Gods: The Poverty and Potential of Religion in Canada,* Toronto, Irwin 1987.

economy, polity, or science.[25] It is precisely the highly selective nature of the specializations that makes these systems so effective, allowing them to spread around the globe in relative disregard for pre-existing cultural boundaries. Religion cannot follow suit: theoretically because it is too diffuse a mode of communication and therefore tends to be broadly rooted in particular cultures; but also, it seems, empirically. Whereas globally, economic, political, scientific, health, and educational communication is becoming more and more homogeneous; religion's diversity is continuing or even increasing. The challenge for religion is to turn this circumstance to its advantage.

In light of religion's functional peculiarity, it is unlikely that we are going to see the development of a global religious system like the world capitalist economy or the system of sovereign states, at least not during the current phase of globalization.[26] This does not mean, however, that no global religious system is possible or that religious communication will shrink to the realms of pious public platitudes and the private concerns of a minority. The holistic starting-point of religion points to these, but also to other possibilities, above all particularistic and usually politicized 'fundamentalisms'; and what I am here calling liberal religion that seeks to address the severe problems engendered by the global system, but on the basis of the prevailing global values and not in opposition to them.[27] As noted in the introduction, it is this latter portion of the religious spectrum that is the specific focus of this paper.

[25] Here I depart somewhat from Luhmann's assessment of the same problem. In at least one of his publications ('Society, meaning, religion – based on self-reference', in *Essays on Self-Reference,* pp. 144–64), Luhmann states that religion has made incorrect choices in response to the development of modernity, thus contributing to its own maladaption. This, I suggest, is too much a judgement with the benefit of hindsight. What I am essentially arguing here is that responses by certain segments of the religious system to environmental problems may be seen as the symptoms of an 'adaptive' response.

[26] The use of the word 'phase' here does not imply anything like a precise periodization of the globalization process, but merely that globalization or, perhaps better, globality is not a stable state that has, in whatever sense, arrived. For just such precise periodizations in the economic world-system literature, see e.g. Christopher Chase-Dunn and Richard Rubinson, 'Cycles, trends, and new departures in world-system development', in Meyer & Hannan (eds), *National Development and the World System,* pp. 276–96; Albert Bergesen and Ronald Schoenberg, 'Long waves of colonial expansion and contraction, 1415–1969', in Albert Bergesen (ed.), *Studies of the World-System,* pp. 231–77; and Philip Robert Weber, 'Cyclical theories of crisis in the world-system', in Albert Bergesen (ed.), *Crises in the World-System,* Beverly Hills, CA, Sage 1983, pp. 37–55.

[27] See Beyer, 'Privatization and the public influence of religion in global society'.

Within the meaning of the word, immanence, religion includes all those matters about which the other functional systems communicate, plus all that they leave out. As I noted above, these systems are effective, globalizing, and totalizing; but there is much that they exclude. Among these are the meaning and thematization of the social whole, the 'private sphere' or 'life-world' and – critically, in the context of this paper – many problematic effects of their operation. Religion, as the one mode of communication that is in principle both totalizing and encompassing, can and does serve as a kind of system specializing in what, from the perspective of the dominant functional systems, are residual matters. Religion's view, under modern and globalizing conditions, is therefore typically 'anti-systemic' in the sense that religious adherents, professionals, and leaders tend to see their communication as essential because it addresses the problems that the dominant systems either leave out or create without solving. I stress, however, that 'anti-systemic' may mean against the dominant structures and values of emerging global society, but need not. As noted in the above discussion of the tension between systemic values and systemic effects, communication in this society can be anti-systemic and pro-systemic at the same time. This also applies to religion, especially (but not exclusively) what I am here calling liberal religion. More precisely, given the functional peculiarities of religion and the structural characteristics of global society, we should expect the emergence of a relatively prominent form of religion that sees among its central religious tasks 'anti-systemic' action based on central 'pro-systemic' values, yielding a somewhat ambiguous attitude to the global social system.[28]

A final point before I move on to the specific question of religion and environment. Although religion has affinity for what I have just called residual matters, social communication outside the dominant systems is not simply therefore religious. Nonetheless, the affinity does make it likely that communication about residual matters such as personal or collective identity, thematization of global society, and the various problematic effects of the dominant systems will quite often take on seemingly religious forms even when it is not what

[28] The distinction between 'anti-systemic', 'pro-systemic', and 'ambiguous' implied here is intentionally parallel to the distinction Dieter Rucht, see 'Themes, logics, and arenas of social movements: a structural approach', in Bert Klandermans, Hanspieter Kriesi, and Sidney Tarrow (eds), *From Structure to Action: Comparing Social Movement Research Across Cultures, International Social Movement Research: A Research Annual*, vol. 1, Greenwich, CN, JAI 1988, pp. 305–28, makes between reactive, proactive, and ambivalent social movements.

most observers would call religion.[29] The sociology of religion abounds in examples ranging from analyses of Marxism as religion and the vexed civil religion debate to the observed similarities between religion and new social movements.[30] Such manifestations, I suggest, are virtually religious: that is, they are religious by virtue of the affinity between religious holism and residual matters.

Religion and the global environment

Much more clearly than others, environmental issues concretize the problematic effects of the global system. For instance, the degree to which Third World underdevelopment is a product of First World development may be a matter for debate; the radioactive fallout in Britain, Scandinavia, and elsewhere as a result of the Chernobyl disaster far less so. In this regard, the most far-reaching example is undoubtedly the dilemma of global warming, a result not just of specific destructive activity but of the general level of human activity everywhere in the world: even clean-burning automobiles, like sheep, still contribute simply because we have produced so many of them. The sheer volume of social communication, in other words, is as much at issue as the type. Environmental issues therefore raise the question of the consequences of human activity as such. There are always unintended effects, unforeseen results.

Historically, religions have concerned themselves with this root indeterminacy. They have postulated a way to circumvent the normal, the everyday, the profane, and communicate a transcendent realm that will ground and guarantee our choices 'in this world'. Whether it is remaining true to the ways of the ancestors, attaining mystical insights into the true nature of reality, living according to the true revelation, or any of a host of other forms, there exists for religion an essentially non-empirical way of knowing what is the right way. The unintended and unforeseen are in this mode indicators of both the necessity and the reality of the transcendent. Religion gives

[29] The question of when religious becomes religion is a very difficult one and here cannot be the place for a thorough examination. Above, I pointed out that we must adopt a broader conception of religion that is not historically limited. Yet we must also avoid allowing the concept to lose all contours. The present study is also, in part, a contribution to the uncertain task of finding the balance between the two.

[30] On Marxism, see e.g. Talcott Parsons, 'Religion in postindustrial America: the problem of secularization', *Social Research* 41 (1974), pp. 193–225. On civil religion, see James A. Mathisen, 'Twenty years after Bellah: whatever happened to American civil religion?' *Sociological Analysis* 50 (1989), pp. 129–46. On social movements, see Beckford, *Religion and Advanced Industrial Society,* pp. 129ff.; and Hannigan, 'Apples and oranges...'.

them meaning and promises the power to overcome them. The nature of environmental crisis is therefore just the sort of problem religion addresses: it is virtually religious.

Contemporary evidence of this relation is not hard to find. As I pointed out earlier, religious people – including theologians – have been concerned with environmental issues since their advent in the 1960s;[31] and recently that concern has become a central issue for major religious organizations as well. The connection is, however, also made by secular environmentalists. The publications of environmentalists and environmental organizations are replete with religious interpretations and explicit recognition that (at least some) traditional religions address this matter at the core of what they are all about.[32] One might even speak of a mutual fructification as secular environmentalists adapt religious language to conceptualize their concerns, while representatives of various religions highlight or even refashion those elements of their traditions that seem to resonate with secular environmental concern.[33]

---

[31] In addition to the sources cited above, see, as a selection of recent examples, Thomas Berry, *The Dream of the Earth,* San Francisco, CA, Sierra Club Books 1988; John Carmody, *Ecology and Religion: Toward a New Christian Theology of Nature,* New York, Paulist 1983; Matthew Fox, *The Coming of the Cosmic Christ: The Healing of Mother Earth and the Birth of a Global Renaissance,* San Francisco, CA, Harper & Row 1988; David G. Hallman, *Caring for Creation. The Environmental Crisis: A Canadian Christian Call to Action,* Winfield, British Columbia, Wood Lake Books 1989; Sean McDonagh, *To Care for the Earth: A Call to a New Theology,* Santa Fe, CA, Bear 1987; and Jürgen Moltmann, *Creating a Just Future: The Politics of Peace and the Ethics of Creation in a Threatened World,* London, SCM 1989.

[32] As examples of the former, see many of the contributions in 'How we can save it', *Greenpeace* 15:1 (January/February, 1990). Some examples can also be found in 'The environment and environmentalism: our progress, problems and prospects', *Probe Post* 11:4 (1989), pp. 10–39; although far fewer, reflecting, perhaps, the less 'anti-systemic' orientation of this publication and its parent organization. See also Farley Mowat, *Rescue the Earth!* Toronto, McClelland & Stewart 1990. As regards the latter, the works just cited include several examples of the appeal that particularly pre-literate religion has for many environmentalists. This attraction probably has more to do with the fact that these religions have not desocialized the non-human environment than some inherently greater sensitivity to the deleterious effects of humans on the world around them. On this point, see Thomas Luckmann, 'On the boundaries of the social world', in Maurice Natanson (ed.), *Phenomenology and Social Reality: Essays in Memory of Alfred Schulz,* The Hague, Mouton 1970, pp. 73–100. For an environmentalist's assessment of various religions in this regard, see the series of articles by Peter Timmerman in *Probe Post* 'God is closer to you than your jugular vein', 12:1 (1989), pp. 24–6; and 'Holding the world together', 12:3/4 (1989), pp. 26–9.

[33] In this latter regard, see Harris, 'How environmentalist is buddhism?' (note 5).

What one might call the 'theodicy' factor in environmental issues does not exhaust their virtual religiousness. Global environment issues in particular also point to the question of holism. One of the abiding themes of the overall environmental debate is the fact that all action is interconnected, that 'to pluck a flower is to trouble a star'.[34] From nuclear fallout and global warming to ozone depletion and waste disposal, local action creates problems that affect the planet as a whole. The holism of religious communication, discussed above, offers a logical social perspective from which to address this aspect. Moreover, because global environmental problems are a result of the power of the globalizing functional social systems, they also point to the globalization of society and to the problem of conceiving that society. This again is a religious task: the meaning of the whole as immanence profiled by positing transcendence.[35] A direct result of this connection is that environmental theology will often contain a decidedly global thrust.[36] It also means that pro-systemic religion (especially if, as noted above, it also includes significant anti-systemic elements) will in all likelihood take up environmental issues as a fundamental theological concern. We arrive here at the close relation among the liberal religious goals of, as the World Council of Churches phrases them, 'justice, peace, and the integrity of creation'.

Peace and justice have for some time been key terms for more liberal, especially Western religion.[37] As religious concepts, they

[34] From the title of Michael McAteer, 'To pluck a flower is to trouble a star', *The Toronto Star* (30 June 1990), p. M15, which includes a report of a letter by eminent scientists calling for co-operation between science and religion: 'Efforts to safeguard and cherish the environment need to be infused with a vision of the sacred, said the scientists, who acknowledged the power of religion to motivate'.

[35] Self-conception of society is, of course, not exclusively a religious task. The globalization debate among social-scientists also has this as part of its agenda. See Robertson, 'The sacred in the world system'; 'Mapping the global condition: globalization as the central concept'; Luhmann, 'The self-description of society'; 'Tautology and paradox in the self-descriptions of modern society'. Even here, however, the results are often virtually religious, as exemplified in the function of 'socialism' among the Wallersteinians. See, for instance, Wallerstein, *The Capitalist World-Economy*, pp. 269–82.

[36] See R. A. Ambler, *Global Theology: The Meaning of Faith in the Present World Crisis,* London, SCM 1990; and McAteer, op. cit.

[37] Here cannot be the place for a detailed proof of this assertion. See, as typical examples, Walsh & Davies, op. cit.; John R. Williams, *Canadian Churches and Social Justice,* Toronto, Lorimer 1984; David M. Paton (ed.), *Breaking Barriers;* and David Gill (ed.), *Gathered for Life,* Official Report VI Assembly World Council of Churches, Vancouver, Canada 29 July–10 August 1983, Geneva & Grand Rapids, MI, World Council of Churches/Eerdmans. These sources also exemplify the interpretation in the text that follows.

indicate both acceptance of the core values of modernity – equality, progress, etc. – and rejection of what are deemed the negative consequences of modernity. We can describe the logic roughly as follows: More than the absence of open conflict, peace implies the existence of community, globally speaking, world community. The word points to a self-conception of a global society which harmoniously includes all people. Justice is a strictly complementary term referring to the relations that must exist among people if community is to be realized. These ideal relations incorporate several core modern values, including equality, human rights, progress, individual and collective self-determination, and tolerance – even celebration – of diversity. Various forms of marginalization or exclusion are accordingly manifestations of injustice. Among these are racial/ethnic discrimination, poverty, political powerlessness, individual alienation, religious intolerance, gender bias, and the vast disparities between rich and poor regions of the world. For there to be peace, there must be justice first. Translated into the terms of the globalization debate used here, the continued elaboration of the global system depends on pursuing the key cultural values that resonate with that system.

The liberal religious concepts of peace and justice are not, however, simply an accommodating confirmation of emerging global social order. Contained within both notions is the assertion that the injustices are to a significant degree the result of the operation of the globalizing, instrumental systems.[38]

The pro-systemic/anti-systemic combination discussed above manifests itself in this kind of religion. In Weberian terms, it is both priestly and prophetic. It attempts to conceive the global whole (peace) and does so by concentrating on the problems that the more dominant functional systems generate but do not solve (justice).

Global environmental issues are then a religiously logical comp-lement to the peace/justice pair. Like peace, environmental issues point to the whole, in Abrahamic faith terms, creation. Like justice, they also point quite specifically to the problems generated by the same globalization. The World Council of Churches rubric expresses the combination nicely: integrity (justice) of creation (peace). Indeed, beyond the logical parallel, the two are frequently tied together explicitly. For example, in his recent message,[39] the pope places part

---

[38] Just as one example, see the critique of 'capitalism' (globalizing functional system) in John Paul II's encyclical, 'Laborem exercens', in Walsh & Davies, pp. 271–311.

[39] See note 1.

of the blame for the Third World's contribution to environmental problems on the injustices of the global economic system.[40]

Although peace/justice and environmental concerns thus seem to imply each other, there is also a certain amount of tension between the two. This derives from the pro systemic attitude of much liberal religion, namely that the cornerstone of injustice is the marginalization or oppression of the majority of people in the world by a minority; and that the solution lies in the elimination of these inequalities. Without going into the matter in great detail, simple redistribution of power and wealth will not work because the effectiveness of the major functional systems depends on a significant concentration of communicative resources. Continued growth of the same systems, on the other hand, even assuming that it will eventually spread the benefits to increasingly larger segments of the human population, carries with it the environmental problems typified by the issue of global warming. In this sense, solving the problem of injustice would imply exacerbating the problem of environmental degradation.

A few examples can illustrate the dilemma. In Canada, environmental activists were successful in effectively ending the hunting of harp seal pups. The brunt of the economic cost was borne by the chronically underemployed Maritime fishermen and, indirectly, various Aboriginal communities of the far north. Attempts to save virgin timber stands in various parts of Canada constantly pit those wishing to preserve endangered jobs against those battling further environmental destruction. In Brazil, the desperately poor flock to the Amazon region in hopes of a better life, contributing to the destruction of the rainforest. Various Third World countries are hesitant about co-operating in international environmental efforts for fear that their own development would be hurt and they would become even more dependent on First World technologies and expertise.

To be sure, each of these cases has its own complexities; and one could argue that the core areas of the global system contribute far more to these problems than the peripheries. The point, however, is

---

[40] See also Hallman, *Caring for Creation*, pp. 129–42. Among more secular environmentalists, the connection is even more explicit. Animal rights advocates, for instance, as the name implies, trace environmental problems to injustice (denial of 'human' rights) toward animals. Occasionally one encounters the wider argument that the environment itself has rights. See Christopher D. Stone, *Earth and Other Ethics: The Case for Moral Pluralism*, New York, Harper & Row 1988. For potential problems with such a simple extension of rights to non-humans, this time from a philosophical perspective, see Paul W. Taylor, *Respect for Nature: A Theory of Environmental Ethics*, Princeton, NJ, Princeton University 1986, pp. 219ff.

not who is to bear greater responsibility for both the mess and the clean up, both the injustice and the restitution; but rather that both the globalizing systems and the core values that resonate with them – in particular equality and progress – have spread to virtually all corners of the globe. And this implies the further growth or intensification of precisely the instrumentalities that are at the root of the environmental crisis.

Religious people concerned about both marginalization and the environment are, for the most part, aware of this tension.[41] The responses, of course, vary a great deal; but most call for some 'new understanding of who we are and how we fit in'.[42] Such vague formulations are indicative. They are a call to what, in effect, is a religious conversion, a change of heart, a *metanoia*. The purely religious content of this conversion, while important for a more detailed understanding, is of less interest here. More germane is the implicit attitude to the global system. Among various formulations of the supposedly proper religious responses to environmental problems, one often finds an ambiguous attitude that, in the light of the present analysis, we can see as typical of liberal religion with its combination pro-systemic/anti-systemic outlook. In this regard, the following report of a debate at the 1975 World Council of Churches conference in Nairobi is worth quoting at length:

> ... after a chillingly detailed analysis of the threats to human survival, ... [Professor Charles Birch] asked what positively we could do, for if we cannot permit technology to have its head, we cannot do without it. Our goal, therefore, must be a just and sustainable society; and this demands a fundamental change of heart and mind about humankind's relation to nature ...
>
> Metropolitan Paulos Gregorios drew a sharp distinction between the Limits to Growth People (LGPs) and the Technological Optimism People (TOPs). They could, however, agree to put their best minds and efforts together to control the four elements of population explosion, resource depletion, environmental deterioration, and nuclear war. But success will depend on a new economics and a new science and technology; and these can only grow in a climate of thought and life which takes seriously the deep religious questions

[41] See Carmody, *Ecology and Religion,* pp. 39–52; Hallman, *Caring for Creation,* pp.129ff.; John B. Cobb, Jr, 'Christian existence in a world of limits', in Eugene C. Hargrove (ed.), *Religion and Environmental Crisis,* pp. 172–87.

[42] Daniel Martin as quoted in McAteer; see also Cobb, pp. 184ff.; and Jay McDaniel, 'Christianity and the need for new vision', in Hargrove (ed.), *Religion and Environmental Crisis,* pp. 188–212.

about our relationship with the Transcendent, with one another, and with nature.[43]

The ambiguity is particularly clear in this quote. In the theological literature on this topic, however, the 'LGPs' (anti-systemic) dominate: pure 'TOPs' (pro-systemic) seem not to be present at all. By contrast, more anti-systemic voices are not difficult to find.[44] Environmental problems, after all, result from the unprecedented power of the globalizing systems, and not from their fragility. Global economy, polity, and science hardly need religious legitimation.

Conclusions

The ambiguity inherent in at least many liberal religious responses to environmental issues illustrates an important aspect of the dilemma of religion in globalizing society. Religion is a relatively diffuse mode of human communication that in many respects thrived better in smaller, more clearly bounded societies lacking the potent functional specialization of instrumentally oriented systems. As the contemporary world shows, however, this feature does not mean a crude form of secularization in which religion simply declines, inevitably to disappear. In the globalization theory terms used here, it is unlikely that religion can become a specialized system like the global economy or polity; but a functionally differentiated system it can become and to a great extent is. Nonetheless, the characteristic disadvantages of religion vis-à-vis other systems, rooted as they are in the very nature of religious communication, point to a different, more indirect way of making its influence felt in global society. The response of religion to environmental issues illustrates this.

Religion cannot do anything direct about environmental problems. To be sure, various individuals may convert to a thoroughgoing environmental ethic, perhaps on the basis of their own traditions, perhaps in switching allegiance to another. But these are likely to be a minority. As with peace and justice issues, many religious people and organizations will become deeply involved in the problems, but the proffered solutions are going to be political, educational, scientific, economic, and medical – assuming, of course, that the global system does not collapse along with its biological environment. Put slightly differently, as with other negative effects of the global system, religion can offer significant organizational, ideological, and motivational resources which primarily religious, but also non-

[43] *Breaking Barriers,* p. 23f.

[44] See Berry, *The Dream of the Earth;* and McDonagh, *To Care for the Earth.*

religious, people can use to conceptualize 'residual' problems and mobilize to deal with them. The temples and the synagogues, the churches and the holy places, however, are not going to be filled to overflowing as a result; but they will undoubtedly survive.[45]

[45] James Beckford comes to a similar conclusion on the basis of a very different analysis: 'The partial freeing of religion from its points of anchorage in communities and natural social groupings has also turned it into a resource which may be invested with highly diverse meanings and used for a wide variety of purposes. Religion can now be put to varied use both within and outside the framework of religious organizations. ... Health care, movements for the protection of the environment or the promotion of peace, and the institutions of human rights are ... spheres in which religious symbolism is increasingly being appropriated' (*Religion and Advanced Industrial Society*, p. 171).

Acknowledgements

Grateful acknowledgement is made to the following sources for permission to reproduce textual material within this book:
'World charter for nature', 1982, Center for International Earth Science Information Network/United Nations; Burgess, J.P. (1997) 'Theologians and the renewal of institutions', *The East German Church and the End of Communism*, Oxford University Press, Inc.; Mernissi, F. (1998) 'A feminist interpretation of women's rights in Islam', in Kurzman, C. (ed.) *Liberal Islam: A Sourcebook*, Oxford University Press; Gupta, L. (1991) 'Kali, the saviour', in Gooey, P.M., *et al. After Patriarchy: Feminist Transformations of the World Religions*, Orbis Books; Beyer, P. (1992) 'The global environment as a religious issue: a sociological analysis', reprinted from *Religion*, vol. 22, pages 1–19, copyright © 1992 Academic Press Limited.

Index